Studies on the European Union

Series Editor:

Wolfgang Wessels
Jean Monnet Chair *ad personam* for Political Science
CETEUS | Centre for Turkey and European Union Studies
University of Cologne

Volume 12

Stefan Becker | Michael W. Bauer
Alfredo De Feo [eds.]

The New Politics of the European Union Budget

Nomos

Co-funded by the
Erasmus+ Programme
of the European Union

The Deutsche Nationalbibliothek lists this publication in the Deutsche Nationalbibliografie; detailed bibliographic data are available on the Internet at http://dnb.d-nb.de

ISBN 978-3-8487-3500-6 (Print)
978-3-8452-7803-2 (ePDF)

British Library Cataloguing-in-Publication Data
A catalogue record for this book is available from the British Library.

ISBN 978-3-8487-3500-6 (Print)
978-3-8452-7803-2 (ePDF)

Library of Congress Cataloging-in-Publication Data
Becker, Stefan / Bauer, Michael W. / De Feo, Alfredo
The New Politics of the European Union Budget
Stefan Becker / Michael W. Bauer / Alfredo De Feo (eds.)
297 p.
Includes bibliographic references.

ISBN 978-3-8487-3500-6 (Print)
978-3-8452-7803-2 (ePDF)

1. Edition 2017

Acknowledgements

This book emerged from the workshop “EU budget politics – Experiences, dynamics, reform options”, held at the European Parliament, Strasbourg, France, in October 2015. The workshop was organized by the Chair of Comparative Public Administration and Policy Analysis at Speyer University and the European Parliamentary Research Service (EPRS). We would like to thank the EPRS staff, in particular Katerina Vavrova, and Andrea Arendt at Speyer University for helping us organize the event.

The workshop and this book are part of a research project on the role of the European Parliament in the EU budget system funded by the European Commission in the Jean Monnet Chair program.

We would like to thank the European University Institute, in particular Brigid Laffan, Director of the Robert Schuman Centre for Advanced Studies, for her advice and support, Dieter Schlenker, Director of the Historical Archives of the European Union, for facilitating the access to archival holdings of the European Union Institutions, Paivi Vainiomaki and Alexandra Devantier of the Historical Archives of the European Parliament, for their support in the selection of documents of the European Parliament, and last but not least Julia Lynch for her linguistic revision. We are also grateful to Johanna Dietrich and Jana Pöhler for editorial assistance.

Table of Contents

List of Tables and Figures

List of Abbreviations

AFET	European Parliament Committee on Foreign Affairs
ALDE	Alliance of Liberals and Democrats for Europe
AO	Authorising Officer
AOD	Authorising Officer by Delegation
AOSD	Authorising Officer by Subdelegation
BReg	Bundesregierung (German Federal Government)
BUDG	European Parliament Committee on Budgets
CA	Commitment Appropriation
CAB	Cyclically Adjusted Balance
CAP	Common Agricultural Policy
CAPB	Cyclically Adjusted Primary Balance
CDU/CSU	Christlich Demokratische Union Deutschlands/Christlich-Soziale Union in Bayern (Christian Democratic Union of Germany/Christian Social Union in Bavaria)
CE	Compulsory Expenditure
CFSP	Common Foreign and Security Policy
COFOG	Classifications of the Functions of Government
CSDP	Common Security and Defence Policy
DAB	Draft amending budget
DG	Directorate-General
DNA	Discourse Network Analyzer
EAGGF	European Agricultural Guidance and Guarantee Fund
EC	European Community
ECA	European Court of Auditors
ECB	European Central Bank
ECJ	European Court of Justice
ECOFIN	Economic and Financial Affairs Council
ECR	European Conservatives and Reformists
ECSC	European Coal and Steel Community
EEC	European Economic Community
EFSI	European Fund for Strategic Investments
EIB	European Investment Bank
EP	European Parliament

EPP	European People's Party
ERDF	European Regional Development Fund
ESF	European Social Fund
ESI	European Structural and Investment Funds
EU	European Union
FDP	Freie Demokratische Partei (Free Democratic Party Germany)
FP/MFF	Multiannual Financial Planning
GAC	General Affairs Council
GDP	Gross Domestic Product
GNI	Gross National Income
GNP	Gross National Product
GUE-NGL	European United Left-Nordic Green Left
HI	Historical Institutionalism
HLGOR	High-level Group on Own Resources
IIA	Interinstitutional Agreement
IMF	International Monetary Fund
MCA	Monetary Compensatory Accounts
MEP	Member of the European Parliament
MFF	Multiannual Financial Framework
MFFR	Regulation on the Multiannual Financial Framework
MRI	Maximum Rate of Increase
MSA	Multiple Streams Approach
NCE	Non-compulsory Expenditure
NIC	New Community Instrument for Borrowing and Lending
OBB	Operating Budgetary Balance
OECD	Organisation for Economicy Co-operation and Development
OLAF	European Anti-Fraud Office
PA	Payment Appropriation
PDB	Preliminary Draft Budget
PiS	Prawo i Sprawiedliwość (Law and Justice, Polish party)
RAL	Outstanding Commitments
R&D	Research & Development
S&D	Socialists & Democrats
SEA	Single European Act
SME	Small and Medium-sized Enterprise

SPD	Sozialdemokratische Partei Deutschland (Social Democratic Party of Germany)
SURE	Special Committee on Policy Challenges and Budgetary Resources for a Sustainable European Union after 2013
TEU	Treaty on European Union
TFEU	Treaty on the Functioning of the European Union
TOR	Traditional Own Resources
UK	United Kingdom
US	United States of America
VAT	Value-added Tax

The New Politics of the European Union Budget: Background, Key Findings, and Outlook

Stefan Becker, Michael W. Bauer and Alfredo De Feo

After over a decade of relative stability, the years between 2007 and 2016 showed new momentum in EU budget politics. Regarding the institutional and political environments, the Treaty of Lisbon introduced the broadest reform of budgetary procedures since the 1970s, while the general political climate, affected by financial and economic crisis, has turned toward exceeding skepticism of European integration. As a result, the preferences and strategies of budgetary actors have changed, and the potential for conflict has grown—evidenced by the three temporary breakdowns of annual budget negotiations since the Treaty of Lisbon took effect. Meanwhile, budgetary outcomes have taken unprecedented shapes. The latest Multiannual Financial Framework (MFF) has been the first plan to reduce EU spending in real terms, and annual budgeting practices have caused serious problems in fulfilling financial commitments. Finally, decision-makers have entered uncharted waters with new flexibility arrangements and funding instruments, such as the so-called Juncker Plan. Hence, the EU budget has become more challenged, more flexible, and more fragmented.

Some of these developments, such as an eroding consensus and increasing fragmentation, resemble Wildavsky's observations of the United States, laid down in *The New Politics of the Budgetary Process* (1988). For him, the "new" politics are more complex and less stable than the "old" politics (Wildavsky 1964). The vast differences between arrangements in the US and the EU notwithstanding, dynamics between 2007 and 2016 suggest that an EU version of "new" budget politics is emerging. This raises empirical and theoretical questions, which join the plethora of older, yet still unresolved issues regarding the revenue system, spending priorities, and accountability deficits, to name a few. This volume brings together contributions from scholars and practitioners that address present-day EU budget politics, taking stock of budget making and implementation in the context of the Lisbon Treaty and the financial and economic crisis. This introduction outlines the context of the volume, summarizes the key findings, and offers an outlook on future challenges in the theory and practice of EU budget politics.

Background: The EU budget and its study

By allocating and redistributing resources, public budgets deliver tangible answers to the classic question of politics according to Harold Lasswell (1936): Who gets what, when, and how? It follows that, as Wildavsky (1992, p. xi) argues, "Those who wish to understand politics must acquaint themselves with budgeting if they want to know what is going on." Indeed, US budget politics have been an important focus of public policy research since its inception (e.g., Wildavsky 1964; Fenno 1966; Wildavsky 1988; Rubin 1991). By contrast, studies of the EU budget, once it was established, have taken longer to materialize (but see the work of Strasser, e.g. 1975). This asymmetry can be primarily attributed to three factors. First, the EU budget has always been small compared to national budgets. It currently stands at roughly one percent of its members' combined gross domestic product (GDP). By contrast, the members' national budgets on average amount to almost fifty percent of GDP. The overall effect of EU spending has therefore been called into question. Second, while allocation and redistribution at the EU level have remained moderate, integration in regulatory matters has advanced greatly (Majone 1994). Perceived as the areas where the EU makes the most difference, these regulatory policies have attracted the attention of the scientific community. Third, budget politics elsewhere have often appeared to be more contentious, and therefore more interesting. In the US, for instance, where budget studies are more frequent, government shutdowns are more than a mere possibility. In the EU, the rules—such as the stipulation that all budgets shall be in balance (Art. 310 Treaty on the Functioning of the European Union – TFEU), and the provisional twelfths system (Art. 315 TFEU) that governs EU spending if no budget is agreed upon—have prevented similar meltdowns.

While these circumstances still hold, a more nuanced understanding of the EU budget has emerged in the 2000s and 2010s. It has become apparent that allocation and redistribution at the EU level can have significant economic and political effects. On the one hand, the effective size of the EU budget is more than one percent of the GDP due to co-financing obligations for the member states. The mobilized funds are roughly double of the nominal budget (Núñez Ferrer/Katarivas 2014). Over time, specific clientele and poorer member states in particular have greatly benefitted from EU funds. On the other hand, budgetary decision-making has been of more political importance than often presumed. Conflicts related to EU finances have been frequent, and often they are connected to larger debates about the general trajectory of integration. In this regard, several important contributions have brought EU budget politics into the spotlight (e.g., Laffan 1997; Begg/Grimwade 1998; Lindner 2006). These studies have also identified key dynamics and issues that provide the empirical and theoretical background for this volume.

The first proposition is that, at EU level, budgetary conflicts are as much political as they are institutional. Spending priorities are discussed along national or party ideological lines, but the European Council, the European Commission, and the European Parliament (EP) also have clear institutional interests. The supranational bodies, specifically, have long fought for larger budgets, as they would also increase their spheres of influence (Lindner 2006, p. 31, 43). With more resources to allocate, the EP would have a voice in more issue areas, while the Commission's role in managing the budget would also grow in importance. Meanwhile, the Council tries to keep both institutions at bay by limiting increases in spending. Repeatedly, institutional interests overshadowed political concerns, such as during the budgetary battles of the 1980s (see De Feo 2017a). However, major conflict had all but subsided and budget politics had become a rather routine process—up until 2007, when the Lisbon reforms, along with the economic crisis, provided catalysts for new conflict.

Furthermore, EU budget politics extends beyond just allocation and redistribution. While this is true for any political system, the potential for logrolling and package deals is enormous in the EU due to the number and diversity of actors. The member states have, for instance, used the budget to facilitate cooperation in other areas, such as enlargement or economic integration. One result was the establishment of structural funds (Allen 2010). The Parliament, for its part, has used the budget as a vehicle for influencing legislative processes (Laffan 2010, p. 216). It has been able to strengthen existing programs or even introduce new ones even if the Council had not yet passed the respective legislation (Pollack 2008, p. 26). As the budget manager, the Commission has also pursued its own preferences, such as in facilitating subnational mobilization through cohesion policy (Hooghe/Keating 1994), or subtly influencing higher education policy (Batory/Lindstrom 2011).

All of these activities had long taken place in an unstable environment. Even though the budgetary procedures had in principle not been changed since the budget treaties of 1970s, incremental reform was frequent. Prominent examples are the introduction of multiannual financial planning in the 1980s, following a proposal by Commission President Delors, and the EP's strategy of opportunistic rule interpretation, such as regarding the spending categorizations of compulsory and non-compulsory (in the non-compulsory category the Parliament had more influence) (Lindner 2006). Apart from this institutional instability, EU budget politics were further affected by the political dynamics resulting from external crises, enlargement rounds, and the overall trajectory of integration. Given budget politics' institutional dimension and its utilization for different purposes, these dynamics often had immediate effects. The accession of the United Kingdom (UK) in 1970s had, for instance, been a strong stimulus for budgetary reform and more spending; the European Regional Development Fund (ERDF) was established to compensate the UK, which hardly benefited from subsidies in the agricultural sector (Bauer 2001). Again, conflicts had almost subsided up until the early 2000s, although the Eastern enlargement only brought in net recipients. But even through this period of relative stability, some issues have remained on the EU budget agenda.

The first issue is the prevailing dominance of *juste retour* logic among member states in the Council. Despite their more or less pronounced vows to an ever-closer union, when negotiating budgets, governments are focused on minimizing contributions and maximizing receipts. As a result, conflict is inevitable, and revenue decisions as well as allocation outcomes are criticized as suboptimal and unstable. The overall financial autonomy of the EU is thus limited. The increasing share of national contributions in the own resources system further aggravates problems resulting from *juste retour* logic. Calls for reform are widespread; the system is considered overly complex, nontransparent (due to many rebates), and regressive in nature, as it disadvantages poorer member states (Cipriani 2014).

Another long-standing issue pertains to the accountability structure in EU spending. National authorities spend most of EU funds, with the Commission supervising the system and acting as the politically responsible party. For decades, these formal expectations were not met by actual capacities, and the Commission failed to fulfill its managerial role effectively (Laffan 1997). Several reforms have been undertaken in the first decades of the twenty-first century, most of them triggered by the Santer Commission resigning amid allegations of fraud and mismanagement, but financial management reform in particular has proven particularly hard and inconclusive (Levy et al. 2011; Bauer 2008; Kassim 2008). Furthermore, the EP, which grants discharge to the Commission in regard to the implementation of the budget, has long been unable (and partly unwilling) to focus on this problem.

Budget reform, in general, has been on the agenda for a long time, but hardly any initiatives have gained significant momentum. The revenue system especially has come under criticism; however, the status quo orientation in the Council has prevented meaningful reform. Given the complexity of the own resources system, with its many rebate mechanisms, governments have been hesitant to engage with this issue. Transparency and legitimacy concerns have also been repeatedly voiced. This, inter alia, relates to the effective inclusion of the Parliament in revenue questions. Budgetary rights are widely considered to be cornerstones of democratic systems; regarding the role of only directly elected institutions at EU level however, Begg (2009, p.43) refers to "representation without taxation."

Before the Lisbon Treaty and the financial and economic crisis, EU budget politics seemed to have reached a rather stable equilibrium. The time of big budgetary battles was over, and most conflicts were, if not solved, latent. Budget politics had almost become routine. The focus of decision-makers was on improving management and control; revenue and spending reform, while not thoroughly forgotten, were put on the backburner. Since 2007 however, this phase of stability has come to an end.

Key findings: New dynamics and issues

The new politics of the EU budget that emerged are characterized by several dynamics addressed in the contributions to this volume. Although the authors take different perspectives, their analyses amount to three general findings on current EU budget politics: the environment is more volatile, the actors have changing preferences and strategies, and novel outcomes are resulting.

A more volatile environment

The period of institutional and political stability after the budgetary battles of the 1980s was unsettled by two, almost parallel developments—the implementation of the Lisbon Treaty, which took effect in budgetary matters in 2011, and the onset of the financial and economic crisis in 2010. Regarding the institutional environment, the Lisbon Treaty reforms have significantly altered the balance of the budget authority (i.e., the Council and the Parliament) in terms of spending decisions. In his historical review of EU budget politics, Alfredo De Feo shows that while the Lisbon Treaty seemed to merely codify previously informal procedures, the effects were groundbreaking.

Initially, scholars were divided about how these formal changes would affect the budget authority in practice. Hix and Høyland (2011, p. 243) have, for instance, stressed that the EP is now "equally influential under all budgetary headings." By contrast, Benedetto (2013, p. 366) has argued that, "in budget policy [the EP's] powers have generally weakened." Indeed, as Corbett et al. (2011, p. 272-276) have pointed out, "Lisbon has unfrozen a situation that had appeared immutable and opened up a new era in budgetary history of the European Parliament and its relations with other institutions, in particular the Council." Budgetary actors therefore had to grow into their new roles. In this regard, Anne Vitrey's contribution outlines the interinstitutional frictions in the first MFF negotiations under the new rules. As for the formal balance of power after the Lisbon reforms, the contributions by De Feo, Vitrey, as well as Michael W. Bauer and Stefan Becker agree that the EP has indeed suffered a formal loss of influence in spending decisions.

At the same time, the effects of the financial and economic crisis on the political environment altered the logic of budget politics in two important ways. First, as the economic fundamentals changed, so did the debate on the EU's finances. While one side considered the budget a suitable vehicle for anticyclical economic policy to stimulate growth, the other side argued for austerity. According to the latter position, most member states had taken great pains in efforts to consolidate their finances; increasing the EU budget would therefore be inappropriate. At the EU level, the Parliament was the most ardent supporter of the stimulus approach, but its arguments for more spending failed to resonate, as the contribution by Bauer and Becker demonstrates. As Linn Selle shows in her chapter on the MFF negotiations, the budgetary discourse has generally been lopsided in recent years. This applies not only at the EU level; even the left-leaning opposition in the German Bundestag found it hard to argue against the austerity-dominated mindset.

Second, the financial and economic crisis has aggravated the decline of trust in the EU institutions and fueled a Eurosceptic sentiment. European integration was already politicized, but the crisis took the "constraining dissensus" (Hooghe/Marks 2008) to unprecedented levels. The rapid establishment of new lending facilities to offer financial support to ailing countries, the conditionality attached to this support, and the timid attempts to address employment and social issues have caused unease in creditor and debtor states alike. This has not only fueled the debate about what the EU budget should be for, but it has also called into question the democratic credentials of the EU in general. While the need for common action has grown, the room for political maneuver has declined. This trend was intensified by the refugee crisis that unfolded in 2015. Budgetary actors have taken the dynamics in the institutional and political environment into account, but with different effects.

Changing preferences and strategies

In view of budget making, profligacy is not something any actor wants to be associated with, especially under the current circumstances. The national governments in the Council eventually seek re-election, for which they have to show what they have accomplished at EU level; the Commission needs political capital to further its influence, so it must avoid allegations of being an unaccountable bureaucracy; and even the EP, paradoxically once fairly detached from electoral pressure with respect to EU budgetary decisions, is now more aware of the current predicament of EU integration—the influx of Eurosceptic representatives in the 2014 election is a forceful reminder. At the same time, regarding budget control, changes in the political environment, entailing a stronger focus on the effectiveness of EU spending, have provided fresh momentum. Changing preferences and strategies mark the new politics of the EU budget.

Among the budgetary actors, the two intergovernmental institutions, the Council and the European Council, can be considered the most constant. Traditionally, the member states have been status quo-oriented in budget matters, in terms of both numbers and procedures, compared with the Commission and the EP (Lindner 2006). The member states' actual position has, however, been dependent on the power balance between net contributors and net recipients, as they bargained with each other for *juste retour*. This logic still shapes decision-making in the intergovernmental institutions; however, as Manuele Citi shows in his contribution, the *juste retour* rhetoric has not yet altered the redistributive function of the EU budget. Whenever a member state has requested a rebate or a correction mechanism, the effect on its net budgetary balance has been insignificant or has even produced an effect that is paradoxically contrary to the original intention. In accounting for this puzzle, Citi finds a "dissociation" between the two levels of the budgetary game: Domestic politics with its rhetoric about regaining control over fiscal resources and the complex supranational mechanism that leads to the adoption of the EU budget. The differences between national talk and supranational outcomes, he goes on to argue, can be considered a positive feature, as it grants the EU institutions some financial independence and allows the EU budget to make a difference in the less developed regions of Europe.

Lately, however, the net contributors have all but dominated the budget negotiations, leading to intergovernmental bargaining positions far from the Parliament. In doing so, the member states have also put the brakes on far-reaching reform initiatives. As Peter Becker argues in his contribution, meaningful reform of the MFF is arduous but not impossible. Criticism has accumulated over the years, not least from the member states themselves. During the latest negotiation cycle (for the MFF 2014-2020), however, the member states—or more specifically, the net contributors to the budget, organized in the Friends of Better Spending group—remained unimpressed by calls for reform and effectively limited the window of possible change.

While the member states' stance on the budget's size was adamant, they proved more open in terms of procedures, conceding a more flexible MFF, including a midterm review, and the establishment of a High Level Group on Own Resources (HLGOR) to the EP, which threatened to veto the multiannual planning process. Overall however, the sacrifices made were largely on the Parliament's side, and this also applies to annual budgets. The intergovernmental institutions have principally followed their traditional preference patterns and strategies, even though the institutional and political environments have changed.

By contrast, the EP (the second arm of the budget authority) has emerged as a more dynamic actor, as the contributions by Vitrey as well as Bauer and Becker point out. It has repeatedly called for budget reform and has used its veto power to achieve minor successes, as mentioned above. These developments thus fit the Parliament's traditional preferences and strategies. Other than that, however, its internal politics have resulted in less stable positions. The quest for an ever-larger budget is increasingly contested in the EP, and even if a majority favors the traditional line, the growth of internal disputes weakens the Parliament's bargaining position. While its assertiveness in procedural matters is often interpreted as evidence for influence, the EP has, at least temporarily, retreated from battles on the budget's size.

The changing preferences of the EP relate to the loss of its paradoxical status. While it is the only directly elected institution at the EU level, representatives used to enjoy considerable autonomy as they faced little pressure in the "second-order national elections" that EP elections long represented (first, Reif/Schmitt 1980). The Parliament is acutely aware of the critical sentiments in the broader political environment; it is under stronger pressure from national governments, which increasingly use their party channels to discipline members. As Parliament's rise to power has been facilitated by normative arguments (Rittberger 2003), parliamentarians are intent on not fueling criticism that the EU and its elites are remote or dysfunctional. By being overly confrontational on budgetary matters and thus risking deadlock, the EP could lose political capital.

Its increasing focus on better (instead of just more) spending is in line with this challenge. Some of its efforts, institutionally underpinned by the establishment of a Directorate for Impact Assessment and European Added Value in 2012, arguably have a double purpose. They are, true to the Parliament's traditional preferences, aimed at providing justification for additional spending, such as in the case of the "cost of non-Europe" reports. But the EP is also adjusting to the scenario that in the years to come, the EU budget will remain at the same level of spending, or even shrink. Flexibility, evaluation, and control are thus likely to remain on the top of the Parliament's budgetary agenda for the years to come.

This also reflects the recommendations made by Uwe Wagschal and Georg Wenzelburger. Their contribution elicits determinants of successful budget consolidation at national level. While the EU budget cannot be in deficit, consolidating the revenue and the spending side can nevertheless be beneficial in that it expands the room for maneuver in budget politics. In this regard, Wagschal and Wenzelburger recommend several reforms: Improving economic forecasts, increasing budget reserves, using a 'golden hamster' rule, i.e., unexpected surpluses must be used to set other priorities, establishing independent fiscal institutions that can help to plan the budget and strict auditing systems. Increasing spending efficiency by benchmarking and controlling implementation are also essential.

The Commission takes center stage in the latter phase of the budget process. After all, it is the central manager of the budget. According to Article 317 TFEU, it shall fulfill this role "in cooperation with the Member States," but "on its own responsibility," and with "regard to the principles of sound financial management." As Gabriele Cipriani shows in his contribution, the current accountability framework for the EU budget still exhibits several flaws and gaps, despite long-standing criticism and some efforts at financial management reform. He argues that the Commission, partly to protect itself from political difficulties, *de facto* reduces its responsibility for budget implementation. But the input-orientation and the focus on compliance in the control of the EU budget go beyond the Commission; they are systemic. A shift towards more results-oriented control is difficult in a "shared management" system with national authorities.

Cipriani argues that the Commission should not control everything, but rather certify a system of delegations that also focus on results. As a result, the Commission would be in a position to responsibly respond to the actual use of funds and the results, and the discharge procedure would be more meaningful.

This new focus on implementation would intensify the Commission's shift from policy entrepreneur to manager (Laffan 1997; Becker et al. 2016), which also applies to the budget. Throughout most of the history of European integration, the Commission could be expected to present budget drafts that (usually close to the EP's position) favored more spending (Pollack 2008). After 2007, however, it has become more restrained. As Becker shows in his contribution, the Commission's MFF proposal, which called for a slight spending increase, was criticized by the net recipient member states and the Parliament for failing to address the economic and social impacts of the crisis (i.e., it was deemed too modest in terms of spending). Rather than following a supranational agenda in an entrepreneurial fashion, the Commission is increasingly perceived as merely moderating the budget negotiations, as Bauer and Becker argue in their contribution. This affects the budget processes to a considerable extent, and it disadvantages the EP, long considered the Commission's natural ally in the pursuit of supranational solutions. The Commission's newfound restraint in ordinary matters of the budget should, however, not obfuscate its endeavors in new areas, such as in the establishment of the European Fund for Strategic Investments (EFSI) in 2015. It could very well be that the Commission, having realized how little room there is for maneuver in the MFF and annual budget negotiations, will increasingly resort to other options to further allocation and redistribution in the EU.

Novel outcomes

The EFSI is a key outcome of the new politics of the EU budget. In fact, the scheme to provide guarantees to mobilize investment among other public and private investors has already been used in the Project Bond Initiative, launched in 2012. In that case, the reallocation from the EU budget was rather modest (230 million euro). The EFSI was realized with an eight billion euro reallocation from the budget—after Commission President Juncker's initial idea to transfer unused funds from the European Stability Mechanism was turned down by the member states. Although the reallocation of five billion euro from existing EU funding programs was controversial in the EP (the other three billion euro came from the margins of the EU budget), it eventually conceded. Although Commission President Juncker boasted the agreement was evidence of his assertiveness, much remains unknown. The effectiveness of the fund remains to be seen. It is already clear that the accountability structure is problematic, in that the Commission again avoids taking political responsibility, as Cipriani argues in his contribution. Since the fund is formally established within the European Investment Bank (EIB), the Commission claims that it has no control over the investment decisions, although it has majority representation on the steering board and, as a member of the board of directors, is consulted before EIB approval of each financing and investment operation. Even this novel instrument thus comes with old problems.

Meanwhile, the old, if reformed, budgetary procedures have produced a novel outcome in the form of abnormal payment backlogs. The asymmetry between payment demands and authorized appropriations peaked at the end of 2014. As Alessandro D'Alfonso and Magdalena Sapała indicate in their contribution, these backlogs are not merely a technical problem, but also a symptom of diverging views in the budget authority on the amount of resources that the union needs to achieve its policy objectives. While the Parliament has repeatedly called for higher payment appropriations, the Council has cut the Commission's proposals. When amending budgets to address shortfalls in payments have been discussed, the Council has often called for proceeding first with redeployments of payment appropriations from other budget lines, even if all potential redeployments have already been explored and exhausted. The implications of the payment crisis, D'Alfonso and Sapała argue, are visible in most of the spending areas, and directly affect the beneficiaries on the ground—thus the achievement of the EU's goals. Moreover, with interest paid on delays, in addition to the abstract cost of lower credibility among stakeholders and citizens, they also represent a measurable material cost for the EU.

It must be reiterated that the establishment of the EFSI and the emergence of abnormal payment backlogs took place in a context of decreasing spending. The expenditure forecasted in the MFF 2014-2020 was, for the first time, lower than in the previous agreement—about 3.5 percent in real terms. At the same time, spending became more flexible. At the behest of the EP, the MFF now allows for adaptability between headings and budget years, and there is a revision clause that stipulates a comprehensive midterm review and potential adjustment. The dynamics that lead to these outcomes can all be partly traced back to the intergovernmental dominance in the new politics of the EU budget. The governments' position on payment appropriations facilitated abnormal backlogs, while their stance on spending in general encouraged the Commission to expand innovative financing instruments and led the EP to emphasize budgetary flexibility in an attempt to do more with less.

The stable equilibrium that governed the EU budget for well over a decade before the Lisbon Treaty and the financial and economic crisis has thus been replaced by the volatility and change of the new politics of the EU budget. As a result, budget politics have become more challenged, more flexible, and more fragmented. This poses challenges for scholars and practitioners alike.

Outlook: The challenges ahead

The issues raised in this volume suggest that the budget should have a prominent place in EU studies. Allocation and redistribution are indeed at the heart of politics, as Wildavsky once argued. Even at the EU level, where regulation is widely considered to be the most important, is no exception. Here, budget issues have often related to major questions of the integration project, and the challenged, flexible, and fragmented nature of the new budget politics reflects the EU's overall trajectory. Scholars are thus well-advised to pay attention to the developing dynamics in the budgetary field. Beyond the specific issues raised in this volume, there are general trends to be acknowledged. When outlining a new research agenda for budget politics, Rubin (2014) urges scholars to recognize and reexamine key assumptions. Three of these can be adapted to the EU context, providing empirical research avenues, theoretical suggestions, and methodological advice.

The first relates to the effects of fiscal stress in multilevel systems—an issue of utmost importance as the EU is, in parts, still struggling with the aftermath of the global financial and economic crisis. The respective research questions relate to the mechanisms established between the different levels to prevent and deal with budget problems. Although the EU member states still have budgetary sovereignty, economic integration has created complex interdependences, and recent disruptions have caused further integration in budgetary matters. Despite the "no bailout" clause, several lending facilities with enormous resources have been established. Furthermore, serious proposals for a eurozone budget, which could be used to remedy asymmetric shocks or facilitate domestic reform, have materialized (see, for instance, Núñez Ferrer et al. 2010, p. 144-156). Further budgetary fragmentation, along with differentiated integration, is conceivable. This entails not only analytical questions, but also normative concerns regarding effectiveness and legitimacy. The design and politics of this emerging multilevel budgetary field are thus important objects of inquiry in EU studies.

The same is true for the informal processes of budgets politics, a second area Rubin highlights in her research agenda article. The importance of these processes in EU policy-making has already been well-established (Farrell/Héritier 2003). The contributions to this volume suggest that budget politics is no exception. Further research is needed to fully grasp how formal and informal processes interact in the making and the control of the budget. How does internal and interinstitutional bargaining beyond the formal script affect the course and outcome? This requires profound qualitative research with expert sources that may be difficult to access. However, with a dominance of formal analysis, EU budget research runs the risk of oversimplification, especially now that preferences and strategies have become more fluid.

This relates directly to the third of Rubin's (2014, p. 8) suggestions, that budget politics should have more of a conflict orientation, "How do various interests frame issues? How do battle lines form, with whom on each side, and with what impact on budgeting?" For EU studies, this advice calls for a more sophisticated understanding of institutional and interinstitutional decision-making. While the study of single issue areas has been well developed, political interdependence and the wider context of European integration should be acknowledged—more so as the near future offers a myriad of challenges for the EU in general, and its budgetary decision-makers in particular.

The EU is in turmoil. Apart from the persistence of the financial and economic crisis, EU institutions must grapple with the Brexit fallout, the refugee crisis, instabilities in neighboring countries, its general relations with Russia, its commercial relations with the United States, and the reduction of emissions to limit the climate change—to name but a few of the most pressing issues. At the same time, Eurosceptic or outright nationalist movements and parties are on the rise in many countries, while EU decision-makers have difficulties outlining a new vision for European integration.

The budget may not be at the core of these problems, but it could be a part of the solution. In this regard, three areas deserve special attention by practitioners (see also the final contribution to this volume by Alfredo De Feo). First, meaningful reform of the revenue system could help to develop new strategies and policies, and thereby demonstrate to citizens what Europe is able to accomplish. Second, a more effective use of EU funds (i.e., with a stronger focus on results) could prove beneficial, increasing the added value of financial redistribution. Third, enhancing the monitoring and scrutiny of EU policies could remedy deficits of accountability, which is one of most important criticisms leveled against the EU. In all three areas, reform options abound, but their political feasibility is in question.

The politics of the budget, with both old challenges and new dynamics, thus promises to remain an important part of EU integration. In a more volatile environment, actors will frequently adapt their preferences and strategies, and outcomes will be even more flexible and fragmented. This volume has raised a number of important issues that will keep both scholars and practitioners occupied for the years to come.

References

Allen, D. 2010. The Structural Funds and Cohesion Policy. Extending the Bargain to Meet New Challenges. In *Policy-Making in the European Union*, Eds. Wallace, H., Pollack, M.A., and Young, A. R., 229-252. Oxford: Oxford UP.

Ackrill, R., and Kay, A. 2006. Historical-institutionalist perspectives on the development of the EU budget system. *Journal of European Public Policy* 13(1): 113-133.

Aksoy, D. 2010. Who gets what, when, and how revisited: Voting and proposal powers in the allocation of the EU budget. *European Union Politics* 11(2): 171-194.

Batory, A., and Lindstrom, N. 2011. The Power of the Purse: Supranational Entrepreneurship, Financial Incentives, and European Higher Education Policy. *Governance* 24(2): 311-329.

Bauer, M. W. 2008. Diffuse anxieties, deprived entrepreneurs: Commission reform and middle management. *Journal of European Public Policy* 15(5): 691-707.

Bauer, M. W. 2001. *A creeping transformation? The European Commission and the management of EU structural funds in Germany*. Dordrecht: Kluwer Academic Publishers.

Bauer, M.W., and Becker, S. 2017. Assessing the European Parliament's Power of the Purse: Rights, Capabilities, and Strategies. In *The New Politics of the European Union Budget*, Eds. Becker, S., Bauer, M.W., and De Feo A., 173-194. Baden-Baden: Nomos Verlag.

Becker, P. 2017. Reforming the European Multiannual Financial Framework – Looking for a Policy Window in a Path-dependent Environment. In *The New Politics of the European Union Budget*, Eds. Becker, S., Bauer, M.W., and De Feo A., 103-132. Baden-Baden: Nomos Verlag.

Becker, S., Bauer, M. W., Connolly, S, and Kassim, H. 2016. The Commission: Boxed in and constrained, but still an engine of integration. *West European Politics* 39(5): 1011-1031.

Begg, I. 2009. *Fiscal Federalism, Subsidiarity and the EU Budget Review*. Swedish Institute for European Policy Studies, Report No. 1, April 2009.

Begg, I., and Grimwade, N. 1998. *Paying for Europe*. Sheffield: Sheffield Academic Press.

Benedetto, G. 2013. The EU budget after Lisbon: rigidity and reduced spending? *Journal of Public Policy* 33(3): 345-369.

Benedetto, G., and Høyland, B. 2007. The EU Annual Budgetary Procedure: The Existing Rules and Proposed Reforms of the Convention and Intergovernmental Conference 2002-04. *Journal of Common Market Studies* 45(3): 565-587.

Benedetto, G. and Milio, S. (Eds). *European Union Budget Reform. Institutions, Policy and Economic Crisis*. London: Palgrave Macmillan.

Corbett, R., Jacobs, F., and Shackleton, M. 2011. *The European Parliament*. London: John Harper.

Cipriani, G. 2014. *Financing the EU. Moving Forwards or Backwards?* Brussels: Centre for European Policy Studies.

Cipriani, G. 2017. The EU Budget, the Accountability Gap and a Possible Way forward. In *The New Politics of the European Union Budget*, Eds. Becker, S., Bauer, M.W., and De Feo A., 225-256. Baden-Baden: Nomos Verlag.

Citi, M. 2013. EU budgetary dynamics: incremental or punctuated equilibrium? *Journal of European Public Policy* 20(8): 1157-1173.

Citi, M. 2015. European Union budget politics: Explaining stability and change in spending allocations. *European Union Politics* 16(2): 260-280.

Citi, M. 2017. EU Budgetary Politics and the Paradox of *Juste retour*. In *The New Politics of the European Union Budget*, Eds. Becker, S., Bauer, M.W., and De Feo A., 83-102. Baden-Baden: Nomos Verlag.

Crombez, C., and Høyland, B. 2015. The budgetary procedure in the European Union and the implications of the Treaty of Lisbon European Union Politics. *European Union Politics* 16(1): 67-89.

D'Alfonso, A., and Sapała, M. 2017. Abnormal Payments Backlog as a New Problem in the Implementation of the EU Budget. In *The New Politics of the European Union Budget*, Eds. Becker, S., Bauer, M.W., and De Feo A., 195-224. Baden-Baden: Nomos Verlag.

De Feo, A. 2017a. The European Budget: Motor or Brake of the European Integration? A Walk through 40 Years of Budgetary Decisions. In *The New Politics of the European Union Budget*, Eds. Becker, S., Bauer, M.W., and De Feo A., 33-82. Baden-Baden: Nomos Verlag.

De Feo, A. 2017b. EU Budget Politics: Looking Forward. In *The New Politics of the European Union Budget*, Eds. Becker, S., Bauer, M.W., and De Feo A., 281-294. Baden-Baden: Nomos Verlag.

Farrell, H., and Héritier, A. 2003. Formal and Informal Institutions under Codecision: Continuous Constitution-Building in Europe. *Governance* 16(4): 577-600.

Fenno, R. F. 1966. *The power of the purse: Appropriations politics in Congress*. Boston: Little, Brown and Co.

Giuriato, L. 2009. Reforming the EU Budgetary Procedure: Is Codecision a Step Forward? *CESifo Economic Studies* 55(1): 57-93.

Hix, S., and Høyland, B. 2011. *The Political System of the European Union*. London: Palgrave Macmillan.

Hooghe, L., and Marks, G. 2008. A Postfunctionalist Theory of European Integration: From Permissive Consensus to Constraining Dissensus. *British Journal of Political Science* 39 (1): 1-23.

Hooghe, L., and Keating, M. 1994. The Politics of European Union Regional Policy. *Journal of European Public Policy* 1(3): 367-393.

Kassim, H. 2008. "Mission Impossible", But Mission Accomplished: The Kinnock Reforms and the European Commission. *Journal of European Public Policy* 15(5): 648-668.

Laffan, B. 1997. From policy entrepreneur to policy manager: the challenge facing the European Commission. *Journal of European Public Policy* 4(3): 422-438.

Lasswell, H. D. 1936. *Politics: Who Gets What, When, How*. New York: Whittlesey House.

Levy, R. P., Barzelay, M., and Porras-Gomez, A. 2011. The reform of financial management in the European Commission: a public management policy cycle case study. *Public Administration* 89(1): 1546-1567.

Lindner, J. 2006. *Conflict and Change in EU Budgetary Politics.* New York: Routledge.

Majone, G. 1994. The Rise of the Regulatory State in Europe. *West European Politics* 17(3): 77-101.

Núñez Ferrer, J., Le Cacheux, J., Benedetto, G., and Saunier, M. with Candau, F., Emonnot, C., Lachet-Touya, F., Mortensen, J. Aymeric Potteau, A., and Taranic, I. 2016. *Study on the Potential and Limitation of Reforming the EU Budget*. Expertise commissioned by the European Commission on behalf of the High Level Group on Own Resources.

Núñez Ferrer, J., and Katarivas, M. 2014. What are the effects of the EU budget: Driving force or drop in the ocean? *Centre for European Policy Studies Special Report* No. 86/April 2014.

Pollack, Mark A. 2008. *Member-State Principals, Supranational Agents, and The EU Budgetary Process, 1970–2008*. http://dx.doi.org/10.2139/ssrn.1119108.

Reif, K., and Schmitt, H. 1980: Nine second-order national elections: A conceptual framework for the analysis of European election results. *European Journal of Political Research* 8(1): 3-44.

Rittberger, B. 2003. The Creation and Empowerment of the European Parliament. *Journal of Common Market Studies* 41(2): 203-225.

Rittberger, B. 2014. Integration without Representation? The European Parliament and the Reform of Economic Governance in the EU. *Journal of Common Market Studies* 52(5): 1174-1183.

Rubin, I. 2014. Past and Future Budget Classics: A Research Agenda. *Public Administration* Early View: Doi 10.1111/puar.12289.

Rubin, I. 1991. *The Politics of Public Budgeting. Getting and Spending, Borrowing and Balancing*. Chatham: Chatham House.

Rubio, E. 2011. The "added value" in EU budgetary debates: one concept, four meanings. *Notre Europe Policy Brief* 28, June 2011.

Selle, L. 2017. What Multi-level Parliamentary System? Parliamentary Discourses in EU Budgetary Negotiations (MFF 2014-2020). In *The New Politics of the European Union Budget*, Eds. Becker, S., Bauer, M.W., and De Feo A., 149-172. Baden-Baden: Nomos Verlag.

Strasser, D. 1975. La nouvelle procédure budgétaire des Communauté européenes et son application á l'établissement du budget pour l'exercise 1975. *Revue du marché commun* 182: 79-87.

Vitrey, A. 2017. The First Multiannual Financial Framework under the Lisbon Treaty: The Dynamics in the European Parliament from the Perspective of an Insider. In *The New Politics of the European Union Budget*, Eds. Becker, S., Bauer, M.W., and De Feo A., 133-148. Baden-Baden: Nomos Verlag.

Wagschal. U., and Wenzelburger, G. 2017. Budget Consolidation and National Budget Policy Instruments. In *The New Politics of the European Union Budget*, Eds. Becker, S., Bauer, M.W., and De Feo A., 259-280. Baden-Baden: Nomos Verlag.

Wildavsky, A. 1964. *The Politics of the Budgetary Process*. Boston: Little, Brown.

Wildavsky, A. 1988. *The New Politics of the Budgetary Process*. 1st ed. New York: Scott, Foresman & Co.

Wildavsky, Aaron B. (1992): *The New Politics of the Budgetary Process*. 2nd ed. New York, NY: Harper Collins Publishers.

The European Budget: Motor or Brake of European Integration? A Walk through 40 Years of Budgetary Decisions

Alfredo De Feo

Public policy and politics find their *raison d'être* in budgets. Budgets allow policies for public welfare and to acquire public goods to be developed. This rule also applies to the European project, but the European project is not only public spending. The regulatory policy of the European Union, legislative harmonization, the creation of a single market, and the European presence on the world scene have a high impact even if not linked directly to financial support. Discussions on the role of the European budget, its financing and the institutional balance have been as important as discussions about its size and the expenditure mechanisms (see, among others, Laffan 1997; Benedetto/Milio 2012; Lindner 2006).

This chapter aims to read the institutional development of the European project from the perspective of the budget. The budget is understood here as the dynamic part of the policy, but also inter-institutional relations, as part of the power game to influence political choices. In particular, the link between budget politics and institutional development will be highlighted over the whole period. Three phases can be identified:

1975-1987:	the institutions in search of supremacy;
1988-2008:	the inter-institutional cooperation drive for institutional progress;
2009 on:	a new balance of power: Council leadership and the European Parliament's (EP) new role.

My "walk" through this period will be taken not through the eyes of a rigorous academic, but through those of a modest practitioner who has had the chance to meet and discuss with some of the actors during this period and to directly follow some of the developments.

Narrating the European budget over time should not be an aim in itself but also the key to understanding if there is still space for a European budgetary policy capable of bringing public goods, added value, efficiency and effectiveness to European construction: a European budgetary policy which can be better understood by citizens.

These reflections will take into account the current political situation in which the European project is put into question by a growing part of public opinion. European construction is no longer in an ivory tower, protected from criticism. Ironically, attempts to disaggregate the European project are developing when the challenges facing our countries have a transnational dimension that has probably never been reached in the last 50 years. The answers to problems such as economic stability, security, management of migration flows, energy, environment and climate changes cannot be given efficiently by individual Member States but by a united Europe.

This chapter does not pretend to give answers to these problems but to stimulate reflection based on our history by analysing possible developments of the budget as the motor of the European project.

To conclude, this introductory chapter presents an overview of the evolution of budgetary powers from the entry into force of the 1975 Treaty until now. The research questions which will be addressed are:

a) How have EU budget politics contributed to the European integration process and to the institutional balance?
b) What have been the drivers influencing the evolution of budgetary procedures?
c) After the Lisbon Treaty, how can the EU budget contribute to European integration?

The chapter will be divided in two parts; the first will outline the history of the European budget from the entry into force of the 1975 Treaty until 2009, from the shaping of procedures to the conflicts of power between the institutions and the development of soft law. The second part of the chapter will analyse the current situation since the entry into force of the Lisbon Treaty and will draw lessons from the past and outline some scenarios for the evolution of EU finance in terms of resources and of expenditures and its contribution to the numerous challenges facing the European project. The chapter will be mostly based on official documents and factual experience, supported by interviews and references to academic literature.

A last introductory consideration: why 40 years? The project for this edited volume started in October 2015 with a workshop held in Strasbourg on EU budget politics – experiences, dynamics, reform options. The volume is being compiled in 2016 and it will possibly be on the market for the following years. The period 1975-1979 was particularly important in shaping the future of the European project. There was the finalization of the budgetary reform with the 1975 Treaty, with a recognition of a role for the EP, its entry into force during 1977 in parallel with the preparation for direct elections and finally the first direct election in 1979. The 40-year anniversary is therefore not referred to a specific year but to the period 1975-1979, which represented a milestone in the construction of the European Union.

The European budget in search of democracy

The Coal and Steel Community (ECSC)

The ECSC created a very original model inspired by the principles of a federation with a fiscal capacity, the ability to borrow and lend, and a budgetary decision-making process concentrated in a supranational body, the High Authority, with a limited role of the Council and a mere ex-post control by the Assembly.

The ECSC benefitted from very special circumstances: the necessity not only to re-launch the steel and coal industry but also to maintain control over German production; the existence of a European tax, the levy, imposed on production; the redistribution of its revenue to the same sector; financing for the modernisation of the industry and improvement of the social conditions of the workers. The ideal world constructed around the ECSC did not last long, and, after the defeat of the European Defence Community due to the non-ratification of the Treaty by the French National Assembly in 1954, Jean Monnet, President of the High Authority, understood that a fear of supranational infrastructure was spreading among Member States. He therefore started to involve, although informally, the Member States, seeking the agreement of the Council ahead of major decisions. The informal opening to the Council led to a change in the relations between the High Authority and the Assembly. The Assembly became more present in the decision-making process and influential, with consultation ex-ante on major decisions (De Feo 2015). The Assembly was composed of Members appointed by their national parliaments. Generally, they were senior members with much parliamentary experience and they raised the necessity of rendering the European process more democratic. In spite of this, the Assembly's position did not influence the negotiations on the European Community (EC) Treaty.

The EC Treaty

The Treaty establishing the EC was signed in March 1957. The Member States regained a central position with respect to the ECSC Treaty. Some competences were transferred to the EC, but with no effective democratic control at the European level. Nevertheless, an entire chapter of the Treaty was dedicated to financial provisions, with the appearance of a role for the Assembly, which would be consulted on the draft budget adopted by the Council and which could propose modifications which would be submitted to the Council before the final vote.

In the early 60s the issue of real democratic control was on the table, together with the need to expand resources to finance new policies, in particular the common agricultural policy (CAP), while reinforcing the Parliament's role in budgetary matters (De Feo 2016).

The Assembly had the support not only of the national parliaments, which had lost control of a number of competences to the European Communities, but also of some national governments. The close relations between the Assembly and the national parliaments were facilitated by the members' double mandate: the members appointed to the Assembly had long parliamentary experience and helped to shape the Assembly along the same lines as their national parliaments. These Members then used their influence back home in their national parliaments to support a strengthening of the powers of the Assembly, pushing their respective governments to defend a reinforcement of the competences of the European Assembly.

In March 1962, the Assembly decided autonomously to call itself the European Parliament, anticipating the change of name which was formalised only in 1987 by the Single European Act (SEA; Art. 6).[1] Talks on strengthening the powers of the Assembly had already begun during the preparatory work for the Treaty of Rome, but they had failed. The matter was taken up again during discussions on the merging of the executives under the Merger Treaty. Even then, the Treaty was adopted with no reference made to strengthening the powers of the EP. On the contrary, as all the budgetary procedure was modelled on the EC Treaty the Assembly lost its influence on administrative expenditure. Under the ECSC Treaty the administrative expenditure of all the institutions had been established by the Committee of four Presidents.[2] This Committee acted as the budgetary authority for administrative expenditure. Its decisions constituted authorisation of expenditure. To change the allocation of authorised appropriations, the institution concerned had to make a request for a transfer to the Committee of Presidents. This gave the President of the Assembly quite an important negotiating role, which was suppressed by the merger Treaty of 1965.

The Treaty of April 1970

After the "empty chair" crisis, a favourable wind of reform started to blow in 1965, following the mandate given by the Council on 15 December 1964. The Hague Declaration (European Summit, 1-2 December 1969) produced a spectacular acceleration of events, which led to the new Treaty.

The Commission updated its 1962 proposals.[3] The new proposal was quite ambitious and foresaw the reinforcement of the EP's competences in a two-step approach linked to the replacement of national contributions with own resources from the EC fiscal mechanism:

- First phase: the Council maintained supremacy, as the resources remained covered by the Member States;
- Second phase: Parliament had more competences and the final say on the budget once the EC's financing was totally covered by own resources.

At the Council meeting of 22 December 1969, all the delegations except France substantially supported the Commission proposal. The French delegation deployed all its efforts and diplomacy between 22 December and 19 January to introduce the concepts of compulsory (CE) and non-compulsory expenditure (NCE) into the discussion. The French Delegation, led by Maurice Schumann, Foreign Affairs Minister and Valery Giscard d'Estaing, Finance Minister, convinced the reluctant delegations and on 6-7 March 1970 a final agreement was reached in the Council, with final adoption on 22 April.

The Treaty of 1970 recognized a role to the EP in the annual procedure, giving a right of amendment only for part of the expenditure (NCE) and introducing a mechanism to limit the Assembly's margin for manoeuvre, as proposed by the French government. With this mechanism, Parliament could not intervene in the financing of decisions taken by the Council in enforcement of the Treaties, in particular to secure agricultural policy.

The Treaty itself provided a definition of CE as "expenditure necessarily resulting from this Treaty or from acts adopted in accordance therewith." This definition was rather obscure and gave rise to numerous conflicts of interpretation in the following years.

In the 1970s, CE represented about 97 percent of expenditure and NCE three percent, including staff salaries and rent, which limited the political room for manoeuvre of the Assembly.

The second limitation introduced by the Treaty aimed to prevent EP from increasing the budget. The mechanism (the maximum rate of increase of non-compulsory expenditure – MRI-NCE) allowed Parliament to increase NCE only by a limited percentage, beyond which the Council's consent was necessary. The MRI of NCE was to be fixed annually by the Commission.[4]

The Treaty of July 1975

In June 1973 the Commission presented a proposal to further strengthen the budgetary powers of the EP (Commission of the European Communities 1973). The proposal was articulated around the following three elements:

- Budget revenue: the EC should have the capacity to autonomously create (Community method) new resources, with a global ratification by the national parliaments, and not on a case by case basis. The final approval should be by the EP. A procedure to raise loans was also proposed.
- Budgetary procedure: the proposal foresaw an inversed majority of the Council for modifications by the EP, introducing the distinction between a) expenditure compensated by a reduction, which could be rejected by the Council with a qualified majority; b) expenditure increases without compensation, which could be approved by the Council with a qualified majority. The proposal also introduced the possibility of establishing during the budgetary procedure a new *maximum rate of increase of non–compulsory expenditure* with the agreement of the two arms of the budgetary authority. The Commission proposed that all new expenditure should be classified as non-compulsory.

- Budgetary Control: the proposal created a Court of Auditors as an external auditor of EU finances with the obligation to present an annual report. The Commission also proposed to transfer the discharge competence to the EP.

The EP did not hide its ambitions, proposing innovative solutions, which, in some cases, were followed years later.[5] Concerning own resources, the Parliament required the final word after unanimous agreement by the Council, an elegant way to establish a sort of co-decision while leaving intact Member State prerogatives. Concerning the approval of expenditure, Parliament proposed the suppression of the distinction between CE and NCE and in the case of disagreement between the two arms of the budgetary authority proposed calling a "coordination committee". The conclusions of this committee would be submitted to the two arms of the budgetary authority, which would be empowered to adopt them by qualified majority. In the case of non-agreement, the EP's decisions could only be modified by the Council acting unanimously. The EP's proposals for the budgetary procedure only found full implementation forty years later in the Lisbon Treaty. Concerning the creation of the Court of Auditors, Parliament asked to approve the appointment of the Members, and to create a rotation system for the appointments to give continuity to the work of the Court and to guarantee its independence, establishing the Court as an independent institution.

After several informal contacts with EP delegations, the Council took into account some of the EP requests. Finally, the Treaty adopted in July 1975 modified the financial provisions, which remained in force until the Treaty of Lisbon (2009).

No change was introduced on the revenue side. The main changes can be summarized as follows:

- A qualified majority in the Council to reject modifications proposed by the EP with no increase in expenditure (i.e. compensated by reductions);
- A qualified majority in the Council to adopt modifications proposed by the EP with an increase in expenditure;
- The EP has the last word on NCE, within the limits of the Treaty;
- Co-decision to establish a new MRI in NCE;
- EP President declares and signs the adoption of the annual budget;

- The EP can reject the budget. Parliament considered this power already implicit in the 1970 Treaty but the Council opposed this interpretation. The new Treaty makes the principle clear;
- Parliament is consulted before the appointment of the members of the Court of Auditors;
- The members of the Court of Auditors are appointed with a rotating system;
- The EP is entrusted with the sole authority for discharge.

The period was particularly intense in the building up of the *sui generis* financial system. Far from the autonomy conceded to the ECSC, the EC Treaty followed the step by step method inspired by Jean Monet: the growing competences and financial needs of the EC favoured reform of the decision-making process, allowing a more direct involvement of the EP.

The adoption of the 1975 Treaty marked the beginning of a new period with new responsibilities, competences and powers of the EP. The budgetary competences were nevertheless the second-best option. As indicated in the conclusions of the Vedel group,[6] the strengthening of the European Parliament was the result of a legislative decision, as in most parliamentary democracies (Commission of the European Communities 1972). It should not therefore be a surprise that on many occasions the EP has used its budgetary competences to gain influence over the political and legislative domain, in some cases even pushing the interpretation of its budgetary powers to the extreme. Concrete examples of this parliamentary attitude will be examined in the following paragraphs.

Budgetary policy and politics in the 80s: Institutions in search of supremacy

The 70s saw most of the political and institutional debates concentrated on the modification of the Treaties for a new inter-institutional balance in the budgetary domain. The procedures for adopting the annual budget remained instrumental in carrying out the policies that the Member States, Council and Commission wanted to develop.

The presence of an elected EP introduced a change of culture in the attitude of the Council, Commission and Member States, even if its influence on the substance of budgetary policy remained marginal. The security net created by the Members States in the Treaties – distinction between CE and NCE, a MRI – made it difficult for the EP to translate its priorities into substantial budgetary amendments. In spite of this, the Parliament's political influence grew more each year.

In the first years of the EC, expenditure was concentrated on the building up of an independent administration, and later in the 60s on the common agricultural policy. From the mid-70s, the budget started to finance the development of new policies to enhance the European integration process.

This chapter will go through the evolution of the European budget with this double perspective: the budgetary policy to support the development of common policies; and the budgetary politics of the institutions, the inter-institutional relationships and influences, elements which cannot always be separated.

The budget and the Common Agricultural Policy (CAP)

The CAP was the first integrated policy created by the Treaty. The Member States transferred all the competences to the European communities. The federalists considered this transfer of competences a supplementary step in the integration process after the integration of the coal and steel industry. In the 60s agriculture was a key strategic sector, not only because of the number of employees in the sector but especially for the well-being of countries in a period when international trade and tariffs added uncertainty to food security.

The CAP was developed with a protective shield towards imports and with the guarantee of high prices within the EC. This policy encouraged farmers to produce with an eye more to subsidies than to the market or food security. European consumers paid twice, indirectly to finance the subventions and directly paying a high price for agricultural products. It was equally difficult for farmers in third countries, in particular in developing countries, who found it difficult to accede to the European market due to levies.

Highly subsidised and protected agriculture was not only a characteristic of the European communities. In the 60s and 70s, most industrialized countries (e.g. the US, Norway, Switzerland, to name a few) had comparable, or even higher, subsidies for their agriculture. The main objective for these countries was to ensure food security for their citizens and maintain agricultural production in their countries. It was only later that public funding of agriculture had a more environmental objective and was more market-oriented.

Expenditure on agriculture not only exploded but went out of control due to the automatic mechanisms. The only solution would have been a reform of the principles of the CAP to reduce its cost and open it to the market. The need for a reform already appeared less than 10 years after the beginning of the CAP.

The Mansholt (attempted) reform

History proves that once a policy has been created it is very difficult to dismantle it or even reform it. Sicco Mansholt, European Commissioner for agriculture, faced such a difficulty. After presenting the "success of the CAP" in two paragraphs, the Memorandum of Agriculture reform (1968) demonstrates in the next 80 pages the disastrous consequences, for European public finances and for agricultural production, in the case of non-reform (Secretariat General of the European Commission 1968).

A fierce reaction by the agriculture sector[7] and the French government blocked the reform process. As a result, only three directives, which did not change the course of the CAP, were adopted in 1972, concerning the modernisation of agricultural holdings, the abandonment of farming and the training of farmers (Division for Agricultural Information 1972).

The problems of the CAP were not solved and its budgetary cost continued to grow. Moreover, the CAP produced important distortions in the agricultural markets.[8] Between 1975 and 1982 the cost of agriculture increased at an average rate of 15.5 percent per year and accounted for about 65 percent of the whole budget (Strasser 1984, p. 283). The situation was aggravated by monetary instability and the different exchange rates between Members States, artificially attenuated by monetary compensatory accounts (MCA). Agriculture expenditure was considered a sort of free cash machine: much of the production was only to obtain EU subsidies.

The impact of monetary instability[9]

The burden of the CAP on the budget was not only due to the market organisation, export refunds and stocks, but also MCAs. When the French franc was devalued in 1968 (by eleven percent) the system of common prices collapsed. The situation was aggravated by a revaluation of the D-Mark a few months later. Following the monetary crisis of 1971, MCAs were created as a temporary measure. However, they were only abolished in 1993 with the creation of the single market (Council of the European Union 1971; European Commission 1988).

The creation of a "green rate" artificially maintained common prices in spite of the monetary differences, and to avoid countries with devalued currencies being able to benefit from a competitive advantage to export into countries with a stronger currency (i.e. Germany and the Netherlands) MCAs were introduced, creating a complex system of "levies and refunds" at the borders. This mechanism encouraged the so-called "carousel" of agricultural products travelling between borders to benefit from the payment of MCAs. This was a supplementary concern for the European budget. Table 2.1 below shows the impact of MCAs on the total cost of the CAP.

Table 2.1: Budgetary impact of MCAs on total cost of the CAP

Year	1968	1973	1975	1978	1980	1984
Total CAP	1,259	3,614	4,327	8,679	11,292	16,500
Of which MCA		147	336	880	298	368
MCA/CAP (%)		4.1%	7.8%	10.1%	2.6%	2.2%
Total Budget	1,487	4,505	5,817	12,041	15,857	25,361
Total Budget (%)	84.7%	80.2%	74.4%	72.1%	71.2%	65.1%

Sources: Commission documents and Strasser (1984)

The figures above show the net impact on the budget. In fact, there were both negative and positive MCAs and they were budgeted as an exception to the principle of universality of the budget. The "revenue" side of MCAs was entered in the expenditure part of the budget as a "negative" expenditure – a technique which was used in other circumstances too (e.g. penalties for dairy quotas).

The impact of the MacSharry reform

After the failure of the Mansholt proposal, the budgetary situation of the CAP worsened. The export refunds for dumping overproduction aggravated the situation, bringing the EC budget close to collapse. This was the main driver of the reform which started in the mid-80s and the Member States accepted a number of effective decisions (dairy quotas, budgetary stabilisers and maximum guaranteed quantity). More generally, a decision was taken to cap the yearly agriculture expenditure to three quarters of the

Gross Domestic Product (GDP) increase (agriculture guideline). The measures taken, and a favourable market situation, were effective in budgetary terms but did not change the approach of the CAP. Increases for other policies gradually reduced the value of agriculture in the overall budget.

Table 2.2: Evolution of agriculture expenditure 1968-1990

Year	Total CAP	Total Budget	% CAP/total Budget
1968	1,259	1,487	84.7%
1973	3,614	4,505	80.2%
1975	4,327	5,817	74.4%
1978	8,679	12,041	72.1%
1980	11,292	15,857	71.2%
1984	16,500	25,361	65.1%
1988	27,500	45,433	60.6%
1989	27,761	46,423	57.6%
1990	26,522	46,716	56.8%

Sources: Commission documents and Strasser (1984)

Table 2.2 and Figure 2.1 above show that the trend in the market related to agricultural expenditure increased more slowly, with a stabilization which started with the first financial perspectives of 1988. The MacSharry reform achieved its main objective of stabilising agricultural expenditure.

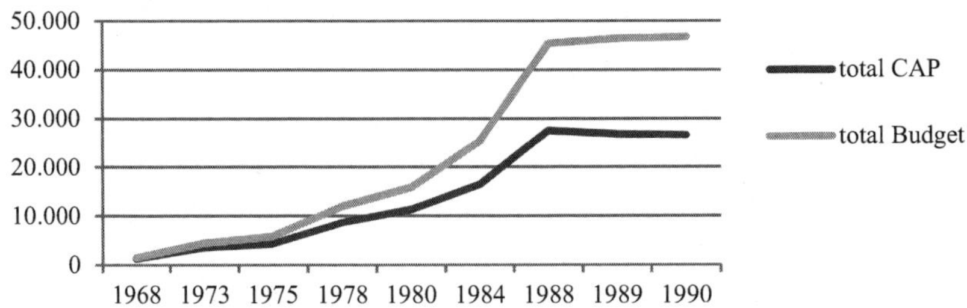

Figure 2.1: Evolution of agriculture expenditure 1968-1990

Source: Data from EC, Financial Report 2008.

The development of new policies

The European project could not survive with only the integration of agriculture, and other policies started to develop, even if with limited resources.

In 1958 the European Social Fund (ESF) started its activity of supporting professional training. In 1965 the budget started to contribute to the development of the agriculture structure. The Guidance sector of the European Agricultural Guidance and Guarantee Fund (EAGGF) opened in 1975 with the creation of the European Regional Development Fund (ERDF), which represented about four percent of the EC budget in 1975. At the end of the 70s the research, industry and energy policies appeared in the budget, but it was only in the mid-80s that they received more substantial resources.

Following the positive results of the ECSC, already from 1961 the European Investment Bank (EIB) invested about 70 percent of its resources in support of regional development. In 1978, a new community instrument was created (New Community Instrument for Borrowing and Lending, NIC) to allow lending and borrowing by the Community to increase economic convergence with the guarantee of the EC budget (European Council 1977).

The EP played an important role in proposing and supporting the development of the new policies, and the new budgetary procedure opened the way for the influence of the Parliament. The EP's margin for manoeuvre was limited and quasi symbolic but it was wisely used to support the development of new policies. Although the EP's decisions were timid and modest until 1978, already with the 1979 budget on the eve of the direct elections it started to use the budgetary procedure to force decisions by the Council. The Council rapidly realized that the Parliament could no longer be treated as a simple "procedural step" to be taken but that it had become an institution with concrete influence, even though with limited power. The Council realized that a qualified majority was necessary to reject a Parliamentary amendment and sometimes this majority could not be reached (as in the case of the doubling of regional funds in 1978).

At the Paris Summit of 19-21 October 1972, the European Council gave a decisive impetus for the development of new policies to complement the CAP. An important role in this decision was played by the new Member States, in particular the UK (European Council 1972).

During this decade, the Regional Fund started to develop and take shape, as did the Social Fund and that for energy and industry. Figure 2.2

below gives an overview of the budgets implemented (payment allocations) during this period for policies other than agriculture.

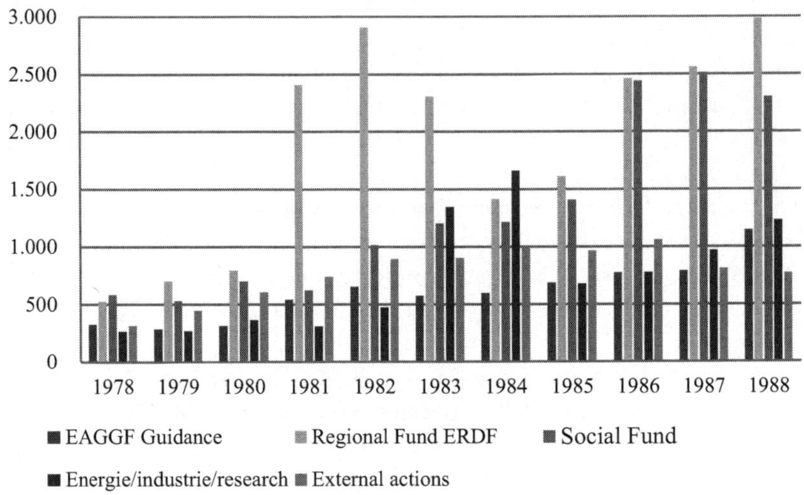

Figure 2.2: Budget implementation for policies other than agriculture 1978-1988

Source: data from EC, Financial Report 2008

A season of conflicts

The decade 1978-1988 was characterised by a high level of conflicts and problems. During these years, the adoption of the budget became a nightmare, especially for the Commission, which had the responsibility to implement a budget with the provisional twelfths procedure. Looking back from a distance in time, this period was dynamic and rich and established the basis for a new vision of EU public finances which started in 1988.

The direct election of the Parliament, and the fact that the EP was deprived of legislative power, certainly played a role in these conflicts, but other elements favoured the situation: the ambiguity of the text of the Treaty, which was the result of a last-minute compromise, the will to develop new policies under pressure from the new Member States, which had the direct consequence of a lack of resources, and last but not least the problem of budgetary imbalances and requests for correction mechanisms.

Without attempting to be exhaustive, this chapter will try to explain the main reasons for the different types of conflict and present the solutions which were found in some cases after 1988. It will not be difficult to see that the problems mentioned below are part of the history of the EU institutions and will remain topics of budgetary debates for many years.

The conflicts between institutions

The first conflict between institutions was over agriculture. The Commission already understood in the late 60s that the CAP expenditure could go out of control and introduce a distortion of the markets, but the Council and the Member States, under the leadership of France, limited the impact of the various reforms. The situation gave rise to other conflicts internal to each government between Finance and Agriculture Ministers. It was only at the end of the 80s that the Finance Ministers strongly supported the introduction of a cap on agriculture expenditure: the "agriculture guideline". In spite of the fact that agriculture limited the development of other policies, the Assembly was relatively absent from this conflict due to the compulsory nature of the expenditure, and probably also because of pressure from the agriculture "lobby".

The fact that during this period four budgets (1980, 1985, 1986 and 1988) out of ten were not adopted in time is a concrete sign of the profound mistrust between the institutions. Even in the cases where the budget was adopted according to the Treaty calendar, tensions and conflicts existed between the two arms of the budgetary authority, the Council and the EP.

The Treaty definition of CE – "expenditure necessarily resulting from this Treaty or from acts adopted in accordance therewith" (Art. EC/272, par. 4) – was vague and ambiguous. The Council was convinced that the EP could easily be obliged to accept its definition of CE, but the definition influenced the results for the MRI in NCE, and then the EP's powers directly.

Behind these struggles there was also a difference between the EP and the Council on the role of the budget as a legal act. The Council considered that any budget line could only be implemented with a specific legal basis adopted by the Council. The EP considered, instead, that the budget was a legal basis sufficient to implement appropriations for an action entered into the budget. With this in mind, Parliament created a number of budget lines initiating new policies. At the same time, the Council systematically entered amounts in the legal acts with NCE, a practice contested by the EP. In theory, the issue was settled with the joint Declaration of

1982. The Council recognized that to preserve the budget procedure "the fixing of maximum amounts by regulation must be avoided, as must the entry in the budget of amounts in excess of what can actually be expended" (European Parliament et al. 1982, point IV, 3b), and Parliament recognized that a "legal basis, separate from the budget, is required for the utilization of appropriations for any significant action" (point IV, 3b).

After the declaration, The Council continued to enter the amounts into the legal act but with the mention *amounts deemed necessary,* and Parliament gave quite an extensive interpretation of "significant action". A definitive solution to this issue was then given by the European Court of Justice (ECJ, no expenditure without a legal act) and completed with the interinstitutional agreements (IIAs) of 1999 (see below), which determined the exceptions to the rules, later formalised in the Financial Regulation. This is an example of how during this period each institution tried to stake out its territory to affirm its own supremacy.

Budgetary conflicts: a few examples

The few examples below outline some of the recurrent reasons behind budgetary conflicts. The 1980 budgetary procedure had a particular relevance as it was the first after the first direct EP election in June 1979. The EP articulated its strategy around three pillars:[10]

- Modifications to reduce CE in the milk sector introducing a levy to limit milk expenditure – a similar measure was introduced years later;
- Increasing expenditure for the Regional Fund and energy policy within the MRI, as calculated by the EP;
- A request to include all the lending/borrowing information, together with the European Development Fund, in the same budget (principle of unity of the budget).

As the Council disregarded the EP's requests (resolution 7, November 1979), the EP rejected the budget in December.[11] Beyond the budgetary arguments, this decision only a few months after the direct election aimed to show the other Institutions, and also public opinion, that an elected Parliament was much stronger and wanted to be treated with more respect. The 1980 budget was operated, for the first time, under the provisional twelfths rule until its final adoption in July 1980. An amending letter was presented to the Preliminary Draft Budget (PDB) with a number of new elements in June 1980. The EP presented a limited number of amendments, which where all adopted by Council. The 1980 budget was finally adopted in July 1980.

In December 1981, the 1982 Budget was declared adopted by the President of the EP without the explicit agreement of the Council on the new MRI in NCE. The Council brought the case before the ECJ for annulment of the 1982 budget. A political agreement was reached in June 1982 with a Joint Declaration which laid down a list of expenditure as compulsory or non-compulsory and defined the respective powers of the two arms of the budgetary authority. The legal action in front of the Court was then withdrawn. This Joint Declaration inaugurated a new era in budgetary relations with soft law to resolve conflicts. But "soft law" could not be enforced by the ECJ, so not infrequently the institutions later had difficulties in respecting their own commitments. This Declaration was no exception, and some of the principles were disregarded in later procedures:

- The Commission was invited to make a proposal to the budgetary authority for the classification of new budget lines, but in the case of disagreement the Presidents of the three institutions "[*should*] *endeavour to resolve any disagreements before the draft budget is established*";
- The three Presidents also called for a solution to be found in the case of disagreement on the establishment of a new MRI;
- There was agreement that the EP would maintain its half rate of increase in NCE whatever the Council decided. A difference in the interpretation of this point appeared during the procedure for the adoption of the 1978 budget.

The Joint Declaration was not sufficient to conclude the 1982 budget with good cooperation and the EP rejected an amending letter to mark its disagreement with the arrangements then in force for correcting the budgetary imbalances of the United Kingdom (the UK rebate). The correction mechanism was then included in the 1983 budget.

The President of the Parliament refused to sign and declare adopted the 1987 budget, obliging the Council to come to a compromise. The budget was then adopted in February with a "creative" interpretation of the mathematical rule to calculate the MRI.

The first conflict, at the end of 1979, was more of a political nature. The newly elected EP found in the budgetary procedure the ideal ground on which to mark its presence. The second and third conflicts show that the

EP was now a full actor on the budgetary scene, and that the Council was not the only institution on board. The fact that the Council preferred to conclude a political agreement without waiting for the decision of the Court was another signal of a new inter-institutional balance. This was not the "*equal footing*" claimed by Members of Parliament but the EP had a powerful negotiating tool which allowed it to build up its influence not only on the budget but also in the legislative domain.

The ECJ and the budget

After the adoption of the 1986 budget, the Council brought an action before the ECJ to annul the budget as adopted by the EP on 12 December 1985 on the grounds that the EP had unilaterally exceeded the MRI. This was the first time that the Court ruled on a "budgetary case." Two other cases on budgetary matters went before the ECJ (1995 and 2011) and they will be related here.

The Court declared the 1986 budget void but refused to rule on substance, indicating that the two arms of the budgetary authority should find a solution in the frame of the inter-institutional cooperation defined in the Joint Agreement of 1982. The Court renounced its role of interpreting the Treaty and/or Financial Regulation and reinforced the negotiating capacity of the EP (ECJ Case 34/86).

The same approach was taken by the Court in Case 41/95. The MRI was only a secondary aspect of this case. The EP challenged the classification of a number of budget lines in the agriculture and fishery sector which, in its opinion, did not have any compulsory element. The Council on its side considered that all the expenditures where the EP had introduced amendments on the figures and on the remarks were compulsory. The EP, which had provoked the case, in fact wanted a decision by the Court on the definition of classification and on some of the legal acts related to the contested lines to ascertain whether they could be considered compulsory or not. For instance, the EP did not agree that credits set aside for the international fishery agreement, which was not yet concluded, could be compulsory. Ultimately, the EP wanted to expand its influence in that area and show how obsolete the distinction was.

At the end of December 1995 the Court decided to annul the 1995 budget act with no practical effects on its implementation. It did not come as a surprise that once again, as in Case 34/86, the Court gave the budgetary authority the responsibility to find a solution.

In case 34/86, the Court did not want to enter into a more technical discussion on the calculation of the MRI in NCE. In Case 41/95, the Court again left the responsibility to find a compromise to a political agreement between the two arms of the budgetary authority and refused to give a legal interpretation of the Treaty and of secondary legal acts. This approach was surprising, to say the least.

To complete this short overview of the conflicts between the EP and Council, in Case 77/11 the ECJ confirmed the role of the President of the EP in signing the EU budget at the end of the annual procedure. The case was brought by the Council, which contested that in the Lisbon Treaty the budget was the result of a co-decision and as such should be co-signed by the Council and EP. The Parliament defended the interpretation that the signature of its President was "founded on a power which is particular to the President of that Institution … It is an independent act which does not reflect a parliamentary majority and may be regarded as verification on the part of the President of the EP that the budgetary procedure complies with the FEU Treaty" (ECJ Case 77/11, 36). The Court accepted the EP's argument and rejected the appeal by the Council.

The correction mechanisms

Soon after the enlargement of the European communities, the structural imbalance of the UK contribution to the EC became a recurrent problem. At that time the Commission was correctly reluctant to openly give figures for net balances. In fact, the benefits of belonging to a community cannot be synthetized in a balance sheet (Richter 2008). The UK imbalance was particularly important as the budget was absorbed by the CAP, where the UK had no advantage. The first correction mechanism was already agreed in 1975 and confirmed in 1984 at the Fontainebleau summit and again in 1987 (European Council 1975, 1984). The correction mechanism was then extended to other net beneficiaries (i.e. Germany, Austria, the Netherlands and Sweden), which received a rebate on the financing of the UK rebate.

The correction mechanisms had some grounds in the past, but now they represent a source of distortion and complexity in the own resources system. In spite of the Commission's proposals, only a global reform system could overcome this problem. This problem will be discussed in more detail in the sections on own resources.

The contraction of resources

A number of combined factors created a serious reduction in resources in the second half of the 80s, which caused concern for the development of EC policies:

- A reduction in the revenue from the traditional own resources, levies and custom duties, due to the generalised tendency to liberalize the world market (trade rounds);
- A reduction in agricultural imports due to the self-sufficiency reached by the EC;
- The limit reached by the value added tax (VAT) contribution to the budget;
- The enlargements to Greece (1981) and to Spain and Portugal;
- The lack of control of agriculture expenditure;
- An increase in the needs of other policies.

The Council tried to face this situation by imposing budgetary discipline limiting the increase in agriculture expenditure (the agriculture guideline) and that in NCE. A decision to increase the proportion of VAT going to the budget from one percent to 1.4 percent entered into force in January 1986. Both measures proved to be ineffective and, as often happens in Europe, the deep crisis led to calls for wider reform – an opportunity which was not missed by the President of the Commission, Jacques Delors.

The period 1975-1987 was particularly intense and dynamic. The first enlargement of the EC not only increased the number of Member States but also inflated new ideas led to a different approach to integration. The direct election of the Parliament changed the balance of power between the institutions. Jacques Delors, at the helm of the Commission, did not limit himself to maintaining the course but in 1992 launched new objectives for the integration of the Single Market, which were approved by all the Member States in the SEA, the first profound revision of the Treaty of Rome (Ludlow 2014).

The institutions adapted to the changes in culture. Each institution tried to expand or maintain its position in terms of its powers and budgetary priorities in order to set the pace for the European integration process. The power of the purse was no more a sole prerogative of the Prince but a more complex exercise with other actors, like the EP, the Commission and also individual Member States, which could choose allies according to their own interests.

The season of conflicts did not alter the institutional balance, but showed the fragility of the budgetary procedure, which could easily be blocked due to the power game among the institutions.

During this decade, the EC budget was the motor of European integration because of the new balance of competences and the development of new policies, but also a brake because of the cost of agriculture, the disputes over the interpretation of the rules and, at the end of the period, a limitation of resources.

The visionary leadership of Jacques Delors as President of the Commission leads us to the third part of this walk through 40 years of the European Budget.

Cooperation and soft law: institutional progress

The arrival of Jacques Delors at the helm of the Commission inflated a new sail in the wind of European integration. Delors found a favourable environment; he had the vision and leadership to indicate the way forward not only to Heads of State and Finance Ministers but his message also reached public opinion. The first step was to launch a revision of the Treaty.

The aim of the new treaty cannot be better summarised than in the words of Jacques Delors himself: "The Single Act means, in a few words, the commitment of implementing simultaneously the great market without frontiers, more economic and social cohesion, [a] European research and technology policy, the strengthening of the European Monetary System, the beginning of [a] European social area and significant actions in [the] environment." The SEA was the conjunction of a number of positive elements:

- The need to reinforce the external role of the EC to respond to initiatives by the Soviet Union (the invasion of Afghanistan in 1979) and the US Foreign policy inspired by Ronald Reagan (elected in 1980), which ignored the European allies. The Genscher-Colombo Plan of the Foreign Affairs Ministers of Germany and Italy called, amongst other things, for reinforced political cooperation.
- The initiative of the directly elected Parliament which adopted the Draft Treaty on European Union in February 1984. Adopted by a very large majority (237 in favour, 34 against), it designed a federal constitution, modelled on the US system. The EP was certainly most active

in inspiring reforms and enhancing integration, but two approaches emerged in the parliamentary arena: the federalist Crocodile group, inspired by Altiero Spinelli, composed mainly of Italian, German and French Members of European Parliament (MEPs); and the Kangaroo group, inspired by a liberalist approach and composed mainly of Dutch and British MEPs. The contribution by the Group for the Recovery of the European Economy, composed of the Chairs of the six committees concerned, should also be mentioned.[12] This group requested contributions from external experts (Ball/Albert 1983).
- The Fontainebleau Summit appointed two groups of experts, coordinated by James Dooge and Pietro Adonnino, to open a reflection on the future of Europe and its people.[13] In particular, the conclusions of the Dooge report (March 1985), even though less ambitious than the Spinelli resolution, paved the way for the SEA.
- An open attitude on the part of Margaret Thatcher after the consolidation of the agreement on the rebate. Probably, the UK Prime Minister saw the opening of the internal market as a European deregulation and not as complex legislation trying to untie the national barriers to an open market.
- Open support by the two true European leaders: Helmut Kohl and François Mitterrand.
- Support by southern countries and Ireland, which saw the possibility of substantially increasing the allocations for structural funds.

All these elements created the momentum for re-launching the European integration process under the leadership of Jacques Delors.

The impact of the Delors Commission

The paragraphs above have shown the acceleration given by the Delors Commission to European integration. The Integrated Mediterranean Programmes aimed to prepare the smooth entry into the EC of Spain and Portugal. In mid-1985 the White Paper on the internal market was launched, and later and in 1985 there was agreement in the European Council on the SEA. President Delors' strategy created a win-win situation where all stakeholders could find a reason to subscribe to the vision proposed. The UK was satisfied to have its right to a rebate recognised in a more formal text and, together with the most prosperous countries, appreciated the opening and launch of new policies, such as those on research and the environment. Other Member States led by France were relieved to see agricultural expenditure ring-fenced, and the so-called club Med and Ireland valued the importance given to the cohesion policy.

The last mile was to convince the Finance Ministers and Heads of State to allocate more financial resources to achieve these objectives. The vision for the development of Europe embedded in the revision of the Treaty of Rome gave support for an increase in financial transfers from the Member States to the EC, which will be examined in the next section.

Reform of the budget

"Making a success of the Single European Act" was the title of the Commission Communication on the reform of the EC Budget (Commission of the European Communities 1987), which can be summarised as follows:

- A new structure for own resources with a global ceiling and the introduction of a fourth resource;
- Binding budgetary discipline;
- An increase in funds, mainly for the cohesion policy;
- A new planning mechanism.

The reform was not only necessary to increase the resources but also to reduce the budgetary conflicts which had polluted the previous decade. The development of new policies needed financial support to aid European integration (Kolte 1988).

Own resources

The reform of the own resources introduced at Fontainebleau was no longer sufficient to sustain the objectives of the SEA. The European Council endorsed the Commission proposal of 17 February 1988 (European Council 1988).

A global ceiling on own resources would guarantee the Member States an orderly evolution of payment appropriations over the 1988-1992 period and annually thereafter. The level was fixed at 1.2 percent of Gross National Product (GNP) for payment appropriations and 1.3 percent of GNP for commitments.[14] The annual ceiling on payment appropriations was established in the own resources decision.[15]

Community Rules determined that VAT would be capped at 1.4 percent for all Member States and applied to a common base. The Member States could deduct ten percent of the final amount of traditional own resources and VAT as collection costs.

The traditional own resources were no longer sufficient to guarantee an increase in resources and a fourth resource, based on a percentage of GNP, was introduced as a final top-up to the other sources of the EC budget.

The reform of the own resources was completed by the correction of the budgetary imbalance for the United Kingdom which was paid by the other eleven Member States, with the exception of Germany, whose contribution was reduced by one third. A temporary special provision also existed for Spain and Portugal.

This measure was welcomed as the only possibility to increase the budget, but in reality it reinforced Member State control not only over the budget but also over the development of European policies. The idea of autonomy of resources, which was one of the specificities of the European model, started to fade into a new system based on direct contribution by Member States. Through this system, the Member States regained full control of the power of the purse. Ratification by the national parliaments was a supplementary protection against unwanted increases in the costs of European integration.

Agriculture and budgetary discipline

The Agricultural reform initiated by Commissioner Fischler started to open European agriculture to the market, but European support was still high and for many market organizations its costs continued to be linked to external factors. The so-called agriculture guideline was confirmed. Thus, expenditure on market-related expenses could not grow by more than 74 percent of the increase in GNP. Supplementary measures decided by the Council aimed to limit the external influence of the costs and control of production (Avery 1988). The introduction of ceilings on own resources obliged a reinforcement of budgetary discipline for agriculture. The stabilizer mechanisms limiting the community guarantee were extended to all market organizations. The "exceptional circumstances" to escape the limitation were reduced to monetary divergences between US-Dollar and European Currency Unit. An early warning system would monitor excesses of production with the possibility of price reduction, co-responsibility levies, and limitation of the intervention measures according to the various market organisations. The financing of set-aside and the early retirement of farmers were all meant to encourage a reduction in production.

Cohesion policy

The enlargement to Spain and Portugal and the creation of the internal market convinced Delors of the importance of launching a more coherent Cohesion policy with substantially increased resources. The three structural Funds (EAGGF-Guidance, Regional and development, and Social) were then integrated (Lowe 1988). Four key principles were meant to guide the political choices for financing: Concentration, Partnership, Programming and Additionality. The Cohesion policy switched from an annual to a multiannual basis. Last but not least, the funds were doubled from 6,4 billion in 1988 to 20,5 billion in 1992 and their share in the budget rose from 16 percent to 31 percent.

The elements above are a fundamental part of the reform of the EC budget of 1988, but the "revolution" came with the planning method introduced into the Community system.

The new procedure

The concept of a multiannual financial perspective was not an original idea in itself, as it had already emerged in the 70s to improve control of agriculture expenditure and had been formally adopted by the Council[16] in a first attempt at multiannual financial programming. This new mechanism, introduced by soft law, was fundamental to guarantee the development of European integration. It lasted twenty years until its codification into the Treaty of Lisbon.

To strengthen the development of European integration, Delors had a clear vision: to reduce structural inequalities, to create a single market and to make progress on economic convergence and on monetary union. To go in this direction, he needed more resources.

The first ten years under the regime of the two budgetary treaties showed progress in the institutional balance, but also weakness on budgetary policy and stability due to the complex and ambiguous rules, which generated frequent conflicts. A new mechanism was therefore necessary. The solution proposed by the Commission and adopted by the Council was to limit the autonomy of the two arms of the budgetary authority, establishing a budgetary discipline which limited in particular the Council (responsible for the agriculture CE) and division of NCE into binding categories with individual ceilings, which limited the EP's prerogatives (Council of European Union 1988).

The advantage for the EP was an increase in the NCE over the period beyond the statistical MRI of NCE, concentrated on two EP priorities: Structural Funds and Research and Development.

The Finance Ministers could appreciate that the proposed mechanism gave them control over the destination of resources, limiting the uncertainties of the annual procedure. The major sources of conflict of the previous decade were thus eliminated.

A final general consideration concerns the legal form of the chosen mechanism. A change in the Treaty was neither necessary nor recommended. A planning mechanism called *financial perspectives* was included in an IIA with no formal legal status but with the political commitment to respect it. Over twenty years of application the IIA was always respected, even though in some cases the EP threatened, as a negotiating tactic, to ignore it. Only in one case, in 1994, did a serious conflict arise between the institutions on classification. This was resolved with a decision by the ECJ.[17] The IIAs were also respected because of the general obligation of loyal cooperation between the institutions, which was established by the Treaty (Art. 10, EC Treaty) and recognized by the ECJ (ECJ Case 65/93).

The formula proposed by the Delors Commission not only achieved the immediate aim of increasing resources for the implementation of the SEA, but also proved its solidity in the negotiations which followed, notably in 1992, 1999 and 2006. Since then, negotiations on the Multiannual Financial Framework (MFF) have become one of the topical moments of European institutional life, as have all the legislative acts with financial implications.

While legislative procedures are generally classified as normal policy-setting decision-making, the negotiations on the MFF are considered a keystone of the institutional life involving the Heads of State, the European Council and its President, the Commission and the EP. The core of the negotiations remains solidly in the hands of Member States but the final deal can only be struck with the consent of the Commission and the EP (see Laffan 2000). The EP's role is concentrated less on the figures but more on the principles (i.e. special procedures) included in the IAA.

The changes in budget politics introduced by the Delors package marked the beginning of a "new era" of inter-institutional cooperation and a new relationship between the institutions. This new method consisted of two pillars: multiannual financial planning (FP/MFF) and the IAA.

If the intergovernmental method prevails in the negotiations FP/MFF, the community method prevails in the definition of the IAA, where the institutions have developed forms of cooperation which generally have increased the EP's influence over the process. The new governance of the EU budget has had an impact on institutional development. The cooperation structure in different areas of interest of the institutions has confined conflicts to tactical positions, mainly in the annual procedure but always framed in a problem-solving structure.

Big bargains

The success of the Delors I package was partly due to efforts made by the German government, which accepted a supplementary financial burden to facilitate the final compromise. The situation was less favourable in 1992 (Delors II package). The approach taken by the Commission in 1988 was maintained but the influence of the Commission diminished. This was somehow in line with the different spirit of the Maastricht Treaty, where the community method was watered down with a more intergovernmental approach. The Commission proposal to increase the own resources from 1.20 percent to 1.37 percent of GNP was rejected, and the increase in resources was limited to 1.27 percent of GNP (Commission of the European Communities 1992). In spite of the minimalist proposals by the UK Presidency, an *entente* between Kohl, Mitterrand and Aznar facilitated the final agreement of the European Council. An effort was made to substantially increase the funds for the Eastern countries to consolidate their independence and economic recovery (European Council 1992).

The bargains became tenser and more complicated in 1999, 2006 and 2013. A group of net payers appeared on the scene, which blocked hopes of increasing resources. The outcome of these tensions and the appearance of veto players on the scene is notably visible in the resources allocated to the European project.

The detailed conclusions of the various European Councils are probably the most visible aspect of the big bargain between the Member States. They marginalise the community method and the role of the Commission and hinder legislative and budgetary procedures. The conclusions contradict the clear provision of the Treaty but the authority of the European Council and its parliamentary majority render any formal challenges to its pragmatic role useless.[18]

Another consequence of the intergovernmental predominance in those negotiations is the appearance of pre-allocated envelopes in many regulations.[19]

Furthermore, the European Council had to concede special "gifts" to obtain the support of some Member States. The conclusions of the European Council in several paragraphs feature such *special allocations* (European Council 2013).[20]

The practice developed by the European Council of concluding political agreements with detailed legislation is well established and has, *de facto*, modified the institutional balance created by the Treaties, reducing in consequence the prerogatives of the Commission and of the EP (see Christiansen 2006a, 2006b). The EP was present in all the phases of the preparation of the MFF, in some cases even ahead the Commission proposals, but the final agreements in the European Council wiped out months of negotiations.

To conclude, the setting up of the MFF reduced conflicts and allowed a dynamic evolution of competences with a right of veto for each arm of the budgetary authority, which was the best stimulus to seek agreements. The possibility that each institution could withdraw from the agreement and go back to the Treaty rules was another guarantee to enhance cooperation between the institutions. The fact that an agreement was always reached over more than twenty years[21] is the best proof of the success of this method.

The budgetary negotiations on multiannual planning are again a combination of intergovernmental interests framed into an institutional method: a *negotiated order* (Laffan: (2000) p.741), part of "European democracy." National governments, in fact, also act on behalf of their national parliaments, to whom they regularly report.

Soft law through IAAs

From 1988 until after the Lisbon Treaty, the "grand bargain", which mostly concerned finance, was accompanied by an IAA. IIAs had been used since the beginning of the European process and often allowed informal practical cooperation between the institutions in a relatively formal setting. Many scholars consider IIAs part of the *European Constitutional model* (Puntscher-Riekmann 2007; Kietz/Maurer 2007). Before the Lisbon Treaty, an IIA was a "legal" act containing the MFF and all the special arrangements necessary to smooth and simplify the annual procedure. The IIAs offered a platform for discussion between the two arms of the budgetary authority and also assumed a relevance in negotiations, as the EP often asked for political concessions on principles which were then included in the IIA in exchange for supporting a more restrictive approach on figures as requested by the Council. The IIAs saw the creation of special procedures – informal arrangements between the institutions which allowed smoother budgetary procedures and prefigured the modifications introduced in the Lisbon Treaty.

The Commission's proposal for an IAA linked to the SEA aimed to change the culture of the two arms of the budgetary authority from confrontation to cooperation. The Council directly saw the advantage of the proposal, which focused more on budgetary support for political priorities and recognised the EP's new role. The EP, after ten years of budgetary conflicts, saw its new role recognised. The EP opened a political dialogue with the Council which was not limited to strict budgetary policy but could also touch aspects of *de jure condido* or *de jure condendo* related to legislation financed by the EC budget. The four IIAs allowed the evolution of the Treaty's financial provisions, enhanced the role of both arms of the budgetary authority, and *de facto* cancelled some of the ambiguity in the Treaties, such as the CE/NCE distinction and the MRI. The period 1988-2009 was not immune from ambiguity and tensions emerged between the Council and EP, but the dialogue structure established in the IIAs always worked and the institutions never again suffered the conflicts of the pre-IIA period. The ambiguity of texts was often the result of different positions of the institutions and an ambiguous formulation in some cases allowed an agreement to be reached. The paragraphs below present the major principles embedded in the four IIAs.

Respect for budgetary discipline and ceilings

Respect for budgetary discipline and the ceilings on various headings was certainly one of the leading principles of the MFF. The three institutions were bound to respect the ceiling on each heading and not to move potential margins from one heading to another without a proper revision procedure. This means that co-decision was necessary to move appropriations between headings (Zangl 1989). The same applied to budgetary discipline, which linked all institutions and all expenditure. Budgetary discipline was a less precise concept and its respect was more a vague political commitment, except for agriculture, where there was a specific legal act (Council Decision 88/377). Under the other headings, each institution gave its own appreciation, but still in respect of the ceilings. Furthermore, budgetary discipline did not apply to the heading of Structural Funds/Cohesion Policy, where the institutions committed themselves to not modify the amounts entered in the FP/MFF.

The obligation for the institutions to leave, *as far as possible,* margins under the ceilings of the various headings was in some cases interpreted in a very flexible way.

NCE were split into two sub-categories: privileged, corresponding to the structural funds; and non-privileged NCE – all other policies. For the first group, the EP committed itself to respect the amounts indicated in the financial perspectives, in other words the EP self-limited its competence to introduce amendments to all privileged NCE. The EP had a full right of amendment on other NCE, within the ceiling under each heading. In return, the Council automatically accepted the MRI of NCE for each year during the period. Respect for the ceilings under each heading was the condition for the Council to accept whatever MRI resulted during the annual procedure.

The ad hoc procedure for agriculture

The 1993 IIA introduced a new chapter on improvement of the budgetary procedure concerning CE (annex II) with respect to the procedure foreseen by the EC Treaty (Art. 203).

The procedure indicated in the 1993 IIA aimed to seek an agreement on CE, notably agriculture, through a special trialogue and conciliation on CE ahead of the Council's first reading with the aim of the Council being able to consider EP requests before the formal vote on the modifications. The Parliament started to vote on a specific report before the Council's first reading with the specific requests on CE (Committee on Budgets 1996). This procedure appeared to be difficult to implement for various reasons: the period between May (when the PDB was presented) and mid-July was too short for evaluations on agricultural forecasts to be made and to fully involve the committee on agriculture. In any case, the Commission had a tendency to revise its forecast towards the end of the year. As seen above, the EP challenged the compulsory nature of some agricultural expenditure and the case went in front of the ECJ. The Decision by the Court reinforced the necessity of a proper agreement between the EP and the Council on the definition of the expenditure. The decision by the Court on 7 December 1995 encouraged the Institutions to go further in the ad hoc procedure for agriculture, and an agreement was reached at the trialogue on 9 April 1997.[22]

The new provisions postponed decisions on agricultural expenditure from mid-July (ahead of the Council first reading) to *before the end of October* so that the Commission could update the forecasts on agricultural production and present a new proposal to the budgetary authority for the financial needs for the Guarantee Section of the EAGGF, as a Letter of Amendment to the PDB. Why the end of October? The calendar for the budgetary procedure when applied to the Letter of Amendment to the PDB did not allow the double reading by the Council and the EP to be completed before the end of December. Then, the Letter of Amendment with the most updated forecasts could be incorporated in the annual budget with a co-decision. The EP presented its requests for CE at the July conciliation and also during the vote on agricultural amendments to the committee on agriculture in September and to the budget committee in October. To facilitate the adoption of the Letter of Amendment, the Commission then had sufficient indications to include elements which could facilitate EP support for this Letter of Amendment. Thanks also to the case brought before the ECJ, the EP gained a veto power on the NCE in the agriculture budget.

This ad hoc procedure on agriculture expenditure, which was informally introduced in 1996, was more formally included in the IIA of 1999. This text again showed the importance of "soft law" through IIAs. The agreement of all the actors achieved a fundamental modification of the procedure, ending more than twenty years of conflict on the classification of expenditure. The success of this procedure convinced the Intergovernmental Conference, in its preparation of the TFEU (Treaty on the Functioning of the European Union), to cancel the distinction between CE and NCE.

The ad hoc procedure for the international fisheries agreement

During the 1996 budgetary procedure an agreement was reached by the three institutions on *improving the information provisions for the international fisheries agreements.*[23] The EP recognized that expenditure to cover the IAA concluded with third parties was classified as CE, but it opposed the Council approach that financial provisions made available for fishery agreements during the negotiation phase ought to be considered compulsory.

The EP split the fishery agreements item into two parts: one for concluded agreements (CE) and another for those in negotiation (NCE). The EP considered recognition of the non-compulsory nature of the fishery agreements in negotiation a priority in the 1997 procedure. A joint statement, which was later incorporated into the 1999 IIA, put an end to this conflict.

It was agreed that appropriations for agreements in negotiations had to be entered in the reserve line (B0-40) attached to the *Fishery agreements* main line (B7-800). The Joint Statement foresaw that the Commission should keep the budgetary authority informed in all phases of the negotiations, and within the procedure established for agriculture the budgetary authority should *seek to agree on the amounts to be entered into the reserve for Fishery agreements.* The EP marked a supplementary step to expand its influence. Once again, the crucial element was not the semantic legal discussion on classification but agreement on discussion of a co-decided position. The Joint Statement, and later the IIA, did not mention classification at all but offered a pragmatic and shared solution which then became more important than a legal dispute on classification.

Financing of the Common Foreign and Security Policy (CFSP)

Another specific agreement was concluded between the institutions in July 1997: an ad hoc procedure on the financing of the CFSP (Committee on Budgets 1997; European Parliament 1997). While the two previous agreements concerned CE, in this case it was the Council that needed – in an area of NCE – some financial freedom to launch and sustain new activities in this sensitive domain. The EP on its part felt frustration at being kept on the margin of this policy and started to reduce the amounts or freeze them in the reserve (B0-40 chapter). The Agreement traded more information and involvement of the EP for some limitation of its competences on NCE and more freedom and predictability for the Council. The agreement was divided into three parts:

- *Financial arrangements.* A structure for this chapter was agreed, with a commitment to decide the amounts in co-decision;[24]
- *An ad hoc procedure* to secure the agreement, to be concluded possibly before the Council's first reading;
- *Consultation with and information for the European Parliament.* In exchange for EP moderation, the agreement established a procedure

for a formal consultation of the EP ahead of the final decisions on the CFSP.[25]

The implementation of the agreement was not as successful as expected. The Council gave the impression that once the procedure on the figures was secured the rest was only a formality. Meetings were agreed on an ad hoc basis, creating political and logistic problems. Due to the lack of planning of the dates it was difficult to get adequate political representation.

A new declaration was then formalised in November 2002 with more precise deadlines and a stricter structure. For the first time, this opened the question of confidentiality (Grossir 2003; Tym 2006). At the same time, another IAA was concluded concerning access by the EP to sensitive Council information in the field of security and defence policy.[26] This agreement gave the Council more confidence in disclosing confidential information to the EP (Rosén 2015).

The development of the CFSP, the budgetary powers of the EP and also the close cooperation of the two parliamentary committees (Committee on Foreign Affairs, AFET, and Committee on Budgets, BUDG) allowed a further improvement in the wording on the democratic scrutiny by the EP on CFSP. These improvements, achieved over the years, were consolidated in the IAAs for the period 2007-2013, and later confirmed in the 2014-2020 IIA. [27]

Parliament managed to pass from words to trust and gained the Council's confidence. The Council appreciated the new interaction with the EP, which gave stability to the financing of the CFSP (Committee on Foreign Affairs 2005).

This section cannot be concluded without mentioning that the EU Budget was not the only source of financing of the CFSP. In 2004, The Council created a special intergovernmental financing mechanism called Athena, with the objective of financing the common costs of EU military operations under the EU's Common Security and Defence Policy (CSDP), part of the CFSP. Athena,[22] which is still in force, can also finance costs borne at the national level, including lodging, fuel and other costs linked to national contingents. The Athena mechanism is financed by 27 Members States (Denmark opted out).

Budget vs legislative acts

During the decade 1978-1988, two conflicts opposed budgetary and legislative decisions: the necessity of a legal base to implement the budget and the *amounts deemed necessary* in legislative acts.

Actions without a proper legal base included in the budget were often considered by the EP, but also by the Commission and the Council, as a playground on which to experiment with new legislative initiatives. The Joint Declaration of 1982 on classification of expenditure mentioned this issue marginally, but a clearer definition appeared in the 1999 IIA. Three exceptions, later included in the Financial Regulation, were introduced to the basic rule of *no implementation without a legal basis* (European Parliament/Council of the European Union 2012, Art. 54; European Commission 2012, Art. 18):

- *Pilot projects:* activities to test the feasibility of a potential community action. Financing can be admitted for a maximum of two years with a maximum amount (today, 50 million euro a year);
- *Preparatory actions:* measures designed to prepare proposals with a view to the adoption of future actions. The financing can be guaranteed for a maximum of three years, the third year on condition that there is a proposal for a legal basis, which should be adopted by the end of the third year. Even in this case, IIAs, and later the Financial Regulation, foresaw an annual ceiling (today of 100 million euro a year with a maximum of 50 million euro per new action). Preparatory actions in CSFP should be approved by the Council;
- *Autonomous operations* conducted by the institutions within their administrative autonomy and capacity.

The 2007 IIA also created a special procedure to facilitate agreement between the three institutions. Before proposing pilot projects or preparatory actions for inclusion in the annual budget, the Commission should evaluate the practicality and possibility of implementing the potential proposals. Therefore, the Council and EP should present their new proposals by mid-June. In practical terms, other initiatives might appear outside of this procedure and a negative opinion of the Commission could not totally prevent a vote on such amendments, but this procedure has created more awareness of the introduction of new initiatives into the budget.

The EP Committee on Budgets organises annual hearings where the Commission should indicate the measures envisaged to execute pilot projects and preparatory actions to avoid the risk of the Commission choosing the ones to implement.[28]

The second point of conflict between the budget and legislation was represented by the financial envelopes of legislative acts. At the beginning this battle was a clear technique by the Council to circumvent EP competences on NCE; this element progressively lost its appeal with the extension of co-decision. These amounts could represent a burden for the budgetary authority, which had to respect the amount in the annual procedure irrespectively of the priorities and performances of the various programmes. In March 1995[29] a joint declaration was agreed, later incorporated in the successive IIAs, which introduced a distinction between acts adopted in co-decision and others. For acts in co-decision the budgetary authority committed itself to respect the amount, *unless new, objective, long-term circumstances arise for which explicit and precise reasons are given.* The IIAs of 2007 introduced some flexibility into the obligation to respect the financial provision of legislative acts: the budgetary authority could deviate from the financial envelope (five percent in 2007 and ten percent in the 2013 IIA) without the need to modify the legislative act. For the second category, acts not adopted in co-decision, the Council may introduce a financial reference which will not affect the powers of the budgetary authority, unless the act is to be adopted under the conciliation procedure provided by the Declaration of March 1975.

MFF: rigidity vs flexibility

Financial planning guaranteed a mechanism where the destination of allocations was known in advance, with limitations on budgetary authority in the annual procedure and in the transfer of appropriations from one heading to another. This mechanism would not have survived without some flexibility mechanisms, which were progressively included in the various IIAs.

In 1988 and 1993, the rigidity of the MFF could be overcome through a revision of the framework. The IIA foresaw that the revision should be limited to within 0.03 percent of GNP.

It was only in 1999 that, under pressure from the EP, a new mechanism was introduced to give some flexibility to the annual procedure. Over the whole period, we can see a connection between the funds allocated to the various headings of the MFF and the flexibility instruments. The Council understood that a restrictive financial framework and a longer period made it necessary to have more flexibility to face unforeseen events and new priorities. The flexibility instruments developed during the various IIA/MFFs were necessary not only for the EP but also for the Council and Commission.

The IIA of 1999 made a distinction between revisions up to 0.03 percent of GNP/Gross National Income (GNI), for which a qualified majority was required, and beyond 0.03 percent of GNP/GNI, for which unanimity was necessary. In spite of these provisions, the Member States within the Council informally committed to always vote by unanimity, which made it very difficult to activate the revision mechanism.

The Flexibility Instrument was introduced for the first time in the 1999 IIA. It amounted to a maximum of 200 million euro a year, with the possibility of carrying over the unused part for three years (it could reach up to 600 million euro if not used). The IIA of 2007 had other flexibility instruments which were outside the ceilings of the MFF, such as the Emergency Aid Reserve (up to 221 million euro), the European Union Solidarity Fund (up to one billion euro) and the European Globalisation Adjustment Fund (up to 500 million euro). An overview of these instruments will be presented in the next chapter.

Mid-term review

The mid-term review clause was inserted in the IIAs of 1993 and 2007 and later in the regulation adopted after the Lisbon Treaty. In practical terms, at least in the past, this clause led to an assessment of the situation but never to a revision of the Financial Framework.

Concluding remarks

During this period, European integration had a particular dynamism, and budget politics modified the institutional balance in favour of the EP, but above all guaranteed stability and mutual political respect between the institutions. The EP was constructive and responsible and facilitated the orderly financing of new policies without missing any possible opportunities to expand its influence. The Council realized that a new balance of power existed and it was obliged to consider the EP no longer as a formality to complete a procedure but a partner necessary to pass legislation.

During this period, the EU budget was certainly more a motor of European integration than a brake. All the changes introduced by the budgetary stakeholders in more than twenty years facilitated the important modifications included in the Treaty of Lisbon, which will be analysed in the next section.

The Lisbon Treaty

For the first time since 1975, the Treaty of Lisbon introduced a modification to the budgetary provisions, by incorporating some of the practices developed in the previous two decades. The codification of pragmatic rules into a legal framework changed the dynamic of inter-institutional relations, modifying the budgetary balance more in favour of the Council. This section will be divided into two parts. The first will assess the changes in terms of powers and politics, and the second the challenges that the EU budget will have to face in the near future.

The Lisbon Treaty: codification of budgetary practice

The financial provisions of the TFEU are grouped in Part VI, title II (Art. 310-325).[30] The major novelties concern:

- *Own resources* (Art. 311). Parliament will give its consent to implementing measures;
- *MFF* (Art. 312). Financial planning is part of the Treaty. The Regulation will be adopted after the consent of Parliament, and unanimously by the Council. A *passerelle* clause for a majority vote is foreseen. The MFF should be established for a period of at least *five years*. In the case that the Regulation is not adopted in time, the last year of the previous programming period will be extended until the new regulation is adopted;
- The *annual procedure* (Art. 314). The CE/NCE distinction is cancelled. The Commission presents its draft budget and the Council adopts its position. The EP then amends the Council's draft. The Council and EP's second readings are suppressed. In the case of non-agreement the two institutions meet in the conciliation committee, where they have to finalize an agreement on the points of difference. The results of the conciliation committee, in the form of a joint text, are then submitted for final approval to the Council and EP
  Several scenarios are foreseen by the Treaty for the approval of the joint text: if both institutions adopt the joint text, the budget is ap-

proved; if the EP acting by majority rejects the joint text, the Commission submits a new draft; if the EP approves but the Council rejects, the EP can reintroduce all or part of the amendments by qualified majority; if there is no agreement on the joint text after the deadline of 14 days, the Commission shall submit a new draft;

- When the procedure is completed, the President of the EP shall declare the EU budget adopted;[31]
- *No budget* (Art. 315). At the end of the procedure, the rule of *one twelfth* will apply: each month a sum may be spent not exceeding the sum in the draft budget. The Council may decide, on a proposal by the Commission, to increase the amounts. The EP can reduce it or accept the Council's modification;
- *Member States* (Art. 317) cooperate with the Commission in implementing the budget, formally recognizing their shared management of about 80 percent of the EU budget;
- *Budget based on results* (Art. 318). The Commission shall present an evaluation of the results achieved from the investment of European funds;
- The *Financial Regulation* (Art. 322) is to be adopted by ordinary legislative procedure (co-decision);
- The *Presidents of the Institutions* (Art. 324) are entrusted with the responsibility to reconcile their positions to facilitate the implementation of the financial provisions of the Treaty.

The fact that a number of these changes were already tested under the IIA regime should not reduce the importance of the modifications introduced by the Treaty. The binding nature of some provisions and a new dynamic of negotiations modify the politics of the EU budget, reinforcing the role of the Council.

The progress of the Treaty

The EP's immediate reaction to the modifications introduced by the Treaty was globally positive. Its resolution welcomed the advances brought about by the Lisbon Treaty in the area of the democratic scrutiny and transparency of the Union's finances and it warmly welcomed the abolition of the distinction between CE and NCE, as a result of which EP now has the right to take decisions concerning all Union expenditure on an equal footing with the Council (European Parliament 2009a).

The recognition of FP/MFF in the Treaty consolidated many years of pragmatic approaches. The EP was disappointed that the adoption of the MFF was not in co-decision and that the Council had to act unanimously, but in the end this was the *de facto* situation before the Treaty. Concerning the length of the MFF, the EP's constant position that the length of the period should be aligned with the institutional calendar was partially accepted in the text as *at least five years,* but it leaves the Council the possibility of setting a longer period (European Parliament 2009b).

The abolition of the CE/NCE distinction was seen as an important step forward as it finally gave recognition to full co-decision on the budget. There is no mention in the EP Resolution of the fact that the Council has gained co-decision power over NCE, where previously the EP had the final word.

The resolution recognized the necessity in the new procedure for the EP to fine-tune its political priorities at an earlier stage and accordingly adapt its operational approach and organisational arrangements so as to enable it to achieve all the objectives set.

This evaluation of the new procedure came after the signing of the Treaty but before its entry into force. No evaluation of the impact of the Lisbon Treaty was made after its first years of implementation.

The EP's role under the Treaty

In spite of the fact that some of the modifications introduced by the Treaty were already in place under the IIAs, some of the new provisions have contributed to weakening the EP's position.

In the pre-Lisbon period, if the EP did not agree with the MFF it could even terminate the agreement and automatically benefit from the application of the MRI of NCE, where the EP would have the final decision (European Parliament et al. 2006, para. 30).

Art. 312 TFEU constitutes a more formal frame, in which a change needs not only the unanimous vote of the Council but also ratification by every Member State. Now that the mechanism is embedded in the Treaty, it is impossible for the EP to renounce and abandon the MFF.

In the case of non-agreement on the MFF, the ceilings for the last year of the previous period will be prolonged without any technical adjustment (in the 2006 IIA there was a fixed deflator of two percent). This might encourage a single Member State to block the adoption of the new framework, which could easily lead to a very difficult situation with no fall-back.

On the positive side, art 312 foresees a Council vote only after the EP's consent, which opens the possibility for the EP to present its requests, which the Council should consider including (at least in part) in its text to gain EP support. In practical terms, the EP was fully involved in the preliminary phases of the process before, but much less after the political agreement in the European Council. In the end, the achievements were rather modest.

EP's frustration with the first MFF procedure under the Lisbon Treaty is reflected in a "post mortem" resolution on *MFF negotiations 2014-2020: lessons to be learned and the way forward,* where the EP denounces the Council's lack of vision and disregard for EP positions in spite of numerous meetings held with the successive Presidencies (European Parliament 2014).

The unanimity imposed by the Treaty for the adoption of the MFF strengthened veto players, so that agreement within the Council can only be concluded at the lowest level with no escape route for EP.

The situation of the annual procedure under the Treaty of Lisbon is no better. The previous rules guaranteed a real negotiation as both actors could set their agendas and priorities in their domain of competence (CE for the Council and NCE for the EP) and each institution was obliged to reach an agreement to secure its priorities.

The Council adopts its draft budget by qualified majority while EP needs the majority of its component members. The absence of an EP second reading obliges the EP to concentrate ambitions (negotiating points) and absolute priorities (red lines) in the same vote. This gives the impression that the EP delegation at the Conciliation has an impossible and unrealistic mandate, as the positions between the two arms of the budgetary authority are usually quite distant. The inflexibility of the procedure and the absence of an effective reversion point obliges the EP to accept a final budget much closer to the Council position than to the EP reading.

The provisional twelfths procedure, in the case of non-adoption of the joint text, also penalises the EP. In fact, the lower of the figures between the previous year's budget and the draft budget can be increased by the Council while EP only has the power to reduce it. In other words, this means that the Council has a tool to secure its priorities while the EP can only play the veto card.

Non-agreement by the EP on the joint text could be a positive negotiating tool and it was used by EP at least three time in the first years. It can offer the EP a supplementary margin for negotiation, provided that the final agreement is secured before the end of the year to avoid falling under the provisional twelfths. This time pressure reduces the advantages that the EP has in the case of non-acceptance of the joint text.

The Treaty seems to offer EP a trigger mechanism in the case of rejection by the Council of the joint text. Art 314, 7, d foresees that the EP, *by a majority of its component members and three-fifths of the votes cast, can decide to confirm all or some of the amendments.* This apparent supremacy is in practical terms an impossible case. In fact, while the EP delegation is composed of 28 MEPs (out of a total of 751) in a wise blend of political groups and committee representation, the Council is represented by the 28 Member States, generally represented by the Ministers. It is unlikely or practically impossible that the Council would accept a joint text and then reject it. Generally, the Council meeting to adopt the joint text is held directly after the conclusion of the agreement.

To reject the joint text, the Treaty requires the majority of the components of the EP, while to approve it a vote by the majority of MEPs is necessary. In the pre-Lisbon period a qualified majority was necessary to vote amendments in the second reading. This element represents a supplementary weakening of the bargaining power of the EP. A simple majority facilitates the adoption of the joint text, especially if we consider that individual governments have their political majority in the EP to support the joint text adopted in Conciliation.

The reduction of the budgetary powers of the EP cannot be seen in isolation from the others changes in the Treaty, in particular the extension of competences in the ordinary legislative procedure.

To conclude this analysis of the texts, the Lisbon Treaty changes the politics of the EU budget: in the case of non-agreement the reversion point reinforces the institution asking for a reduction of the budget and conversely penalises the institution fighting for an increase (Benedetto 2013, 2016). Following this practice, the EP is penalised by the new rules.

Further considerations

The financial provisions of the Lisbon Treaty have increased the intergovernmental mechanisms and reduced the influence of the EP.[32] This reduced role in the budgetary domain was probably not fully evaluated by the EP in the moment of ratification of the Treaty. The suppression of classification and full co-decision was appreciated as an important step forward to expand the EP's budgetary influence but the dynamics of negotiations show a different trend: the so-called *equal footing* has not been reached yet.

The reduced role of the EP in the budgetary procedure should be assessed together with the full legislative role that the EP has reached with the Lisbon Treaty after more than forty years of struggle.

The political groups of the EP have perceived this loss of influence in the budgetary domain, and at the beginning of the eighth term in the negotiations to propose the candidate Chairs for the permanent committees the budgetary committee has fallen behind various other legislative committees.

The EU budget suffers from the absence of real own resources and the rigidity of the expenditure mechanisms. It is more difficult to reduce or suppress an expenditure already in the budget than create a new one. Intergovernmental bargains render any reform of the expenditure structure very difficult.

The budget has proven to be the motor of integration and to have the capacity to adapt and innovate, even outside a rigid legal framework. The Lisbon Treaty has created a more rigid corset which limits the budget's support for European integration and makes it more a brake than a motor. A separate chapter will analyse the challenges that the budget will have to face in the near future, and offer food for thought and some options to follow to possibly reverse the tendency and again make the budget the motor of integration.

Final remarks

This chapter will conclude with some remarks on the research questions raised at the beginning. The EU budget has contributed to the development of European integration and of new inter-institutional relations. In particular, the EP used its limited budgetary power to gain influence over legislation. Now that the Lisbon Treaty has expanded its legislative power there is a reduction in the influence of the EP on budgetary decisions.

Legislative and political influence and the increase in resources have been the major drivers of change in the budgetary procedure. The EP did not hesitate to limit its formal power to gain pragmatic legislative and political influence.

The Lisbon Treaty has changed the institutional balance of power of the EU budget. The new regulation of the MFF has increased the flexibility but not the resources available to respond to new challenges. The Member States have started to develop new instruments outside the EU Budget to increase the resources without touching the limit set in the own resources decision (1.23 percent of GNI). Direct payments and trust funds have, *de facto*, increased the resources available for European policies but ignored the procedures foreseen in the Treaty.

A reform of the EU Budget touching both financing and expenditure should accompany the re-launch of the EU integration process to better respond to citizens' worries. To gain the unanimous support of the Member States and national parliaments, this reform should involve: a concentration of funds on European added value policies, a budget more focused on results, enhanced legislative and budgetary scrutiny of legislation and, last but not least, the progressive introduction of genuine EU own resources.

The outcome of the British referendum should constitute an incentive for EU Leaders to offer a new vision of EU integration. Business as usual is no longer an option. Reform of the EU budget could be the motor for the new approach.

Notes

1 Resolution B0-0012/62 presented by the Members Poher, Pleven and Birkelbach on behalf of their respective groups, European Parliament Historical Archives.

2 The Four Presidents Committee consisted of the president of the Court of Justice (who was also chair of the Committee), and the presidents of the High Authority, Council and the Parliament.

3 Com (1969) 1020 of 30 October 1969, European Union Historical Archives, BAC 38-1984, No. 18, pp. 393-412.

4 The maximum rate of increase in non-compulsory expenditure was fixed with the following three parameters: the trend in terms of volume of GNP within the Community, the average variation in the budgets of the Member States and the trend of the cost of living during the preceding financial year.

5 EP Reports on the preparation of the Commission's proposal to reinforce the role of the European Parliament - 131/73 and 175/73 (Spenale reports) and 167/75 (Aigner report), European Parliament Historical Archives.

6 The Vedel group was a group of experts appointed by the Commission with the mandate to examine all the implications of extending the powers of the European Parliament.

7 On 23 March 1971, Brussels saw one of the first European rallies (about 100,000 persons) against Commission proposals. The results were serious: one person died, 140 people were injured and serious damage was caused. Listen to the RTL audio report, published by the Centre Virtuel de la connaissance sur l'Europe, Luxembourg: http://www.cvce.eu/en/obj/demonstration_by_farmers_in_brussels-_by_jean_charles_de_keyser_rtl_23_march_1971-en-bd7b5e0d-6136-4b59-a2f8-f8912d7528e8.html; 20 August 2016.

8 For abundant literature on the subject, see Swinnen 2008 and Matthews 1996.
9 For details of the Monetary mechanisms, see Strasser 1984, p. 276-283, Feld 1979 and Grant 1997.
10 Rapport Piet Dankert, 458/79, 581/79 EP Historical Archives, Luxembourg.
11 The EP rejected the budget with 288 in favour and 64 against. The European Democrats (the Gaullist group) and the French Communists voted against the rejection.
12 The Group for Recovery of the European Economy was composed of Mr Jacques Moreau, Mrs Hanna Walz, Sir Fred Catherwood, Mr Efstratios Papaefstratiou, Mr Pancrazio De Pasquale and Mr Michel Poniatowski.
13 The Dooge group of experts was composed of Enrico Ferri, Italy, Fernand Herman, Belgium, Maurice Faure, France and Frans Andriessen, Netherlands representing the Commission, later replaced by Carlo Ripa di Meana.
14 The Council decision was translated into the Council decision of 24 June 1988 on the system of the Communities' own resources 88/376.
15 The annual ceilings set in art 3 of Council decision 88/376 were 1.15 percent in 1988, 1.17 percent in 1989, 1.18 percent in 1990, 1.19 percent in 1991 and 1.20 percent in 1992.
16 See Council decision, 5-6 February 1970, doc I/100/1970, Historical Archives of European Union (HAEU), CM2/1970, 0550.
17 See the paragraph Court of Justice and the budget above.
18 Art. 15 TFEU: "The European Council shall provide the Union with the necessary impetus for its development and shall define the general political directions and priorities thereof. It shall not exercise legislative functions." The European Council website is even more explicit: "The European Council defines the EU's overall political direction and priorities. It is not one of the EU's legislating institutions, so does not negotiate or adopt EU laws. Instead it sets the EU's policy agenda, traditionally by adopting 'conclusions' during European Council meetings which identify issues of concern and actions to take" (European Council 2016).
19 That is, rural development, fisheries, cohesion policy and annual agricultural subsidies.
20 For the expenditure side, see points 19, 23, 50 to 52, 72 for a total amount of about 18 billion euro; for the revenue side see point 118 for about seven billion euro.
21 The only exception was the challenge on compulsory expenditure raised by the EP in front of the ECJ (Case 41/95), which touched more the principles than the budget itself.
22 Tillich, Stanislaw, working document 7 in the Report A4-0247/97, p.29 on the 'ad hoc procedure' for the 1998 budget, as provided for in Annex II on interinstitutional collaboration in the budgetary sector to the Interinstitutional Agreement of 29 October 1993 on budgetary discipline and improvement of the budgetary procedure.
23 Joint Statement on improving the information provisions for the international fisheries agreements, OJ EC C 20 of 20/1/1997, p. 109.
24 The agreement defined the budget lines of this special chapter: observation and organisation of elections/participation in democratic transition processes; EU envoys; Prevention of conflicts/peace and security processes; Financial assistance to disarmament processes; Contributions to international conferences and Urgent actions.

25 The Council committed to providing detailed costs of actions, in particular those regarding time frame, staff employed, use of premises and other infrastructure, transport facilities, training requirements and security arrangements.
26 OJEC C 298 of 30/11/2002.
27 The good cooperation between the Committees on Foreign Affairs (Chair Elmar Brok) and Budget (Chair Terry Wynn) was fundamental in the building of the EP position. A crucial role was also played by Thomas Subelack, advisor to the EPP group.
28 Each year the Commission presents a working document dedicated to pilot projects and preparatory actions.
29 Joint Declaration of 6 March 1995 on the incorporation of financial provisions into legislative acts, OJ C 293/1995, replaced by OJ C 102 of 4/4/1996.
30 For abundant literature on the changes introduced by the TFEU, see the references.
31 ECJ Case 77/11 confirmed the prerogative of the President of the Parliament to sign the budget without the co-signature of the President of the Council. See the discussion above.
32 See the contribution by Bauer and Becker in this volume.

References

Avery, G. 1988. Agriculture Policy – The conclusion of the European Council. *Common Market Law Review* 25: 523-539.

Bauer, M.W., and Becker, S. 2017. Assessing the European Parliament's Power of the Purse: Rights, Capabilities, and Strategies. In *The New Politics of the European Union Budget,* Eds. Becker, S., Bauer, M.W., and De Feo A., 173-194. Baden-Baden: Nomos Verlag.

Ball, R.J., and Albert, M. 1983. *Towards European economic recovery in the 1980s. Report presented to the European Parliament.* Working Documents 1983-1984, 31 August 1983. http://aei.pitt.edu/5539/; 20 August 2016.

Benedetto, G. 2013. The EU budget after Lisbon: rigidity and reduced spending? *Journal of Public Policy* 33: 345-369.

Benedetto, G. 2016. Power, money and reversion points. The European Union's annual budgets since 2010. *Journal of European Public Policy* Early View. Doi: 10.1080/13501763.2016.1154589.

Benedetto, G., and Milio, S. (Eds). 2012. *European Union Budget Reform. Institutions, Policy and Economic Crisis.* London: Palgrave Macmillan.

Cipriani, G. 2014. *Financing the EU Budget: Moving Forward or Moving Backwards?* Brussels: CEPS.

Christiansen, T. 2006a. The European Commission: the European Executive Between Continuity and Change. In *European Union. Power and Policy Making*, Ed. Richardson, J., 99-120. Abingdon: Routledge.

Christiansen, T. 2006b. The Council of Ministers: Facilitating Interaction and Developing Actorness in the EU. In *European Union. Power and Policy Making*, Ed. Richardson, J., 147-170. Abingdon: Routledge.

Commission of the European Communities. 1972. Report of the Working Party examining the problem of the enlargement of the powers of the European Parliament – Report Vedel. *Bulletin of the European Communities* 4/72.

Commission of the European Communities. 1973. Strengthening of the Budgetary Powers of the European Parliament. *Bulletin of the European Communities* 9/73.

Commission of the European Communities. 1987. Making a success of the Single Act. A new frontier for Europe. *COM (87) 100 final.*

Commission of the European Communities. 1992. From the Single Act to Maastricht and beyond: The means to match our ambitions. *COM (92) 2000.*

Committee on Budgets. 1996. *Report on the 'ad hoc procedure' for the 1997 budget provided for in Annex II on interinstitutional collaboration in the budgetary sector to the Interinstitutional Agreement of 29 October 1993 on budgetary discipline and improvement of the budgetary procedure.* A4-0246/96. http://www.europarl.europa.eu/sides/getDoc.do?type=REPORT&mode=XML&reference=A4-1996-0246-&language=EN; 21 August 2016.

Committee on Budgets. 1997. *Report on the proposal for an Interinstitutional Agreement between the European Parliament, the Council and the European Commission on provisions regarding financing of the Common Foreign and Security Policy.* A4-0249/9. http://www.europarl.europa.eu/sides/getDoc.do?type=REPORT&mode=-XML&reference=A4-1997-0249&language=EN; 21 August 2016.

Committee on Foreign Affairs. 2005. *Report on the annual report from the Council to the European Parliament on the main aspects and basic choices of CFSP, including the financial implications for the general budget of the European Communities.* A6-0389/2005. http://www.europarl.europa.eu/sides/getDoc.do?pubRef=-//EP//TEXT-+REPORT+A6-2005-0389+0+DOC+XML+V0//EN; 21 August 2016.

Council of the European Union. 1971. Regulation (EEC) No 974/71 of the Council of 12 May 1971 on certain measures of conjunctural policy to be taken in agriculture following the temporary widening of the margins of fluctuation for the currencies of certain Member States. https://publications.europa.eu/en/publication-detail/-/publication/2a9825fb-ed5f-460f-b710-afeef38cb03b/language-en; 20 August 2016.

Council of the European Union. 1988. *88/377/EEC. Council Decision of 24 June 1988 concerning budgetary discipline.* https://publications.europa.eu/en/publication-detail/-/publication/2b16f003-12fd-46c2-a6d6-c4fe7cc4fd93/language-en; 21 August 2016.

Davies, G. 2011. Does the ECB really have a silver bullet? *Financial Times.* http://blogs.ft.com/gavyndavies/2011/11/10/does-the-ecb-really-have-a-silver-bullet/; 18 August 2016.

De Feo, A. 2015. A History of Budgetary Powers and Politics in the EU – The Role of the European Parliament. Part I: The European Coal and Steel Community 1952-2002. *European Union History Series.* http://www.europarl.europa.eu/RegData/etudes/STUD/2015/538883/EPRS_STU(2015)538883_EN.pdf; 20 August 2016.

De Feo, A. 2016. A History of Budgetary Powers and Politics in the EU – The Role of the European Parliament. Part II: The non-elected Parliament 1957-1978. *European Union History Series. doi:*10.2861/604009

De Feo, A., and Laffan, B. (Eds). 2016. *EU Own Resources: momentum for a reform?* Florence: European University Institute. doi:10.2870/176147

Division for Agricultural Information. 1972. *A New Common Agricultural Policy? Social and Structural Reform in Agriculture.* http://ec.europa.eu/agriculture/cap-history/crisis-years-1970s/social-and-structural-reform-1972_en.pdf; 20 August 2016.

European Commission. 1988. *Regulation (EEC) No 3578/88 laying down detailed rules for the application of the system for the automatic dismantlement of negative monetary compensatory amounts.*

European Commission. 2011a. Financing the European Union: report on the operation of the own resources system. *Commission Staff Working Paper* SEC (2011) 876 final/2. http://ec.europa.eu/budget/library/biblio/documents/fin_fwk1420/proposal_-council_own_resources__annex_en.pdf; 18 August 2016.

European Commission. 2011b. The added value of the EU budget. *Commission Staff Working Paper* SEC(2011) 867 final.

European Commission. 2015. Report from the Commission to the European Parliament and the Council on the evaluation of the Union's finances based on the results achieved (Article 318 Report). http://ec.europa.eu/smart-regulation/evaluation/docs-/2014_report_en.pdf; 18 August 2016.

European Council. 1972. Statement from the Paris Summit. *Bulletin of the European Communities* 10/1972: 14-26.

European Council. 1975. *Meeting of Heads of Government in Council in Dublin on 10 and 11 March 1975. Summary of Decisions and Conclusion. R/807/75.* http://www-.consilium.europa.eu/en/european-council/conclusions/1992-1975/; 21 August 2016.

European Council. 1977. Session of the European Council Conclusions. *Bulletin of the European Communities* 12/1977. http://aei.pitt.edu/1423/1/Brussels_dec_1977.pdf; 20 August 2016.

European Council. 1984. *European Council Meeting at Fontainbleau on 25 and 26 June 1984. Conclusions of the Presidency.* http://www.consilium.europa.eu/-en/european-council/conclusions/1992-1975/; 21 August 2016.

European Council. 1988. *Note from the Presidency. Making a success of the Single European Act. Consolidated conclusions of the European Council. SN 461/1/88.* http://www.consilium.europa.eu/en/european-council/conclusions/1992-1975/; 21 August 2016.

European Council. 1992. *European Council in Edinburgh 11-12 December 1992. Conclusions of the Presidency. SN 456/1/92.* http://www.consilium.europa.eu-/en/european-council/conclusions/1992-1975/; 21 August 2016.

European Council. 2013. Conclusions (Multiannual Financial Framework*). EUCO 37/13.*

European Council. 2016. The European Council. http://www.consilium.europa.eu/en/european-council/; 21 August 2016.

European Court of Justice. 1986. *Case 34/86. Council of the European Union vs European Parliament (Budget).*

European Court of Justice. 1995a. *Case 41/95. Council of the European Union vs European Parliament (Budget).*

European Court of Justice. 1995b. *Case 65/93. Judgement of the Court.*

European Court of Justice. 2013. *Case 77/11. Council of the European Union v European Parliament.*

European Parliament. 1997. Interinstitutional Agreement between the European Parliament, the Council and the European Commission of 16 July 1997 on provisions regarding financing of the common foreign and security policy. *Official Journal of the European Communities* 40 (C 286): 80-81.

European Parliament. 2009a. Resolution of May 7 2009 on the financial aspects of the Lisbon Treaty. *P6_TA(2009)0374.*

European Parliament. 2009b. Resolution of 25 March 2009 on the Mid-Term Review of the 2007-2013 Financial Framework. *P6_TA(2009)0174.*

European Parliament. 2014. Resolution of 15 April 2014 on negotiations on the MFF 2014-2020: lessons to be learned and the way forward. *P7_TA(2014)0378.*

European Parliament, and Council of the European Union. 2012. *Regulation (EU, Euratom) No 966/2012 of the European Parliament and of the Council of 25 October 2012 on the financial rules applicable to the general budget of the Union and repealing Council Regulation (EC, Euratom) No 1605/2002.* http://eur-lex.europa.eu/legal-content/EN/TXT/?uri=celex:32012R0966; 21 August 2016.

European Parliament, Council, and Commission. 1982. Joint Declaration by the European Parliament, the Council and the Commission of 30 June 1982 on various measures to improve the budgetary procedure. *Official Journal of the European Communities* 25(C194).

European Parliament, Council, and Commission. 2006. Interinstitutional Agreement between the European Parliament, the Council and the Commission on budgetary discipline and sound financial management. *Official Journal of the European Union* 49(C139/1).

Feld, W.J. 1979. Implementation of the European Community's Common Agricultural Policy – Expectations, Fears, and Failures. *International Organization* 33 (3): 335–363.

Grant, W. 1997. *The Common Agriculture Policy.* Basingstoke: Macmillan.

Grossir, J.P. 2003. Budget 2003. La fin d'une époque. *Revue du Marché Commun* 471.

Haug, J., Lamassoure, A., and Verhofstadt, G. 2011. Europe for growth: for a radical change in the revenue of the European Union. https://www.ceps.eu/publications/europe-growth-radical-change-financing-eu; 18 August 2016.

Heinemann, F. 2016. Strategies for a European EU budget. In *The future of the EU-Finances*, Eds. Buettner, T., and Thöne, M., 91-108. Tübingen: Mohr Siebeck.

High Level Group on Own Resources. 2014. *First Assessment Report.* http://ec.europa-.eu/budget/mff/hlgor/library/reports-communication/FirstAssess-mentReport-December2014.pdf; 18 August 2016.

Kietz, D, and Maurer, A. The European Parliament in Treaty Reform. Predefining IGCs through Interinstitutional Agreements. *European Law Journal* 13(1): 4-26.

Kolte, L. 1988. The Community Budget – New principles for finance, expenditure planning and budgetary discipline. *Common Market Law Review* 25: 487-501.

Laffan, B. 1997. *The finances of the European Union.* London: Macmillan.

Laffan, B. 2000. The big budgetary bargains. From negotiations to authority. *Journal of European Public Policy* 7(5): 725-743.

Lamassoure, A. 2007. Report on the future of the European Union's own resources. *European Parliament Session Document* A6-0066/2007.

Lindner, J. 2006. *Conflict and Change in EU Budgetary Politics.* New York: Routledge.

Lowe, P. 1988. The reform of the Community's structural funds. *Common Market Law Review* 25: 503-521.

Ludlow, P. 2014. From Deadlock to Dynamism: The European Community in the 1980s. In *Origin and Evolution of the European Union.*, Ed. Dinan, D. (Ed), 217-232. Oxford: Oxford UP.

Matthews, A. 1996. The disappearing budget constraint on EU agricultural policy. *Food Policy* 21 (6): 497-508.

Puntscher-Riekmann, S. 2007. The Cocoon of Power: Democratic implications of Interinstitutional Agreements. *European Law Journal* 13(1): 27-40.

Richter, S. 2008. Facing the monster "Juste Retour". On the net financial position of Member States vis-à-vis the EU Budget and a proposal for reform. *EU-Consent EU-Budget Working Paper* 7.

Rosén, G. 2015. EU Confidential: The European Parliament's Involvement in EU Security and Defence Policy. *Journal of Common Market Studies* 53(2): 383- 398.

Schratzenstaller, M. 2013. The EU own resources system: reform needs and options. In *Intereconomics* 48(5): 303-313.

Soros, G. 2012. L'Europe pourrait financer seule sa relance. *Le Figaro.* http://www.lefigaro.fr/conjoncture/2012/04/22/20002-20120422ARTFIG00166-soros-l-europe-pourrait-financer-seule-sa-relance.php; 18 August 2016.

Strasser, D. 1984. *Les Finances de l'Europe.* Charleroi: Éditions Labor.

Swinnen, J. (Ed.). 2008. The Perfect Storm. The Political Economy of the Fischler Reforms of the Common Agricultural Policy. Brussels: CEPS. https://www.ceps-.eu/system/files/book/1718.pdf; 20 August 2016.

Tarschys, D. 2015. Entering a world of footloose tax bases: can the EU generate its own income? *European Policy Analysis* 2015(8).

Tym, D. 2006. Beyond Parliament's Reach? The Role of the European Parliament in the CFSP. *European Foreign Affairs Review* 11: 109-127.

Zangl, P. 1989. The Interinstitutional agreement on budgetary discipline and improvement of the budgetary procedure. *Common Market Law Review* 26: 675-685.

EU Budgetary Politics and the Paradox of *Juste retour*

Manuele Citi

Introduction

The European Union's Multiannual Financial Framework (MFF) and the annual budget are two legislative acts that determine the amount of fiscal resources to be committed to specific policy priorities as well as the amount of revenue that each member state of the European Union (henceforth: EU) is expected to transfer to the EU. The adoption of these acts tends to be fairly contentious, since all member states are generally sensitive to the potential loss of a sizeable amount of fiscal resources to the other member states. Over the years, the concern over the net fiscal positon of member states *vis-à-vis* the EU budget, coupled with a certain degree of domestic political rhetoric, have produced the concept of "*Juste retour*", a general understanding that member states should not pay an unfair price for policies and programmes that mostly benefit other member states. This concern has led some of the member states to negotiate a number of 'correction mechanisms' that allow them to reduce the amount of revenue they transfer to the EU. First among others, the UK rebate allowed the UK to receive a substantial discount on the amount of value added tax-based resources it had to transfer to the EU. Following the UK rebate, several other member states like Germany, the Netherlands, Austria, Sweden and Denmark have obtained different types of correction mechanisms, which have reduced the amount of fiscal resources they transfer every year to the EU.

In this chapter, I investigate the impact of these corrective measures on overall expenditure dynamics, and study the extent to which they have altered on the EU budget's redistributive function. The chapter develops as follows: in the first part, I track the emergence, at the European Council of Fontainebleau of 1984, of a redistributive cleavage within the Council which affected virtually all the negotiations rounds on MFFs and annual budgets ever since. In the second part, I rely on a measure developed by the European Commission – the Operating Budgetary Balance (OBB) – to study the evolution of each member state's net fiscal position *vis-à-vis* the rest of the EU, and evaluate the actual impact of the corrections mechanism on the cross-country redistributive dynamics. Here I show that these rebates have had little if any effect on the OBB dynamics in the long run, and in some cases they have produced a result that is paradoxically contrary to its intended purpose. In the third part, I provide some plausible explanation of this phenomenon, and argue that member states have only a weak and indirect capacity to control their OBB and the overall redistributive dynamics within the EU. In the conclusion, I contend that this weak control is ultimately beneficial, because it allows EU social, structural, and cohesion funds to appropriately address the inequalities created by the common market, and suggest some possible directions of future research.

The emergence of a redistributive cleavage in the Council

The European Union's budget has different functions, which have profoundly evolved since its creation, in parallel with the development of its institutional structure. During the very first years of the European Coal and Steel Community (ECSC) and the European Economic Community (EEC), the budget's almost exclusive function was to provide the necessary resources for the ordinary functioning of the nascent supranational institutions. It was not until until 1962 – with the inception of the common agricultural policy 2– that the budget started to have an additional *distributive* function. Following a typology developed by Lowi (1964), a distributive policy is defined as a policy that either finances public goods (infrastructures, defence, research) or provides resources to specific economic constituencies in a pork-barrel fashion, as in the case of agricultural policy. The fundamental feature of distributive policies is that they are typically Pareto-improving decisions: they can improve the welfare of a social group without necessarily decreasing the welfare of any other group. As such, these policies are characterized by a low level of political conflict. For this reason, in the early years of the EEC when the vast majority of the budget was spent on agricultural policy and other smaller-size distributive programs, the adoption of the Community budget was a relatively frictionless political process.

A third function of public budgets is *redistributive.* The policies that fall under this category aim to rebalance the economic disparities that may develop across social classes, or groups, economic sectors or regions. This is indeed the purpose of fiscal policy in general, which employs the revenue accrued from direct and indirect taxation to compensate for economic inequalities. One defining feature of redistributive policies is that they tend to be inherently more conflictual and politically salient than all the other policies, because any change to the status quo implies a transfer resources across regions, or across social classes, in a fashion that resembles a zero-sum game (Lowi 1964, p. 707-711).[1] Social policy, cohesion policy, and all the welfare-state related policies are therefore the most heavily disputed policies in the EU, because in most cases they involve a redistribution of resources from wealthier member states to the poorer ones, and none of them wants to be on the losing side of redistributional conflicts (Bailer et al. 2015).

The redistributive policies directly financed by the EU budget remained a relatively underdeveloped policy priority until the early 1970s, when the EU member states adopted two important reforms. The first was the reform of the European Social Fund (ESF), a programme created with the Treaty of Rome which remained in an embryonic state for more than a decade. In 1971 the member states decided to dramatically expand the spending on this programme, with the aim of reinforcing the social and employment objectives of the Community (European Commission 2007). The second reform, adopted in 1975, was the creation of a European Regional Development Fund (ERDF). This programme, which came after the first enlargement round to United Kingdom, Ireland and Denmark of 1973, had the purpose of sustaining the regions undergoing a phase of economic downturn. In particular, ERDF financed projects for the industrial restructuring of sectors in decline and the training of the unemployed. The ESF and the ERDF were later unified under the name of "structural funds".

Despite the fact that structural funds were redistributive in nature, they did not create any major political conflict in the Council until the first half of the 1980s. This happened for at least two reasons. The first was that practically all the member states of the time (9), perhaps with the exception of Luxembourg, had regions in need of industrial restructuring that could potentially benefit from these funds. In this sense, the redistributive effect was perceived as taking place between wealthier and poorer regions, not between wealthier and poorer states. The second reason was that structural funds were often used as precious bargaining chips for larger legislative bargains within the Council of the EU. More specifically, the wealthier and more liberal member states would use them in order to convince the more "recalcitrant" member state to accept measures that expanded the internal market. This log-rolling practice is supported by historical evidence and confirmed by numerous studies on EU legislative dynamics (Bailer et al. 2015; Mattila 2006; Moravcsik/Vachudova 2003; Rodden 2002; Thielemann 2005).

It was not until the first half of the 1980s, and in particular with the European Council of Fontainebleau of 1984, that a conflict over the redistribution of EU-level resources started to emerge. This conflict was notoriously sparked by Margaret Thatcher' diplomatic offensive which aimed at reducing the UK's contribution to the EU budget. To be sure, the UK net contribution to the EU budget had been an issue since its accession in 1973, remaining a concern under the Heath, Wilson and Callaghan administrations (Moravcsik 1998, p. 349). However, Thatcher was the first prime minister to use an aggressive retaliatory strategy to obtain a substantial rebate on the UK net contribution to the EU budget. At the European Council of Fontainebleau, she managed to obtain a permanent annual rebate corresponding to 66 percent of its annual net contribution (European Council 1984). The decision created a deep discontent among the other member states, particularly among those (like France) who had to foot the bill of the UK rebate. More to the point, the Council of Fontainebleau marked the introduction of a principle that became widely invoked in all the subsequent budgetary negotiations: the principle of "*juste retour*". This principle is based on the assumption that the part of the revenue paid by each member state to complement the EU's "Traditional Own Resources" (TOR) should be proportional – or at least have a strong degree of proportionality – to the amount of benefits received by the same member state.[2] In essence, it is a fiscally regressive principle (Benedetto 2012, p. 11) based on the understanding that net contributors to the EU budget should only bear a reasonable burden for those EU programmes that disproportionally benefits some member states, like the structural funds.

The UK rebate prompted some member states to react with counterclaims or demands of "correction mechanisms", in order to reduce their net contribution to the budget. The first correction, which was agreed at the same Council of Fontainebleau, allowed Germany to pay only 66 percent of the amount due to compensate the UK rebate. The payment of the remaining 34 percent was therefore shared proportionally among the other states. A second set of corrections was agreed in 2000, when four member states (Austria, Germany, the Netherlands and Sweden) claimed a reduction in the amount they had to pay to finance the UK rebate, and obtained to pay only a quarter of their standard share (Council of the European Union 2000).

Some member states gradually learnt that asking a reduction in their contribution to the budget could somewhat boost their domestic approval rate, especially if they could declare before the national press that they were able to negotiate a great deal for the country. This further encouraged the request of a *juste retour* and spearheaded a third wave of corrections mechanism, agreed in 2007. The Council Decision on the system of own resources of that year allowed some member states to reduce the value added tax (VAT) call rate used to calculate each member state's VAT-based contribution. Hence, the VAT call rate was reduced to 0.225 percent for Austria, to 0.15 percent for Germany, and to 0.10 percent for the Netherlands and Sweden. Moreover, a substantial reduction on national contributions based on the Gross National Income (GNI) was agreed to the Netherlands (605 million euro) and to Sweden (150 million euro, Council of the European Union 2007). The joint effect of these correction mechanisms clearly determined an erosion of the EU revenue (Cipriani 2014).

The last round of correction mechanisms was agreed in 2014. In particular, the VAT-based contribution was set to 0.15 percent for Germany, the Netherland and Sweden (it was 0.30 percent for all the other member states). Moreover, Denmark, the Netherlands and Sweden received a reduction of their (GNI)-based contribution, respectively of 135 million euro, 695 million euro and 185 million euro. Finally, the Austrian GNI-based contribution was reduced by 30 million euro in 2014, 20 million euro in 2015 and ten million euro in 2016 (Council of the European Union 2007). The whole set of correction mechanisms agreed since Fontainebleau is represented in Table 3.1.

Table 3.1: System of own resources – correction mechanisms

Member State	1984	2001	2007	2014
Austria		Reduced contribution to finance the UK rebate: 25% of its standard share	Reduced VAT call rate (0.225%)	Reduction of the GNI-based contribution by €30 m in 2014, €20 m in 2015, and €10 m in 2016.
Denmark				Reduction of the GNI-based contribution: €130 m
Germany	Reduced contribution to finance the UK rebate (66% of the normal share)	Reduced contribution to finance the UK rebate: 25% of its standard share	Reduced VAT call rate (0.15%)	Reduced VAT call rate (0.15%)
Netherlands		Reduced contribution to finance the UK rebate: 25% of its standard share	Reduced VAT call rate (0.10%) Reduced GNI-based contribution: €605 m	Reduced VAT call rate (0.15%) Reduction of the GNI-based contribution: €695 m
Sweden		Reduced contribution to finance the UK rebate: 25% of its standard share	Reduced VAT call rate (0.10%) Reduced GNI-based contribution: €150 m	Reduced VAT call rate (0.15%) Reduction of the GNI-based contribution: €185 m
United Kingdom	Annual rebate: 66% reduction on the VAT-based resource payment.	Annual rebate	Annual rebate	Annual rebate

Sources: European Council (1984); Council Decisions on the system of own resources (various years)

Budget rebates between political rhetoric and real effects

Almost all the rebates and correction mechanism mentioned in the previous section have been agreed after lengthy rounds of hard bargaining, characterized by cross-vetoing and logrolling as a way to extract concessions from the other member states. For instance, in the series of EU summits lading to the Council of Fontainebleau, Margaret Thatcher repeatedly threatened to use her veto, and refused to lift it until the "British budget problem" was resolved (Wyles/Cheeseright 1983). In turn, Germany withheld its support to the UK rebate until a programme for supporting the German farmers was put on the agenda (Dawnay 1984). In the same way, during the negotiations for the MFF 2007-2013, Italy promised a veto in case the structural funds destined to the poorer regions of Southern Italy were cut, and during the talks for the MFF 2014-2020, Denmark publicly threatened to use its veto in case its request for a rebate was rejected (Parker et al. 2005; Jacobsen 2012). There are many other examples that could be mentioned, all of which can be explained by a common factor: the redistributive tension that arises every time EU political leaders have to decide how to allocate the common fiscal resources, and where to collect them.

Undoubtedly, domestic politics plays a fundamental role in the rise of redistributive conflicts within the Council. A veto threat signals domestic constituencies that the government is defending their interest, thereby increasing the chances to boost the government's approval rate. This effect may even be amplified by the national media reporting on the Council's negotiations, especially when the government can show to have a hard line on a deal that will bring a relative gain to the country. The most paradigmatic example of this type of exercise in political rhetoric is the famous quote by Thatcher (1979) at the press conference of the Dublin European Council:

> Broadly speaking, for every £2 we contribute we get £1 back. That leaves us with a net contribution of £1,000 million pounds next year to the Community and rising in the future. It is that £1,000 million on which we started to negotiate, because we want the greater part back. But it is not asking the Community for money; it is asking the Community to have our own money back!

Examples of this type of rhetoric focused on protecting or "repatriating" fiscal resources abound, and quite interestingly, they are evenly distributed across the whole political spectrum. For instance, in October 2012 Helle Thorning-Schmidt, former Prime minister of Denmark and leader of the Danish social democratic party, strongly advocated a significant rebate for

Denmark. In order to signal her hard-line position to domestic constituencies, she took advantage of a talk given to the Danish Parliamentary Committee on European Affairs to trumpet her government's stance before the national press (Jacobson 2013):

> We are going to get our rebate, and if we don't get our rebate, then we will have to use the veto. It's very, very simple.

The theoretical literature on European integration, particularly liberal intergovernmentalism, has widely explored the role of domestic politics in explaining preference formation and EU-level bargaining, including the budgetary bargaining. (Moravcsik 1998). Nevertheless, it remains unclear whether these rebates, and the political rhetoric that surrounds them, have a substantive impact on the EU budgetary dynamics. What is the real effect of these correction mechanisms on the net fiscal position of member states? What is the impact on the EU budget's redistributive capacity? The current literature has not yet answered these questions. Yet, it is crucial to consider them, for at least one reason. Multiple studies have shown that the process of political and economic integration in the long run have determined higher levels of inequality in Europe, both across countries and within countries (Beckfield 2006, 2009; Busemeyer/Tober 2015). An EU budget with enough redistributive capacity is thus necessary to foster cohesion and equality across the different regions of Europe.

In the empirical section of this paper, I evaluate the extent to which the various correction mechanisms and rebates that have been put into place during different negotiation rounds have affected the balance between net contributors and net beneficiaries in the long run. In order to evaluate this impact, I use a measure that tracks the changing net fiscal position of all the member states *vis-à-vis* the EU budget. The measure, developed by the European Commission, is called OBB and is computed as a difference between a country's net contributions of the EU budget (gross contribution minus the administrative expenditure retained by the member state) and the net EU expenditure in the same country. This measure, expressed in million euro, is calculated in such a way that the sum of all the member states' OBBs adds up to a zero. For illustration, the formula is reported below.

$$OBB_i = TAE_i - ADM_i - TNC_i \times \left(\frac{TAE_{EU} - ADM_{EU}}{TNC_{EU}}\right)$$

Where:
TAE_i = Total Allocated Expenditure to state *i*
ADM_i = Administrative Expenditure allocated to state *i*
TNC_i = Total National Contribution of state *i*
TAE_{EU}= Total Allocated Expenditure to EU
ADM_{EU}= Administrative Expenditure allocated to EU
TNC_{EU} = Total National Contribution of all member states

As Cipriani correctly points out, this number represents a mere accounting exercise of certain financial costs and benefits derived from the EU by each member state (Cipriani 2014). It provides no information on the impact it produces on the national economies, and no indication on the extent to which it contributes to the achievement of the EU's social and economic goals. Yet, it remains a solid and reliable measure of the member state's net fiscal position *vis-à-vis* the EU budget. In fact, it is the indicator most frequently used by the member states during the negotiations for the MFF.

In order to have a comprehensive picture of how the OBB evolved in the long run and across the member states, I complied a cross-section time series dataset on the basis of data provided by the European Commission and the European Court of Auditors (ECA). The most recent data points were available online, whereas the earlier data were obtained by the Commission and the ECA upon specific request. The time series start either when the member state joined the EU, or at the earliest available data point provided by the two institutions. In order to make data comparable across time and across countries, avoiding the spurious effect of inflation and the effect determined by the country's economic size, I used a relative measure: OBB as a percentage of GNI. An illustration of a sample of the time series is provided below.

Starting with Figure 3.1, which represents the evolution of OBB in the core EU countries, we notice that they all have a general trend toward a negative net balance. This can be easily seen by looking at how the time series evolve with reference to the horizontal (solid) line departing from 0 and representing the perfect balance. If the time series moves above the line, the country is running a positive net balance, which means that it is transferring to the EU budget less resources than it is receiving from it – for instance in regional funds or agricultural policy. If the time series moves below that line, the country is in negative net balance. The figure is expressed as OBB as a percentage of GNI, hence the effect of the country's economic size is controlled. This adjustment is necessary because otherwise the net budgetary balance of each country would be mostly depending on the relative size of its economy.

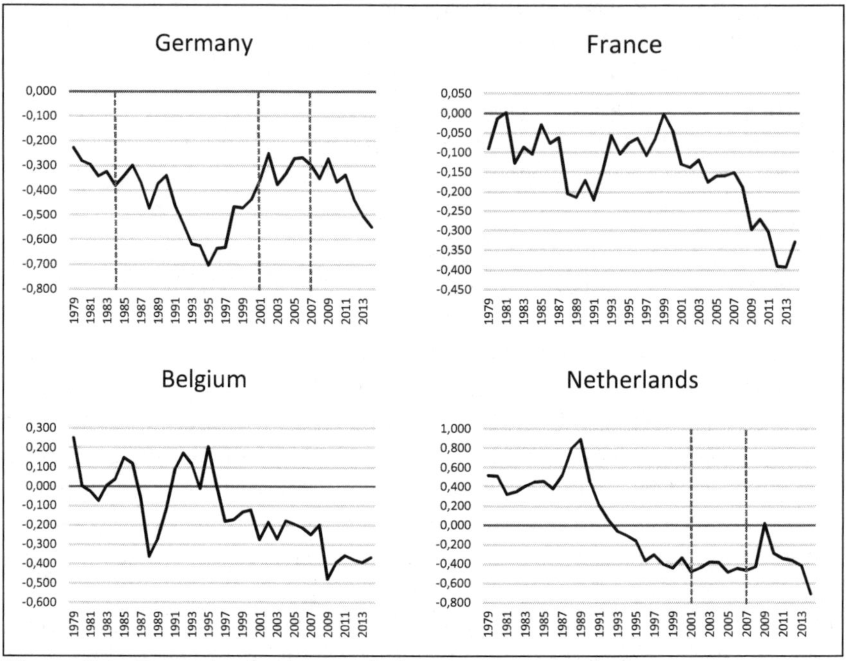

Figure 3.1: Operating budgetary balances: core members
Note: OBB as % of Gross National Income.
Source: own calculations based on data of DG Budget and European Court of Auditors.

Looking at Figure 3.1, we notice that Germany and France have always remained in the negative area, although with some oscillations. This is hardly surprising, given that they are two founding members of the European Union and two of the wealthiest ones. Among them, Germany is by far the strongest net contributor with a negative balance that has historically oscillated between 0.2 percent and 0.7 percent of GNI, whereas France's net contribution has stayed within a band that varies from 0 to 0.4 percent of GNI. The situation is different in Belgium and the Netherlands. In particular, Belgium started as a net contributor in 1979, and then for some years its status oscillated between net beneficiary and net contributor. From 1996, however, Belgium has remained a net contributor with a constant negative trend in its net balance. The Netherlands, on the other hand, show a general negative trend, with a change of status in 1993.

Until then, they were net beneficiary, whereas after 1993 thy became net contributors.

Another feature of Figure 3.1 is the dashed vertical lines appearing on the Germany and the Netherlands charts. These represent the years when they obtained a rebate, or a correction mechanism. Starting with Germany, we can see in 1984 the first correction that was adopted at Fontainebleau as a response to the UK rebate, and the two additional corrections in 2001 and 2007. The first was a lower contribution toward the UK rebate, and the second was a specially reduced VAT call rate applied to TOR collected in Germany. As we can see, none of these corrections reversed the negative trend in the fiscal balance. Quite the contrary, the corrections of 1984 and 2007 appear to have had a "paradoxical" effect. With regard to the Netherlands, Figure 3.1 shows the two corrections agreed in 2001 and 2007, similar in nature (but not in size) to the corrections applied to Germany. The first correction does not appear to have any effect at all on the Netherlands' net balance, while the second one appears to have an effect, although a short-lived one: after an initial inversion of the trend in 2009, the OBB goes back to its general negative trend. All in all, the lengthy negotiations Germany and the Netherlands have embarked upon to gain these concessions, and the political rhetoric employed to justify it do not appear to have produced much of an effect.

The OBB dynamics in southern Europe is remarkably different. Looking at Figure 3.2, we see that Italy has changed its status over the years from net beneficiary to net contributor, in a general negative trend although with many oscillations. Together with Belgium and the Netherlands, Italy is the paradigmatic example of a state that developed its economic growth within the EU, and once grown, it started to "give back" to the rest of the EU, contributing with a negative OBB to the growth of the other countries. In this sense, it is a success story of EU redistributive politics.

The other southern European states represented in Figure 3.2 have maintained, with some oscillations, a positive net balance, mostly due to the EU expenditure in regional policy, agricultural policy, and the European Social Fund. However, starting from 1996, Spain has seen a progressively declining net balance, to the point that in most recent years it has almost reached the zero point. Portugal and Greece, on the other hand, have seen their positive balance slowly decline over the 1990s and the 2000s, until they reached the outset of the economic and financial crisis, when their net balance inverted its direction toward a more positive balance. This dynamic is extremely interesting because it shows that the EU budget is indeed very responsive to the changing economic conditions of member states. The numbers on the y-axis show the how important the EU redistributive policies are for these countries, even in terms of capacity. The net EU funding toward these countries, for instance, represents about two percent of Portugal's GNI, and about three percent of Greece's GNI.

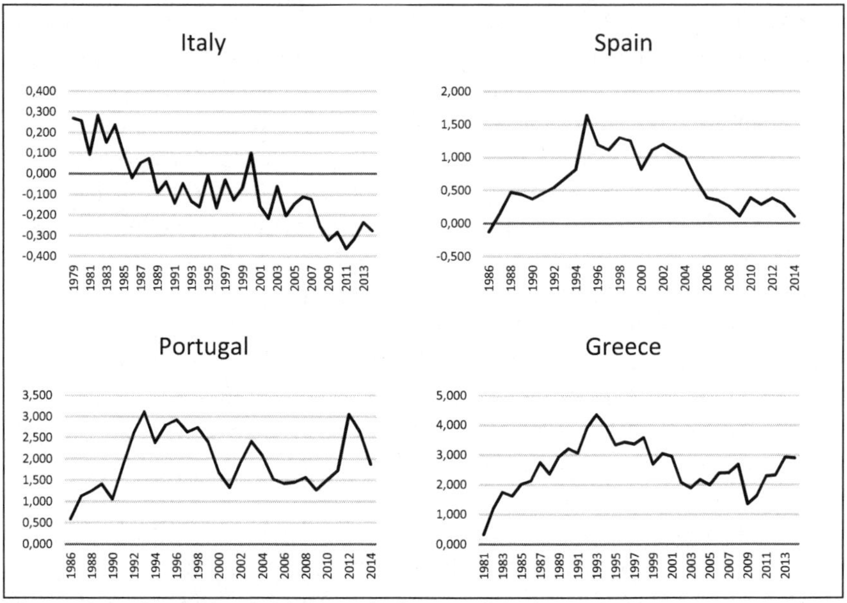

Figure 3.2: Operating budgetary balances: Southern Europe
Note: OBB as % of Gross National Income.
Source: own calculations based on data of DG Budget and European Court of Auditors.

The eastern European countries share a consistent positive trend in their net balance, as shown in Figure 3.3. This is mainly due to their limited contribution to the EU budget, and to the relatively high EU spending in these countries, in the form of regional, cohesion, social and agricultural funding. Indeed, the numbers on the Y axis show that the EU budget has a relevant capacity here, accounting for 3.5 percent of Polish GNI, and almost six percent of Hungarian GNI.

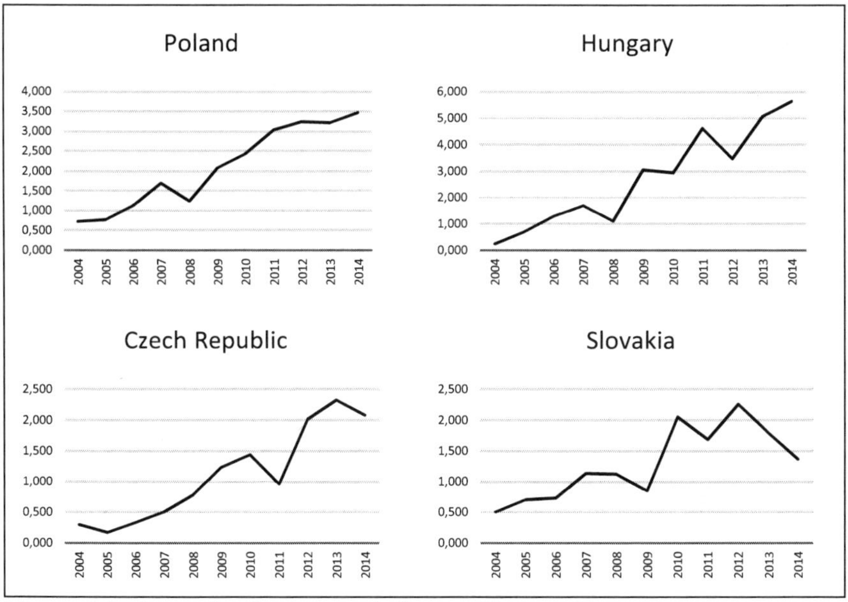

Figure 3.3: Operating budgetary balances: Eastern Europe
Note: OBB as % of Gross National Income.
Source: own calculations based on data of DG Budget and European Court of Auditors.

Let us now turn to Figure 3.4, representing the OBB dynamics in the northern European countries. Starting with the UK, we notice that the general trend is quite oscillatory, although the net balance generally tends to remain in the negative area. What is really striking about this chart is that it shows that the Thatcher's bold political campaign to 'bring the money back' has not produced much results. Quite the contrary, it has made the UK's net balance even more negative. We can see this from the dashed vertical line placed on 1984, in correspondence with the Fontainebleau agreements. In the aftermath of Fontainebleau, the time series markedly turns to negative, after a brief inversion in 1986. The trend then gets closer to zero and remains around that area for around 20 years, after which it gets negative again. The case of the UK shows that the gulf between the rhetoric of *juste retour* and the real numbers can in fact be quite wide.

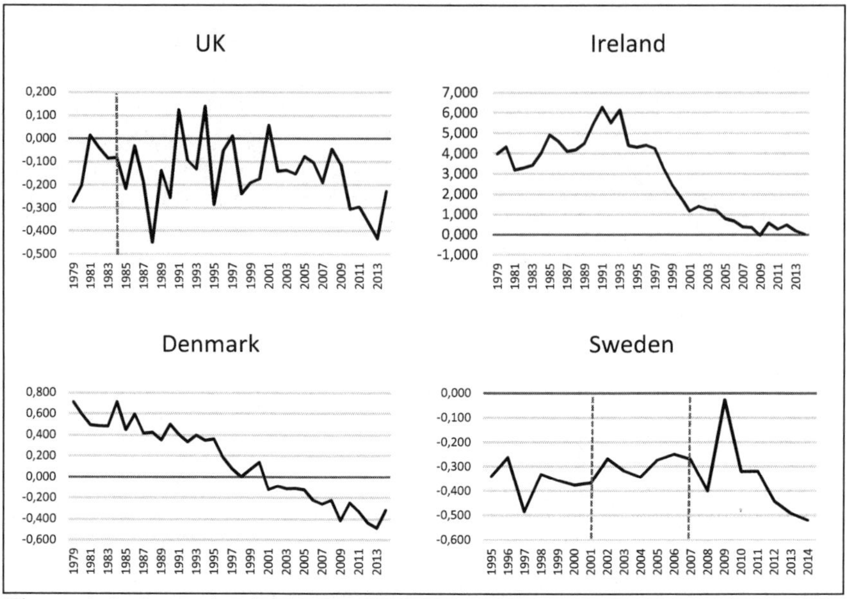

Figure 3.4: Operating budgetary balances: Northern Europe
Note: OBB as % of Gross National Income.
Source: own calculations based on data of DG Budget and European Court of Auditors.

Moving to the other charts of Figure 3.4, we find Ireland and Denmark, which appear to be two additional success stories of EU redistributive politics. Until the end of the 1990s both of them were net beneficiaries, although Ireland benefited much more than Denmark, with a positive net balance reaching a peak of six percent of GNI in the early 1990s. With the end of the decade, Ireland reached an almost perfect balance, whereas Denmark entered the area of negative balance, contributing more to the EU budget than it receives from it. Once more, these figures present evidence that the EU redistributive mechanism is very sensitive to the changing economic conditions of the member states, and proves to be more responsive than generally believed.

Finally, the chart on Sweden shows that the country has always kept a negative balance since its accession to the EU, with some remarkable oscillation. Again, it is interesting to see how the two corrections negotiated at different points in time (represented by the dashed lines) affected its net balance. The first adjustment, negotiated in 2001 (a significant reduction on the UK rebate) only had a very small effect. The second adjustment, composed of a reduction on the VAT call rate plus a reduction on the GNI-based contribution, had the paradoxical effect of reinforcing the negative balance, after a brief inversion of trend in 2009.

Overall, the empirical evidence presented in this section show some recurrent patterns in EU redistributive politics, some of which are quite puzzling and require further explanation based on our theoretical understanding of the budgetary process. Whenever a member state has requested, and thoroughly negotiated, a rebate or correction mechanism, the effect on its net budgetary balance has either been insignificant, or has produced an effect that is paradoxically contrary to the original intention. How do we explain this? And how do we account for this contrast between the rhetoric of *juste retour*, played in domestic political arenas, and the reality of actual numbers?

Explaining EU redistributive politics: the two-level game

Some recent empirical literature on decision-making in the Council has shown that member states are remarkably unwilling, and generally unlikely, to make generous concessions to the other states, particularly the core members of the EU (Naurin 2015). In his extensive empirical analysis of permanent representatives' attitude toward the other member states, Naurin found that the consensual style of decision making in the Council does not determine an "upgrading" of national interest into a common interest. Quite the contrary, state power is found to be the most influential factor in explaining legislative outcomes. Other studies prove with a strong empirical evidence that there are multiple cleavages in the Council, and among these, the cleavage between the net contributors and the net beneficiaries is one of the most powerful ones, leading to conflicts along distributional coalitions (Bailer et al. 2015). This cleavage is not surprising, considering that political unions with a highly decentralized fiscal and redistributive policy are generally very unlikely to redistribute resources across regions (Beramendi 2007, 2012).

In light of the latter theoretical and empirical literature, the finding that the EU budget's redistributive function works in accordance with its original purpose and is relatively immune to national campaigns to reduce fiscal redistribution is quite puzzling. How can we explain it?

There are at least three plausible explanations. The first is related to the way the EU institutions calculate revenue that each member state is requested to transfer to the EU, in particular the GNI-based resource. As Cipriani points out (Cipriani 2014, p. 7, 8), each year the EU budget revenue is determined in relation to expenditure – not the other way round as in most public budgets. Hence, expenditure is calculated first, and then the

GNI resource is adjusted accordingly to reach budgetary equilibrium. Since expenditure in annual budgets is based on EU-wide programmes and priorities (where the precise net benefit of member states is very hard to determine) and since the European Parliament (EP) is very influential in determining budgetary expenditure, the member states have only a weak control of their OBB.

A second factor is related to the way the composition of the EU expenditure has changed over the years. As Citi shows (2013), the EU spending priorities have shifted, particularly after 1985, toward regional, cohesion and social spending, which disproportionally benefit the poorer members of the EU. Incidentally, these are also the spending areas that were once classified as "non-compulsory spending", i.e. areas in which the Parliament, not the Council, had the last word. Hence, the defence of a national preference in these areas could only have a limited impact. The combined effect of these two factors caused the net balance of the beneficiary countries to continue to grow in the positive area.

The third factor is related to member states' legislative behaviour in the Council. Some recent contributions have shown that there is an intensive log-rolling activity taking place in the Council, whereby wealthier member states "trade" more spending in redistributive programmes in exchange for more liberal market-opening regulatory measures (Aksoy 2012; Bailer et al. 2015; Konig/Junge 2009). This effect is amplified by the smaller member states' disproportionate voting power, which obviously has a significant influence on the EU budget allocations (Mattila 2006; Rodden 2002).

These three factors produce a "dissociation" between two levels of the budgetary game: on the one hand domestic politics with its rhetoric about regaining control over fiscal resources, and on the other hand the complex mechanism that every year leads to the adoption of the EU budget, which severely constraints the ability of the net contributors to curb the redistributive effect of the EU budget.

Conclusion

One of the key functions of the European Union's budget is to operate as a redistributive mechanism to contrast the cross-national and cross-regional inequalities created by the common market. Despite the fact that the principle of "*juste retour*" traditionally animates the intergovernmental negotiations in the Council, the EU budget's original redistributive function has not been altered, even in the long run. Using a novel dataset containing the OBB of all the member states during the timeframe 1979-2014, I have shown that the wealthier members of the EU have constantly maintained – and in some cases increased – their negative budgetary balance toward the rest of the EU, whereas the poorer ones have received a constant flow of resources, which has helped, and in some cases is still helping, their economic development. Interestingly, this dynamic has remained unchanged even in the case of governments taking a strong position against the increase of national transfers towards the rest of the EU, and negotiating rebates and correction mechanisms to their advantage (such as the UK in the 1980s). In this paper, I argued that this seemingly paradoxical effect is determined by the fact that EU redistributive politics is played on two levels, which only have a weak connection: the national level and the supranational level. On the national level, domestic political actors typically push for a reduction of fiscal resources transferred to the EU, because this position typically increases the government's approval rate and the chance of being re-elected. The rhetoric of *juste retour*, in this sense, is used to echo the diffused anti-redistributive policy preferences of national constituencies. On the supranational level, however, the national governments have a weak ability to control both the sources of revenue and expenditure, because the budgetary process is a complex legislative procedure that involves several other veto players, both on the side of revenue and on the side of expenditure. All in all, the separation between these two levels is to be considered a positive feature, because it allows the financial independence of the EU institutions, and allows the EU budget to make a difference in the less developed regions of Europe.

What remains unclear is whether the other known cleavages in the Council, namely the positioning of national governments on the left/right and the pro-/anti- EU continuums have an influence on the redistributive cleavage. Are governments on the left side of the political spectrum more likely to support the EU investment programmes aimed at poorer member states? Are governments that support the deepening of European integration more likely to support a sustained expenditure in regional, cohesion and social policies? These are certainly some legitimate and relevant questions that EU scholars will need to address in future research.

Notes

1 The distinction between distributive and redistributive policies belongs to a typology introduced by Theodore J. Lowi in 1964, which is commonly discussed in

the public policy literature. In essence, redistributive policies consist in the transfer of fiscal resources from the wealthier social groups to the poorer ones, or from wealthier states/regions to the poorer ones, and as such is typically represented as a zero-sum game. In distributive policies the zero-sum game is instead generally absent, either because all the states/regions have an equal chance of getting financed (for instance funding for research and technology development like the framework Programme) or because they finance public goods that are beneficial for all the countries/regions within a political union. Both of them are public investments which will produce social and economic returns in the long term, hence they are not just a mere form 'distribution' or 'redistribution' of public resources.

2 It is worth mentioning that the logic of *juste retour* has at times been coupled with an element of distrust with regard to how EU resources are spent within the member states. This element can be found, for instance, in the implementation method that was specifically devised for the Integrated Mediterranean Programs, which involved a stronger oversight power for the Commission together with 'trilateral partnerships' between regional, national and supranational executives (Bauer 2001). This method was later adopted in the framework of the European Regional Policy.

References

Aksoy, D. 2012. Institutional Arrangements and Logrolling: Evidence from the European Union. *American Journal of Political Science* 56(3): 538-552.

Bailer, S., Mattila, M., and Schneider, G. 2015. Money Makes the EU Go Round: The Objective Foundations of Conflict in the Council of Ministers. *Journal of Common Market Studies* 53(3): 437-456.

Bauer, M. W. 2001. *A Creeping Transformation? The European Commission and the Management of EU Structural Funds in Germany*. Dordrecht: Kluwer Academic Publishers.

Beckfield, J. 2006. European Integration and Income Inequality. *American Sociological Review* 71(6): 964-985.

Beckfield, J. 2009. Remapping Inequality in Europe: The Net Effect of Regional Integration on Total Income Inequality in the European Union. *International Journal of Comparative Sociology* 50(5-6): 486-509.

Benedetto, G. 2012. Introduction: A History of the Europan Union Budget and the Possibilities for Reform. In *European Union Budget Reform: Institutions, Policy and Economic Crisis*, Eds. Benedetto, G., and Milio, S., 1-20. Basingstoke: Palgrave Macmillan.

Beramendi, P. 2007. Inequality and the Territorial Fragmentation of Solidarity. *International Organization* 61(4): 783-820.

Beramendi, P. 2012. *The Political Geography of Inequality: Regions and Redistribution*. Cambridge: Cambridge UP.

Busemeyer, M.R., and Tober, T. 2015. European integration and the political economy of inequality. *European Union Politics* 16(4): 536-557.

Cipriani, G. 2014. *Financing the EU Budget: Moving Forward or Backwards?* London: Rowman & Littlefield.

Citi, M. 2013. EU budgetary dynamics: incremental or punctuated equilibrium? *Journal of European Public Policy* 20(8): 1157-1173.

Council of the European Union. 2000. Council Decision of 29 September 2000 on the System of the European Communities' Own Resources. *Official Journal of the European Communities* L 253/42.

Council of the European Union. 2007. Council Decision of 7 June 2007 on the System of the European Communities' Own Resources. *Official Journal of the European Communities* L 163/17.

Dawnay, I. 1984. Bonn Threat to Deal on UK Rebate – The European Community Summit. *Financial Times* 26 June 1984.

European Commission. 2007. *European Social Fund: 50 Years Investing in People.* Luxembourg: Office for Official Publications of the European Communities.

European Council. 1984. *European Council Meeting at Fontainebleau. Conclusions of the Presidency.* http://www.consilium.europa.eu/en/european-council/conclusions-/pdf-1992-1975/fontainebleau-european-council,-25-and-26-june-1984/; 15 September 2016.

Jacobsen, H. 2012. *Denmark Ready to Veto EU Budget Unless it Gets a Rebate.* http://www.euractiv.com/section/eu-priorities-2020/news/denmark-ready-to-veto-e-u-budget-unless-it-gets-a-rebate/; 15 September 2016.

Jacobsen, H. 2013. *Denmark Receives € 134 million rebate in New Budget.* http://www.euractiv.com/section/future-eu/news/denmark-receives-134-million-rebate-in-new-budget/; 15. September 2016.

Konig, T., and Junge, D. 2009. Why Don't Veto Players Use Their Power? *European Union Politics* 10: 507-534.

Lowi, T.J. 1964. Review: American Business, Public Policy, Case-Studies, and Political Theory. *World Politics* 16(4): 677-715.

Mattila, M. 2006. Fiscal transfers and redistribution in the European Union: do smaller member states get more than their share? *Journal of European Public Policy* 13(1): 34-51.

Moravcsik, A. 1998. *The Choice for Europe: Social Purpose and State Power from Messina to Maastricht*. Ithaca: Cornell UP.

Moravcsik, A., and Vachudova, M.A. 2003. National Interests, State Power, and EU Enlargement. *East European Politics and Societies* 17(1): 42-57.

Naurin, D. 2015. Generosity in intergovernmental negotiations: The impact of state power, pooling and socialisation in the Council of the European Union. *European Journal of Political Research* 54(4): 726-744.

Parker, G., Thornhill, J., and Adams, C. 2005. UK and France Clash on the UK Budget. *Financial Times* 10 June 2005.

Rodden, J. 2002. Strength in Numbers? Representation and Redistribution in the European Union. *European Union Politics* 3(2): 151-175.

Thatcher, Margaret. 1979. *Press Conference after Dublin European Council.* 30 November 1979. http://www.margaretthatcher.org/document/104180; 15 September 2016.

Thielemann, E.R. 2005. Symbolic politics or effective burden-sharing? Redistribution, side-payments and the European refugee fund. *Journal of Common Market Studies* 43(4): 807-824.

Wyles, J., and Cheeseright, P. 1983. Thatcher Stresses Fair EEC Budget. *Financial Times* 5 December 1983.

Reforming the European Multiannual Financial Framework – Looking for a Policy Window in a Path-dependent Environment

Peter Becker

Despite classical distribution problems, despite the difficult circumstances, and despite heated conflicts along familiar lines, the European Union has always succeeded in agreeing a compromise for a Multiannual Financial Framework (MFF) of the European Union. Every six years, these difficult and highly conflictual negotiations repeat again. The last negotiation process ended in December 2013 with a compromise on the MFF for the period from 2014 until 2020. And again the compromise, the negotiating topics, and in particular the process were criticized as disappointing and insufficient.

Policy makers and external observers agree that the current system needs to be reformed and a variety of reform options lie on the table for many years, for the revenue as for the expenditure side of the EU budget. However, a reform had not been possible yet, the negotiations still follow the given procedures and institutional structures. The European budget and finance system is obviously strongly resistant to change. This status quo-oriented approach raises inevitably two questions:

1. What will be needed to change this unsatisfactory policy-making and to start a far-reaching reform?
2. Why are EU institutions not capable to start this process to reform the EU budget and what mechanisms are feeding this status quo oriented policy?

So, the question of continuity and change is at the center of this chapter. Rejection and refusal to change political institutions is often explained by the phenomenon of path dependence. A policy process, which begins with a fundamental choice and then follows this direction is described as path-dependent. This policy path becomes irreversible as a result of a sequence of self-reinforcing mechanisms and positive feedback processes, hence "history matters" (Pierson 2004, p. 20). Fundamental changes will not be carried out, despite unsatisfactory decisions and inadequate results because of the high political and economic revision costs for political actors.

However, change is still possible albeit often incrementally and with small steps. One of the best-known approaches for the analysis of policy changes is the Multiple Streams Approach (MSA) by John W. Kingdon (Herweg 2011; Cairney/Jones 2016; Jones et al. 2016). According to this approach policy change or reform takes place whenever a policy window opens, a problem is placed on the political agenda by political entrepreneurs, perceived there by policy makers and coupled with a specific solution. Change or path deviation then is the result of the coupling of the three relatively independent streams of problems, possible solutions and political attention (Kingdon 1995).

This chapter tries first to explain briefly the status quo-orientation of the budget policy of the European Union, i.e. the path dependency. Then, in a second step, the chapter traces back and analyzes why reform and change failed so far by using the MSA. To answer or at least to discuss this question, I will describe and explain the complicated and opaque budgetary policy in the European Union, in particular the recent negotiations on the MFF 2014-2020, the again unsuccessful attempt to reform the policy. Hence, the question will be in the foreground, why a coupling of the three streams has not been possible yet, although a reform window opened foreseeable and although strong political and influential players argued for reform.

It seems that the current impasse and inability to trigger fundamental or off-path change of European budgetary policy is rooted in the failure to define the most pressing problems of the policy. The traditional grouping into net payer and net recipient Member States already shows up in a divergent understanding of the flaws and the problems of the current policy, which have to be tackled. This common understanding and the insight in the necessity to change the policy path has not emerged, neither in the policy nor in the politics stream of European budgetary policy making. Consequently, there is no issue to be placed on the political agenda that could receive the attention of political actors. Without this awareness about the necessity for change in the politics stream it is impossible to deduce alternative solutions, which then can create a new path.

Starting in 2016 the EU institutions, Member States, and the policy community will again review the EU budget and discuss options for reform – the EP made this review process a precondition for its approval during the hard negotiations on the MFF 2014-2020. And already in 2015 a group of experts under the chairmanship of the former Italian Prime

Minister and EU Commissioner Mario Monti has begun to discuss changes in the system of own resources. It is therefore predictable that the European budget and its need for reform will once again be on the Union's agenda next year.

Path dependency and multiple streams as theoretical concepts

Path dependency is the central concept of historical institutionalism (HI) introducing the temporal dimension into public policies (Pierson 1996, Pollack 2004, Thelen 1999). Path dependence refers "to social processes that exhibit positive feedback and thus generate branching patterns of historical development" (Pierson 2004, p. 21). A new path becomes "locked-in" and can shape and constrain the decision-making later in time. A "lock-in" moment means that an institution or policy "becomes entrenched and difficult to change, even in the face of a changing policy environment and changing actor preferences" (Pollack 1996, p. 440). These so created political institutions and policies are more or less resistant to change and generate incentives for political actors to keep them to a great extent unchanged and only to adapt them incrementally. Historically constructed institutions predetermine political decisions and reproduce institutional mechanisms mainly by positive feedback loops. These feedback loops increase the positive returns or rise switching costs. Hence, a path becomes locked-in when these gains are lower or losses are higher than the gains or losses when switching to an alternative path. Path dependent processes hence are self-enforcing; a political decision in one direction evokes further decisions in the same direction and a path is established and locked-in.

Paul Pierson distinguished four mechanisms to increase returns to political actors and hence to strengthen path dependency and finally to facilitate a lock-in moment. He argued that the (a) logic of collective action, (b) the institutional density of politics, (c) political authority and power asymmetries, as well as (d) the complexity and opacity of politics all can increase returns or at least switching costs and so reaffirm the actor's intentions to follow the path. "In each case, there are reasons to anticipate that steps in a particular direction can trigger a self-reinforcing dynamic." (Pierson 2004, p. 40). The self-reinforcing dynamic and self-reproducing process of path dependency will not work automatically but needs process sequencing and policy-making by political actors (Deeg 2005; Howlett

2009). And these political actors are driven mainly by functional and utilitarian, hence rational considerations (Thelen 1999).

Path dependency, however, does not mean that institutions and policies remain completely unchanged (Streeck/Thelen 2005; Mahoney/Thelen 2010). Political institutions are not static or resistant and unwilling to change (Olsen 2009). The path dependency-approach can explain slow and only incremental institutional change resp. institutional continuity and is mainly used to analyze the development of public policies (Kay 2005). “Once created, institutions often change in subtle and gradual ways over time” (Mahoney/Thelen 2010, p. 1).

Change can occur as an evolutionary process, i.e. as gradual modifications of institutions and structures by small, incremental adaptation to a constantly changing environment often triggered or amplified by institutional learning processes (Pierson 2004, p. 137).

Mahoney and Thelen claimed that useful tools to explain this gradual evolution of political institutions are still missing (Mahoney/Thelen 2010). They tried to fill this gap by distinguishing four types of institutional change – displacement, layering, drift and conversion.[1] Displacement means that old rules will be removed and new rules will be introduced instead; layering will keep the old rules unchanged and new rules will only be attached to the existing ones; drift, however, changes the content of rules because of shifts in external conditions while keeping the old rules formally unchanged, and finally conversion occurs when the old rules remain unchanged but were interpreted in new ways. Hence, to differentiate these four types of gradual change Mahoney and Thelen developed two dimensions – the reach and scope of change and the relation to existing institutions and old rules.

However, the question is still open, how to separate incremental adaptations from fundamental change. Johannes Lindner distinguished between “on-path changes”, which he described as “adaptations of the existing path that are in line with the current mechanism of reproduction”, and “off-path changes”, which “replace the existing mechanism of reproduction and introduce a new one” (Lindner 2006, p. 166).

Whereas the path dependency approach focusses on incremental or on-path changes and tries to explain the continuity of locked-in policies, the MSA developed by John W. Kingdon is one of the best-known and most popular approaches to analyze path deviation or off-path changes. While initially developed to explain the agenda setting in the US presidential system, Nikolaos Zahariadis extended the approach to parliamentary systems and to the entire process of policy-making including decision-making processes (Zahariadis 2003). And because MSA focuses on the ambiguity of political processes, the approach seems to be very useful to capture the extraordinary complexity of the EU political system and the ambiguity, which "is an indispensable part of the EU policy process" (Zahariadis 2008, p. 527). So MSA is helpful "in identifying and helping to resolve puzzles of EU policy processes and policy-making" (Ackrill et al. 2013, p. 883).

Political processes or a policy will change only when three streams, flowing independently through the political system, can be "coupled", i.e. when a specific problem is placed on the political agenda, can be connected to alternatives and solutions flowing through the "primeval soup" of ideas in the policy stream, and then can catch the attention of political actors. When the time is ripe for change and a policy window opens, a "policy entrepreneur" can couple the streams. These entrepreneurs are "advocates who are willing to invest their resources - time, energy, reputation, money - to promote a position in return for anticipates future gain in the form of material, purposive, or solidary benefits" (Kingdon 1995, p. 179). Their role is to put an issue to the fore of the political agenda, to prepare the political field and then to couple the streams. However, entrepreneurs cannot open a policy window; the special ability of entrepreneurs is rather to recognize the opening of a window. They are therefore "well-informed and well-connected insiders who provide the knowledge and the tenacity to help to couple the 'streams'" (Cairney/Jones 2016, p. 41). With regard at European policy-making, the European Commission is often perceived as policy entrepreneur in the EU (Crespy/Menz 2015) because of its right to initiate legislative processes and policy changes. However, the Commission is not a homogeneous actor and is not the only potential entrepreneur in the European multi-level system trying to "establish the necessary consensus between the Member States with their policy proposal" (Ackrill et al. 2013, p. 875).

Options to couple the streams are rare and coupling only possible when the time is ripe. Kingdon developed for this moment the concept of "policy windows". The coupling of the streams and thus the possibility for political change is feasible only when a window opens. "Policy windows pose limitations to rational policy-making by framing the context within which choice is made, while the notion of coupling stresses the impact of entrepreneurial politics and strategies in the EU policy-making" (Zahariadis 2008, p. 515). Why and when a window will open (or close) is determined by events in the politics- or in the problem-stream, which is why Kingdon distinguished between problem and politics windows (Kingdon

1995, p. 173). Furthermore, Kingdon differentiated between windows that open foreseeable and unpredictable windows. In addition to this distinction between predictability and origin an additional differentiation criterion is discussed as "non-change windows" and "change windows" (Ackrill et al. 2013, p. 880). Windows hence can be categorized by their objective and functionality to change a public policy or an institution. This means on the other hand to differentiate between various widths and duration of open windows (Howlett 1998; Keeler 1993).

The extension of Kingdon's original theoretical approach to the entire policy-making process and to parliamentary systems of government requires the distinction between two different coupling processes including two windows, which open at different points of time during the policy-making process. This distinction necessitates the analysis of two coupling processes, the "agenda coupling" and then the "decision coupling" (Zohlnhöfer 2016; Herweg et al. 2015; Zohlnhöfer et al. 2015; Herweg 2011). Accordingly, the first coupling is possible when the agenda window opens, either in the problem or in the politics stream. After policy entrepreneurs have used this window successfully to place their preferred solution on the political agenda, the second window opens with the beginning of the formal decision-making process. The window of opportunity, which then will make the decision coupling possible, however, opens out of the policy stream (Herweg 2013, p. 336).

The question if a policy process can successfully change a policy is closely connected with the question from where the off-path change process gets started. Sebastiaan Princen and Mark Rinhard distinguish between agenda setting "from above" and "from below". From above means the political decision-makers in the European Council will open the window of opportunity; from below indicates the working level, i.e. the policy experts of the general directories of the Commission or in the Council working groups (Princen/Rinhard 2006). Problem windows usually open "from below" and follow the technical and administrative procedures of the European policy process. They typically allow only for incremental modifications of the policy and can therefore be classified as "non-change windows". In case, a window opens "from above" political and ideological aspects play a significantly greater role and thus increase the opportunity for fundamental changes. So, the localization of the origin of a change process can influence the width of an opened window and thus predetermine the extent of possible changes.

While the path dependency approach emphasizes the continuity of policy-making the multiple streams framework accentuates off-path changes.

Combining path dependency with multiple streams therefore should provide some hints to explain what is necessary to start far-reaching change, i.e. path deviation, hence what is needed to end the self-reinforcing effects of locked-in institutions and to minimize switching costs.[2]

The European budget in path-dependent streams

The European budgetary and financial system, as we know it today[3], has grown slowly in a more than 25-year-long process with strong signs of path dependency. At the beginning stood the landmark decision to introduce in 1988 new structures with the first financial package, the Delors I-package. This first MFF, or at this time named financial perspective, had been certainly the "crucial founding moment" of a new institutional formation (Thelen 1999, p. 387). The new path had been triggered by the general perception that reforms of the European budgetary policy were strongly needed due to Euro-sclerosis in the European Community in the seventies and eighties. In addition, the Commission had been successful to link its proposal for the first MFF to the project to create the internal market and so to deepen European integration. The new instrument and procedure had been institutionalized by adopting the Delors II-package, the MFF for the years 1993 to 1999. However, the new package had been adjusted and modified for example with the extension of the period from five to seven years. Three MFF followed – the Agenda 2000 for the years 2000 to 2006 and the two subsequent financial frameworks for the years 2007 until 2013 and from 2014 to 2020 (Laffan 1997; Laffan/Lindner 2014; Becker 2014). During these five negotiation rounds on financial packages a European budgetary acquis emerged (Laffan 2000), both concerning negotiating issues and conflicts and with regard at process, procedures and dramaturgy of the negotiation process. This very complex negotiations always require difficult coordination of various negotiating arenas and groups. So, this process allows a variety of options to block or postpone compromises, but also opens up possibilities for package deals and side payments and between Member States, groups of Member States, policies and negotiating arenas (Lindner 2006; Schild 2008).

Each negotiation process on a new MFF package stabilized the process and procedures, reinforced the institutional structures, and at the same time increased the switching costs – even if the outcome of the negotiations had not been satisfactory and less and less convincing. The costs of path switching would affect not only the European Union and its institutions but also and especially the Member States, either as net contributor with increasing payments to the EU budget or as net recipient with rising uncertainty and insecurity about financial benefits and European funding. The Member States seemed to have developed a vested interest in the maintenance of the MFF and the necessary package deals. This process created sunk costs and with each new MFF the price to change the path increased. The suboptimal stability, continuity of procedures, predictability of conflict issues and bargaining power, and finally certain predictability of results outweighs the uncertainty and unpredictability of comprehensive negotiations to create a new, reformed European budget policy (Becker 2012a). Hence, not positive feedback loops with high policy gains, but increasing switching costs and unsecure alternatives created this path of European budgetary policy.

Learning process and the consensus to maintain the negotiation process and to avoid uncertainty had been strengthened by a second lock-in mechanism, the decision-making by unanimity. Although the MFF expires regularly and thus a policy window opens to reform and change the system and the process predictably, unanimity means a very high hurdle because a new system has to find the consensus of all actors. The inclusion of the MFF into European primary law with Article 312 of the Lisbon Treaty including the decision-making by unanimity has been the final lock-in step – the European budgetary system reached a largely irreversible equilibrium.

The European budget in three streams

Nevertheless, decision-makers in EU organs and Member States widely agree that flaws of the system have to be tackled. Therefore, the question is how to overcome the impasse and to start a change process. The MSA is one of the best-known research frameworks to analyze policy change (Rüb 2009) and might be helpful to define the elements needed to start this change process.

Always at the beginning of European MFF negotiations, the European Commission has to forward its proposal in which the institution describes its strategic and financial objectives as well as its political priorities for the next budget. This official start requires intense and often contentious discussions within the Commission. But, once the Commission has presented its ideas and proposals, the Member States dominate the negotiations. These negotiations of the Member States receive a special political momentum when the various dossiers are tied together to form a comprehensive package which is then presented to the European Council for the final round of negotiations and decision-making. There the Member States face the greatest pressure for consensus, because the European Council has to strike the final decision by unanimity.

The compromise struck by the heads of states and governments is the culmination of the negotiations; the result, however, is only a political compromise, which is the starting point and the basis for the subsequent legislation. The legally binding decision-making in which the EP is involved starts only then. The final result is the Regulation on the MFF according to Art. 312 of the Lisbon treaty and additional regulations, especially for European spending policies and the own resources. The negotiations to legally implement the MFF takes place in so-called trilogues between the Council presidency, which negotiates on behalf of the Member States, the representatives of the EP, mostly politicians having a seat in the committee of budgets, and the Commissioner responsible for the budget. In this course of formal legislative procedure on the MFF regulation, the Parliament in its capacity as co-legislator is in a stronger position than earlier in the process.

The problem stream

Experts and political actors discussed the shortcomings and the need to reform the EU budget for decades (Lindner 2006). The most famous (and most quoted) criticism of European budgetary policy came from a group of advisers to the European Commission around the Belgian economist André Sapir. In their report "An agenda for a growing Europe" they noted that the EU budget is a "historical relic": "Expenditures, Revenues and procedures are all inconsistent with the present and future state of EU integration" (Sapir 2003, p. 162).

Moreover, European institutions and political actors themselves stated that the existing budget system needs a reform. In 2005 when deciding on the adoption of the MFF 2007-2013 the European Council asked the Commission, to "undertake a full, wide-ranging review covering all aspects of EU spending, including the CAP [Common Agricultural Policy], and of resources, including compensation to the United Kingdom" (European Council 2005, paragraph 80). The former Austrian chancellor Wolfgang Schüssel remarked, looking back at these negotiations, that the system was at its limits. A fundamental reform was necessary, otherwise "the governments will be 'up in arms'" (Schüssel 2007, p. 3).

The critics always pointed at the structural deficiencies of the existing European budgetary policy. The EU institutions were unable to react flexible to changes in the political environment and to answer quickly on new challenges (Tarschys 2011; Heinemann et al. 2010; Caesar 2006). Fundamental reforms including the comprehensive reorientation of spending priorities and a fairer and more transparent funding system of the EU budget were highly necessary. The wide range of critique can be grouped into four points:

1. The volume of the MFF with currently around one percent of EU Gross National Income (GNI) is too small in order to set a real economic impulse or to achieve political incentives with the EU budget. In addition, critics state that the MFF duration of seven years makes the EU budget highly inflexible. In sum, the EU were unable to act forcefully and quickly to new challenges due to the limited overall volume of the MFF and the nearly unchangeable fixing of the financial resources of policies for seven years.
2. On the expenditure side of the budget, the EU's limited resources are unilaterally concentrated on two, as some critics say, outdated policies, the common agricultural and cohesion policy. This means that only insufficient resources are available to finance other policies or real European public goods. Moreover, these unbalanced European spending priorities, the policies and their funds, are unfairly distributed between the Member States, because even relatively prosperous Member States benefit from grants and subsidies. The distribution of EU funding goes not by the criteria of wealth and indigence but follows the logic of European package deals (Gros/Micossi 2005).
3. The financing of the EU budget is too complicated and too opaque. The revenue side is characterized by numerous special arrangements and rebates that follow no inherent logic, but are also the result of package deals. The most common example is the British rebate, which is, however, not the only special arrangement (Le Cacheux 2007; Heinemann et al. 2008).
4. The current system of European own resources allows the EU only limited budgetary autonomy. The European organs do not decide on the amount and sources of their revenues, the Member States are still funding almost entirely the budget from their national budgets and pay attention to keep the final decision on volume and modalities of financing. The Member States still draw close borders to an autonomous European budgetary policy (Begg et al. 2008).

The policy stream

To start the debate on reform solutions and to collect ideas and options in the policy community, the European Commission launched a public consultation. The Commission argued for more efficiency of European spending policies: "The modernisation of the EU budget must therefore be about targeting, about maximising the benefits from every euro spent, and about setting the budget firmly in the context of the other ways in which the European Union, its institutions and its Member States, can put Europe on the path to growth and jobs for the future" (European Commission 2010, p. 28). This objective coincided with a broad consensus of experts in the policy community, who argued for a fundamental reform and a significantly improved functionality of the European budgetary policy (Benedetto/Milio 2012).

According the policy community, the concept that European spending policies should focus mainly on measures that promise European added value. European added value often serves as an argument to finance European public goods. Financing public goods and tackling common European challenges is taken as a sign of common responsibility, joint policy-making and communality, and identification with the European integration process – and a special sign of real European added value (Rubio 2011). Additionally, the concept of European public goods has to be defined, to be used to justify higher or less spending through the European budget. Usually the CAP is seen as old-fashioned, whereas expenditures for research and development, innovation and education, energy security and climate policy can boost economic growth and thus create added value. Hence, the concept is often linked to economic development, sustainable and intelligent economic growth.

However, Member states, European institutions and also experts in the policy community all use different criteria, to substantiate the concept. The Commission used three criteria to test added value in various policies: (1) effectiveness, where Member States and regions cannot finance a European public good, (2) efficiency, where European actions secure better results and (3) synergy, where pooled resources can generate and complement national activities (European Commission 2011b). Member states developed additional criteria such as incentives for common policies including common interests, transnational measures, economies of scale, critical mass requirements and efficiency. Precise cost-benefit analyses might also be important, as would impact assessments and evaluations of the improved efficiency of European measures. These criteria show that

European added value is not synonymous with enhanced synergies between national and European policymaking and that the principle has a broader meaning than enhanced efficiency and effectiveness (Becker 2012b). There has no common understanding emerged, how to define European added value and what expenditures to capture under this heading.

This, however, opens the definition of European added value to lobbying to influence the content of the definition and the focus of European spending policies. The Member States benefitting from European funds argue that these spending policies are the best and most convincing symbol of European solidarity. Seen from this perspective, often the principle of European solidarity and subsequently European cohesion policy is mentioned as the best example of European added value (Tarschys 2005). Solidarity is one of the core values of the European Union and a guiding principle of the European integration process as a whole and also of the special European budget negotiations. Defining the extent of European solidarity in the context of budget negotiations is a political question and hence part of the budget negotiations. The net contributing Member States argue that the principle of European solidarity is an excuse to secure European transfers. Hence, the two principles of European solidarity and added value are used by beneficiaries and payers in the framework of European MFF negotiations: either to justify high European structural and cohesion funds as symbols of solidarity or to call for added value to limit European funds and refocus European spending policies. Even if the principles of European solidarity and European added value became the guiding principles framing the budget negotiation, both are political concepts for which it is almost impossible to find a common understanding and an agreed set of quantifiable criteria. Over the years, both principles have become catchwords to argue for more or less money, at least as regards European structural and cohesion funds. The discussion is not about the correct definition or the best criteria for measuring European solidarity or European added value. The debate about the content and the relevance of both principles is a kind of shadow boxing – and each government knows how to argue.

Another proposal, discussed in the policy community, is to split the budget into a budget for European public goods and a budget for the current spending priorities (Blankart/Koester 2012; Neheider/Santos 2011; Blankart/Koester 2009). This form of institutional layering is expected to break the deadlock of the negotiations, focused only on national net payments. The proposal to create a separate compensation fund was based on the same idea to smoothen the traditional conflict between net contributors and beneficiaries (Heinemann 1999).

On the revenue side of the budget, some experts proposed to tackle the perceived injustices of burden sharing by limiting the net payments with the introduction of a correction mechanism. This mechanism should define a net payments-limit, for example a percentage of the national GNI. It would cap the national contributions of the net payers at this given threshold and partially reimburse the net contributions exceeding the threshold. An additional proposal on the revenue side is the ending of the value added tax (VAT)-based own resource. The most far reaching proposal to reform the European system of own resources is still the idea to create a new genuinely European own resource, i.e. a European tax, to strengthen the autonomy of the EU budget from national payments (Le Cacheux 2007; Begg et al. 2008).

The political stream

Restricting the conflicts and finding a compromise between the Member States are of primary importance for the finalization of the MFF negotiations, because all actors have one basic interest in common, to conclude the negotiations with a compromise. However, to find this consensus between all Member States and with all organs of the EU is a very difficult task and depends on the willingness to compromise of all actors and stakeholders.

The negotiations follow almost traditional lines of conflict and are largely predictable. Although the conflicts between net payers and net receivers are paramount, there are also distribution conflicts between individual policy areas, especially agriculture and cohesion. Alongside these tensions between the economically strong northern European member states and the traditionally more backward southern European countries, eastward expansion has added an additional distribution conflict. From the Member States perspective, the net balance remains the relevant indicator and decisive point for assessing the final compromise. National negotiating strategies are consequently characterized by the relationship between gross payments into the EU budget via the EU's own resources mechanism and the returns via EU spending programs, especially under the two largest budget headings.

The antagonistic interests of the Member States can be grouped along three conflict lines:

1. The dispute over the total amount of the MFF, which is dominated by the conflict between net contributors and net recipients. National negotiation positions will be determined also by the distribution of European funds and by so the potential flowbacks through the EU spending programs.
2. The conflict over the distribution between the different MFF headings, which means how the European resources are allocated between the different policies. For example, it is important, also for the national net-payments balance, which agricultural products are subsidized with how much European funds or which regions will receive how much European structural funds.
3. The controversy over a just and transparent financing of the Union, in which the question of fair contributions and the variety of special arrangements and rebates are in focus. In particular the British rebate had always been disputed. Moreover, in this context regularly the proposal to introduce an EU autonomous own resources, an EU tax, is discussed.

Furthermore, the EP as co-legislator of the MFF regulation has its own interests, even if it is not a uniform actor (Becker/Bauer 2016, p. 105/106). Nevertheless, according to Art. 312 of the Treaty on the Functioning of the European Union (TFEU) the majority of the Parliament has to give its consent to adopt the MFF regulation. "This increases the agenda-setting power of the EP though the change may not be significant" (Benedetto 2013, p. 355).

To frame these complex negotiations and to achieve consensus a favorable negotiation environment is highly helpful. However, the political situation became worse since 2009/10 because of the massive economic and financial crisis that changed the economic and political environment for the EU budget negotiations fundamentally. The fiscal opportunities were reduced significantly in all Member States and as a consequence also the preparedness and the willingness to provide the EU with greater financial resources. On the other hand, the expectations on European solidarity and assistance from the European funds grew to the same extent.

The problem stream therefore changed the political environment for the policy window that would open predictably, although the criticism of the existing budgetary system and the proposals for reform remained more or less unchanged and the same.

The agenda window and the Commission as policy entrepreneur

The European Commission used its role as entrepreneur early on and tried to use the mid-term review of the MFF 2007-2013 and the associated consultation process in 2008-2010 to consider alternative solutions and to discuss new ideas. The Commission expected to introduce and to formulate a comprehensive reform package for the MFF 2014-2020 (Caesar 2008). This searching for solutions and compromise lines acceptable for all actors and discussing thinkable options with all actors during the consultation process should facilitate the coupling of the streams when the decision window would predictably open. Thus, the Commission prepared not only itself on the upcoming negotiations but activated both the policy community and the policy makers. The entrepreneurship of the Commission had been weakened, however, because the Commission was unable to act consistently and coherently. An internal paper for a comprehensive and far-reaching reform of the EU budget drafted by the Directorate-General Budget (DG Budget) had been leaked and discussed in public very critically. The criticism had been noisy and strong and finally Commission President José Manuel Barroso was forced to distance himself from this uncoordinated draft and hence to sign off from any attempt for a comprehensive reform of the budgetary policy (Funke/Seifert 2011).

The role of the Commission as entrepreneur in preparing the negotiations and in coupling the three streams for a fundamental policy change had been significantly and visibly weakened. The negotiations officially began with the presentation of the Commission proposal for the MFF 2014-2020 on June 29, 2011 (European Commission 2011a). The package included seven communications, legislative proposals and working papers, in total more than 500 pages. In October 2011, the Commission completed the package by tabling legislative proposals for all sectoral policies, in particular for the two largest spending blocks of the EU budget – the cohesion policy and the Common Agricultural Policy. By end of 2011, nearly 60 proposals for new legislation for all European spending programs lay on the negotiating table.

Long before the European Commission had published its proposals, the majority of Member States had expressed their positions and draw first "red lines". The group of net contributors formulated their ideas in a letter dated December 18, 2010 to the President of the European Commission, José Manuel Barroso, even before the Commission had submitted its formal MFF proposal. The leaders of Britain, Germany, France, the Netherlands and Finland called for freezing the EU budget at the spending level of 2013, with the annual growth rate of the next financial framework below the inflation rate. As consequence, the MFF should shrink on the timeline (Prime Minister's Office 2010).

On the other side, some new Member States from Central and Eastern and old Member States from southern Europe joined to the group of the so-called "Friends of Cohesion". They argued that the expenditures for agricultural and cohesion policy should be continued at least at the same level as in 2013. In particular, the share of structural funds in the total budget should remain. Furthermore, the Friends of Cohesion demanded additional funding for European Justice and Home Affairs and for other policies, such as climate or energy policy. Hence, the total volume of the new MFF should increase distinctly (Friends of Cohesion 2012).

Also, the EP tried to define its negotiation objectives very early. It established already on June 16, 2010 a "Special Committee on Policy Challenges and Budgetary Means of the Union for the period after 2013 (SURE)" (European Parliament 2010) and formulated its political priorities for the next MFF 2014-2020. The EP demanded in a resolution of June 8, 2011, hence only a few days before the Commission presented its proposal, to increase the total volume of the MFF by at least five percent (European Parliament 2011).

Because the duration of MFF is limited to seven years, the agenda window opened predictably for all actors. The interinstitutional agreement laying down the MFF for the years 2007-2013 stated that the Commission should present its proposals for a new financial framework before July 1, 2011 (European Parliament et al. 2006). Since the MFF would expire on December 31, 2013 and at least one year is needed in order to complete the preparatory work for the continuation of European funding programs as from January 1, 2014, the window would stay open from mid-2011 by end of 2012 or early 2013. Therefore, the timing of when the window would open and how long it would remain open, had been relatively clearly defined and the further course of the process hence was largely predictable.

The role of the European Commission as entrepreneur and as institution that should formally initiate the process was predetermined. Its task was to submit with the MFF legislative package the starting point for the negotiations. The Commission's interest was not to submit its "pet solution" (Kingdon 1995, p. 123) and to promote it, but to define an acceptable compromise package. The proposal for a new financial framework of the European Commission in June 2011 started with a total volume of around one trillion euro (1025 billion euro at constant prices 2011) or 1.05 percent of the GNI of EU-27. Including the funds outside the MFF the EU budget should comprise a total sum of 1083 billion euro or 1.11 percent of EU GNI. To reform the system of own resources the Commission proposed two new funding categories: a European financial transaction tax and a new VAT-resource. By 2020, these two new own resources should account for almost half of the revenues of the EU budget, while the share of national contributions from Member States should decrease from 75 percent to around 40 percent. Moreover, the special arrangements and rebates in favor of Germany, the Netherlands, Austria and Sweden should be replaced by temporary transitional arrangements. To increase the MFF total volume corresponded rather with the wishes of net recipients and the EP, albeit the proposal to increase the MFF volume was lower than demanded. All actors, the net paying, the net recipient Member States and the EP thus criticized the Commission. The net beneficiaries complained that the proposal failed to tackle the economic and social impact of the fiscal and economic crisis. They argued that the Commission considered the interests of the net payers too clearly and unilaterally. However, the net contributors also criticized the Commission because according to their calculations the proposal was more than 100 billion euro too high. Finally, with its resolution of June 13, 2012 the EP confirmed its previously formulated position and demanded a significant increase of the budget volume (European Parliament 2012).

The following negotiations in the Council were determined by the traditional groups – on the one hand, the net paying Member States and on the other hand the net recipients. After protracted negotiations in the Council working groups the new European Council President Herman Van Rompuy started on 22/23 November 2012 a first attempt to hammer out a political compromise between the heads of states and governments. As with former MFF negotiations, this first effort failed. Only in the second attempt the European Council could in the night of February 8, 2013 agree in a compromise, which foresaw an expenditure ceiling for the EU-28 of one percent of EU GNI, or almost 960 billion euro. For the first time the new MFF thus was significantly reduced by about three percent compared to the MFF 2007-2013.

The decision window and a new entrepreneur

Therefore, the consensus of the European Council provided only the political basis for the following legislative work. With the political agreement of the European Council, the decision window opened in February 2013. Now, the Council and the EP negotiated on the necessary legislative acts for the MFF and the major spending policies. Thus, the European Council took over the entrepreneurship from the Commission. With the European Council's political agreement of February 8, 2013, the Member States adopted a common position to start the legislative negotiations of the Council with the EP. Their interest was to keep the final and finely balanced compromise largely untouched and unchanged in the negotiations with the parliamentarians.

Only one day after the European Council's MFF summit the Members of European Parliament (MEPs) criticized vigorously the Member States' agreement in a joint statement of the chairmen and women of the main political groups. They argued in their joint press communiqué that the Member States' deal provided no answer to the challenges of deep economic and social crisis in the EU. The Parliament should not accept this agreement and should insist on its core demand, a higher total volume and greater flexibility within the MFF between the headings and budget years (Joint Statement 2013).

With the opening of the decision window and the legislative process, the role of the EP changed from the role of a restricted observer to a directly involved actor and co-decisive legislator. To mandate its negotiating team for the trilogue negotiations the EP adopted on March 13, 2013 another resolution (European Parliament 2013a), in which the MEPs dropped the criticism about the reduced total MFF volume. Obviously, the Parliament was not a homogenous actor that stick to its demand to increase the total MFF volume by five percent and to risk the delayed start of the next programming period. The EP position and demands laid down in its prior resolutions had been primarily negotiation positions. The majority of the MEP's did not expect the Council to modify the compromise hammered out by the Heads of State and Government on February 8, 2013 at this crucial point. The EP formulated four main negotiation objectives:

1. Greater flexibility within the MFF between the headings and budget years.

2. The introduction of a revision clause, which should allow approximately after three years, a review and a comprehensive adjustment of the financial framework.
3. A new "real" own resource, which should be incorporated into the current system.
4. A stronger prioritization of expenditures on strengthening growth, competitiveness and research.

In addition, the EP insisted on a supplementary budget to the annual budget 2013 to cover the increased spending as a precondition for its consent on the MFF. It was this combination of negotiations on the financial framework with the demand to increase of the annual budget in 2013, which delayed the start of the usual trilogue negotiations. Only at a meeting on the highest political level, the three presidents of the Council, Commission and EP on May 6, 2013 could achieve a compromise on the link between MFF trilogue and the negotiations on the annual budget.

The MFF trilogues meanwhile remained very difficult and for several times had been close to a break down (FAZ 2013). The German rapporteur of the European People's Party (EPP) Group and long-term budget expert Reimer Böge resigned from the EP negotiation team in protest against the Irish Presidency, who led the negotiations for the Council. Finally and once again, the final deal could only be found on the highest political level of the presidents of the three organs on June 28, 2013. At the end of these long and difficult negotiations with more than ten trilogue meetings from May to June 2013, the European Council's compromise of February had not been questioned in substance. The total amount of the new MFF and the allocation of funds to the budget headings, as had been agreed by the European Council, remained untouched. The institutions compromised on the three key points, which were central to the EP:

1. The compromise on more flexibility includes the option that unused funds in one year can be transferred into the following year. However, Member States were able to establish fixed annual ceilings for these transferred funds, which may total not more than 26 billion euro. The Parliament could push through in addition, that in the year 2017 unused funds of the previous three years can be used for measures to boost growth and jobs. The Member States agreed to more flexibility also, because the European Council in anticipation of the negotiations with the EP already had adopted a formulation on "a specific and maximum flexibility" (European Council 2013, paragraph 109).

2. The Council agreed to review of the functioning of the MFF until end of 2016. A separate article in the new MFF regulation mandates the Commission to conduct this comprehensive review and to submit proposals to adjust if necessary the budget to the economic development. The EP had fought for this review clause to give the next MEPs to be elected in May 2014 the chance to open up the MFF and to assess the spending priorities.
3. The EP had demanded the introduction of a new own resource, but the Member States remained unwilling. However, while the Member States could not agree unanimously on this demand, the Council conceded to set up a high-level expert group to discuss the options and needs for further reforms.

In addition to these negotiations on the MFF regulation, the Council and EP finished their negotiations on the annual budget 2014, a supplementary budget to the annual budget 2013, and on all legislative acts for the various spending policies, in particular the structural funds regulations and the new regulations in the agricultural policy until November 2013.

The EP could achieve some of its goals in these negotiations, which took place in confidential trilogue meetings. It is clear, however, that the Parliament is only forceful when it is negotiating with a single voice and with a strong backing of a large majority of its members. The prior votes in the plenum, however, were more or less votes to mandate and to strengthen the EP's negotiation team. The tactical momentum was immense. With the Lisbon treaty, the Parliament received new rights in European budgetary politics, but the MEPs also received new and higher responsibility. In this institutional power game, the MEPs had to decide between a total blocking of the legislation and negotiating a compromise with the Council. The Council was bound by the deal of February 2013 in the European Council and hence had only a limited room for maneuver and to meet the EP's demands, which nevertheless achieved some of its goals.

On November 19, 2013, the EP adopted with 537 votes in favor, 126 votes against and 19 abstentions the MFF regulation (European Parliament 2013b) and the Council for its part adopted the regulation on 2 December 2013 (Council of the European Union 2013). The decision window was closed.

Conclusion: How to couple path-dependent streams?

To sum up this process: The EU demonstrated its ability and willingness to compromise on a new MFF also in times of severe crisis. However, the EU was unable to reform the existing and often criticized system. Only gradual modifications have been agreed to change the priorities of European expenditure policies, like more flexibility and minor shifts of European funds to promote growth and employment. On the revenue side, the compromise only started a non-binding process to discuss options of reform in an expert group. However, the fundamental conflict between net contributors and recipients, criticized by all observers as well as political actors for many years, remained untouched and unresolved. A significant orientation on the prevailing status quo and path dependency characterized both the negotiation process and the outcome of the negotiations. Even the reform pressure of the deep economic and social crisis in the EU could not persuade the Member States to agree on a comprehensive revision of the EU budget. The crisis remained unused to discuss new forms of European fiscal federalism or the appropriateness of European spending priorities.

The general predictability of European policy-making facilitates the planning of the MFF negotiations for all political stakeholders. Their common interest to achieve at least a timely compromise even though with a suboptimal outcome, works as a self-enforcing feedback loop and creates a European budgetary path that is more and more resistant to change. The fundamental pressure to reach a consensus, to end the negotiations successfully, and to comply with existing procedures, strengthens the dominance of institutions and hence of the well-trodden path of European budgetary policy. The policy follows the logics of muddling through (Lindblom 1959). To reverse these self-enforcing processes in European budgetary policy, i.e. to trigger off-path deviation, Johannes Lindner listed four indications for a "logic of change" (Lindner 2006, p. 167-172):

1. When the bargaining power of a change coalition significantly increases.
2. When the European Council as high-level authority overrules the entrenched interests of lower-level actors and ties up a comprehensive package, which includes the different subfields of the European budget.
3. When the opportunity costs of continuing the existing institutional setting exceeds the switching costs.

4. When smaller reform attempts ease reform pressure and hamper off-path change attempts.

Some of these conditions are already fulfilled, like the dominant role of the European Concil. However, these indications cannot solve the specific problem to separate minor on-path from major off-path changes and, to use Kingdon's formulation, to recognize when the time is ripe for change. Kingdon's MSA offers additional criteria. Florian Spohr analyzes three: (1) changes in the policy stream due to external incentives or internal modifications like learning processes, (2) the right timing when a policy window of opportunity opens and (3) policy entrepreneurs, which are needed to couple the three streams successfully, have to apply techniques of path shaping and blame avoidance (Spohr 2016, p. 258).

In the EU political system, policy entrepreneurs can only seldom be personalized but are usually a European institution. Which institution is able to assume this function, influences the type of policy windows that opens in a specific case. As the European Commission acted as policy entrepreneur when the agenda window opened. Hence, the window opened "from below" at a predictable point of time approximately two years before the expiry of the MFF. The Commission started the negotiation process and forwarded its proposals and draft regulations. Thus, the width and the reform margin of this window were predictable and allowed only incremental reforms. Fundamental reforms would have been possible, when the window had opened "from above", that means when the European Council or a powerful group of the Member States together with the Commission could have assumed political entrepreneurship. The decision window opened predictable, albeit "from above", with the compromise of the European Council. But again, the reform margin, i.e. width of the open window, had been predetermined by the incrementalism of the agenda window. It seems that if one of the two windows is a "non-change window", the likelihood that the outcome of the entire policy process will be limited increases. Since the EU's special political system with its consensus-oriented negotiations tends first to couple the policy with the politics-stream and only then the problem-stream, "providing legitimacy for dealing with societal problems" (Ackrill/Kay 2011, p. 77), incrementalism of European policy-making is more likely than comprehensive reform.

The decision window did not open in the politics stream, for example as consequence of new political mandate after elections, nor in the problem stream because of an external focusing event or internal learning process. Obviously, the economic and social crisis in the eurozone and the problems in European budget policy were not that serious enough to convince the political actors in the Member States that they have to act and to change the policy fundamentally. Instead, the window opened predictably in the policy stream, on a regular basis by the limitation of the MFF duration and the necessity to agree on a new financial framework. The missing reform coalition and the only modest pressure to change in the policy community combined with the predictability of the process strengthened the preference for only incremental adjustments (Kingdon 1995, p. 82/83).

Moreover, European actors proofed unable to find a uniform definition of the problem, neither during the open agenda nor during the decision window, neither in the politics nor in the policy stream. Rather, the traditional groups of net contributors and net recipients with their specific interpretations of the weaknesses and the flaws of the EU budget dominated the process. There had been no common problem description and a deduced idea for a new European budgetary policy, i.e. path deviation, in the policy community or among political actors. Since the Council has to find a legislative consensus with the EP respectively a compromise at the end of the day, the solution is usually the lowest common denominator or the continuation of the status quo with only incremental adjustments. In order to find a way out of this impasse three lessons can be drawn:

1. To enable an off-path change of European budgetary policy, the agenda and the decision window should be opened "from above" and out of the political stream. As long as one window opens "from below", i.e. from the working level inside the Commission or the Council, only incremental adjustments will become possible.
2. "Non-changing windows" are characterized by the lack of a common problem definition as well as of the necessity and urgency to deviate from the well-trodden path. As long as this common understanding is missing and no change coalition develops, no alternative solution will emerge.
3. The EU political system is characterized by functional entrepreneurship to trigger change process. This makes ideas about policy alternatives in the policy community even more important to frame changes in a coherent way.

In a nutshell, any comprehensive reform of European budgetary policy is hampered by the missing of a common understanding of the flaws and main problems of European budgetary policy in the policy community and among political actors. Without this awareness about the necessity for change, it is impossible to deduce alternative solutions which then can create a new path. Policy entrepreneurs are unable to couple the streams, to get the attention of the policy makers and then their willingness to take and to justify the risk of switching costs. The time for an off-path reform had not come and hence the streams have not been coupled yet.

However, off-path changes are often possible as consequence of focusing events, like serious crisis or catastrophes (Kingdon, p. 94), hence an exogenous shock that reveals the boundaries of the existing policy. Obviously, the deep economic and debt crisis in the European Union with worst economic, institutional and political costs could not change the adjusted and accepted negotiation method nor the policy. But maybe, the Brexit referendum on United Kingdom's membership in the European Union could become a focusing event to start a change process of European budgetary policy. The United Kingdom will take part neither in the review process, which will begin this year, nor in the negotiations about the next MFF. This has two consequences:

First, a funding gap will arise because the currently second largest net contributor will be lost. This might increase the pressure to enhance the efficiency of European spending policies and then define a real European added value. On the other hand, the British rebate will be abolished and with this the justification of other rebates and special arrangements. The coherence of the system will grow.

Second, the like-minded net-paying Member States will lose an important and powerful partner. The loss of the sometimes radical and extreme British style to conduct the MFF negotiations will narrow the negotiation margins. However, this specific British style was used by other net contributors to hide behind and enabled some negotiation tactics and a special role deal between London and Berlin, resp. between a radical position and a more moderate negotiation style. But, each Member State means one potential veto-player; the greater their number the smaller the prospect of far-reaching reform (Tsebelis/Chang 2004). With the narrowing of negotiation margins and with member states move closer and a common understanding of the necessity to reform the policy might become more likely. The further apart the negotiating positions the greater the tendency to stick to the status quo. If the opposing positions become more coherent, the likelihood to agree to path deviation can increase.

According to MSA, Brexit could work as focusing event in the politics stream and create there the awareness for a common problem, also in European budgetary policy. This problem awareness could then lead to the opening of the agenda window from above, i.e. the European Council.

And this could then open the change window for the decision-making process. The mid-term review process will show if the time for the coupling of the streams and hence for off-path change will be ripe.

Notes

1 With this approach to differentiate modal types, they follow Streeck and Thelen (2005) who distinguished five modes of gradual change: displacement, layering, drift, conversion and exhaustion.

2 Already Daniel Béland (Beland 2005) and Florian Spohr (Spohr 2016) tried to combine HI and path dependency with MSA, however, both on social policy issues.

3 Adrian Kay (Kay 2005) used the concept of path dependency and Johannes Lindner and Berthold Rittberger recur to HI (Lindner/Rittberger 2003) to analyze and explain the evolution of European budgetary policy, however, before the creation of the multiannual financial perspective in 1988.

References

Ackrill, R., Kay, A., and Zahariadis, N. 2013. Ambiguity, multiple streams and EU policy. *Journal of European Public Policy* 20 (6): 871-887.

Ackrill, R.,and Kay, A. 2011. Multiple streams in EU policy-making: the case of the 2005 sugar reform. *Journal of European Public Policy* 18 (7): 72-89.

Becker, S., and Bauer, M.W. 2016. Horizontale Gewaltenteilung in der EU-Haushaltspolitik – Determinanten des Einflusses des Europäischen Parlaments. *Zeitschrift für Politikwissenschaft* 26 (1): 99-114.

Becker, P. 2012a. Lost in Stagnation. The EU's Next Multiannual Financial Framework (2014–2020) and the Power of the Status Quo. *SWP Research Paper* 2012/RP 14, Berlin.

Becker, P. 2012b. The European Budget and the Principles of Solidarity and Added Value. *The International Spectator: Italian Journal of International Affairs* 47 (3): 116-129.

Becker, P. 2014. *Das Finanz- und Haushaltssystem der Europäischen Union. Grundlagen und Reformen aus deutscher Perspektive.* Wiesbaden: SpringerVS.

Begg, I., Enderlein, H., Le Cacheux, J., and Mrak, M. 2008. *Financing of the European Union Budget.* Brüssel: Study for European Commission, Directorate General for Budget.

Béland, D. 2005. Ideas and Social Policy in institutionalist Perspective. *Social Policy & Administration* 39 (1): 1-18.

Benedetto, G., and Milio, S. (Eds.). 2012. *The European Union Budget Reform. Institutions, Policy and Economic Crisis.* Houndsmill: Palgrave Macmillan.

Benedetto, G. 2013. The EU budget after Lisbon: rigidity and reduced spending? *Journal of Public Policy* 33 (3): 345-369.

Blankart, C. B. and Koester, G. B. 2009. Stillstand trotz Reform – die politische Ökonomie des EU-Haushalts von Rom bis Lissabon. In *Einnahmen- und Steuerpolitik in Europa: Herausforderungen und Chancen,* Eds. Konrad, K.A., and Lohse, T., 13-46. Frankfurt/Main: Peter Lang.

Blankart, C. B. and Koester, G. B. 2012. The Lisbon Treaty, the Financial Crisis and Exit from the Budget Gridlock. In *The European Union Budget Reform. Institutions, Policy and Economic Crisis,* Eds. Benedetto, G., and Milio, S., 79-99, Houndsmill: Palgrave Macmillan.

Cairney, P., and Jones, M.D. 2016. Kingdon's Multiple Streams Approach: What Is the Empirical Impact of this Universal Theory? *Policy Studies Journal* 44 (1): 37-58.

Caesar, R. 2006. Die Finanzwirtschaft der EU – „Historisches Relikt" oder solide Zukunftsbasis? *Zeitschrift für Politik* 53 (3): 333-352.

Caesar, R. 2008. Der „Budget Review" 2008/2009: Durchgreifende Reformen im EU-Haushalt? *Wirtschaftsdienst* 88 (5): 317-321.

Council of the European Union. 2013. Regulation (EU, EURATOM) No. 1311/2013 of 2 December 2013 laying down the multiannual financial framework for the years 2014-2020. *Official Journal of the European Union* L 347: 884-891.

Crespy, A., and Menz, G. 2015. Commission Entrepreneurship and the Debasing of Social Europe Before and After the Eurocrisis. *Journal of Common Market Studies* 53 (4): 753-768.

Deeg, R. 2005. Change from Within: German and Italian Finance in the 1990s. In *Beyond Continuity. Institutional Change in Advanced Political Economies,* Eds. Streeck, W., and Thelen, K., 169-202. Oxford: Oxford UP.

European Commission. 2010. *The EU Budget Review.* COM (2010) 7000 final. 19 October 2010.

European Commission. 2011a. *A budget for Europe 2020.* COM (2011) 500 final. 29 June 2011.

European Commission. 2011b. The added value of the EU budget. *Commission Staff Working Pape*r SEC (2011) 867 final. 29 June 2011.

European Council. 2013. *Conclusion of the European Council* (7/8 February 2013).

European Council. 2005. *Conclusion on the multiannual financial framework 2007-2013.* Doc. 1591505. 19 December 2005.

European Parliament. 2010. *Setting up a special committee on the policy challenges and budgetary resources for a sustainable European Union after 2013, its powers, numerical composition and term of office.* P7_TA(2010)0225. 16 June 2010.

European Parliament. 2011. *Investing in the future: a new Multiannual Financial Framework (MFF) for a competitive, sustainable and inclusive Europe.* P7_TA-PROV(2011)0266. 8 June 2011.

European Parliament. 2012. *Multiannual financial framework and own resources.* P7_TA(2012)0245. 13 June 2012.

European Parliament. 2013a. *Resolution of 13 March 2013 on the European Council conclusions of 7/8 February 2013 concerning the Multiannual Financial Framework.* P7_TA-PROV(2013)0078. 13 March 2013.

European Parliament. 2013b. *Legislative resolution of 19 November 2013 on the draft Council regulation laying down the multiannual financial framework for the years 2014–2020.* P7_TA-PROV(2013)0455. 19 November 2013.

European Parliament, Council of the European Union, and European Commission. 2006. Interinstitutional Agreement between the European Parliament, the Council and the Commission on budgetary discipline and sound financial management. *Official Journal of the European Union*, C 139: 1-17.

Frankfurter Allgemeine Zeitung (FAZ). 2013. *EU-Finanzrahmen droht zu scheitern.* 13 June 2013.

Funke, O., and Seifert, J. 2011. Haushaltspolitik. In *Jahrbuch der Europäischen Integration 2010,* Eds. Weidenfeld, W., and Wessels, W., 157–166. Baden-Baden: Nomos.

Friends of Cohesion. 2012. *Joint declaration on the Multiannual Financial Framework 2014-2020.* http://www.vlada.gov.sk/friends-of-cohesion-joint-declaration-on-the-multiannual-financial-framework-2014-2020/; 3 September 2016.

Joint Statement to the Press by Joseph Daul, on behalf of the EPP Group, Hannes Swoboda, on behalf of the S&D Group, and Guy Verhofstadt, on behalf of the ALDE Group and on behalf of the Greens/EFA Group Rebecca Harms and Daniel Cohn-Bendit. 2013. *MFF: the real negotiations will start now with the European Parliament.* http://www.gruene-europa.de/eu-gipfel-mehrjaehriger-finanzrahmen-gemeinsame-erklaerung-9202.html; 3 September 2016.

Gros, D., and Micossi, S. 2005. A better budget for the European Union. More Value for money, more money for value. *CEPS policy brief* 66.

Heinemann, F. 1999. Der Kompensationsfonds: Eine neue Finanzverfassung für die EU der 21+. *Wirtschaftsdienst* 79 (5): 293-299.

Heinemann, F., Mohl, P., and Osterloh, S. 2008. Reform Options for the EU Own Resources System. *ZEW Economic Studies* 40. Heidelberg: Physica.

Heinemann, F., Mohl, P., and Osterloh, S. 2010. Reforming the EU Budget: Reconciling Needs with Political-Economic Constraints. *Journal of European Integration,* 32(1): 59-76.

Herweg, N. 2013. Der Multiple-Streams-Ansatz – ein Ansatz, dessen Zeit gekommen ist? *Zeitschrift für Vergleichende Politikwissenschaft* 7 (4): 321-345.

Herweg, N. 2011. Multiple Streams Ansatz. In: *Handbuch Policy-Forschung,* Eds. Wenzelburger, G., and Zohlnhöfer, R., 325-353. Wiesbaden: Springer VS.

Herweg, N., Huß, C., and Zohlnhöfer, R. 2015. Straightening the three streams: Theorising extensions of the multiple streams framework. *European Journal of Political Research* 54 (3): 435-449.

Howlett, M. 1998. Predictable and Unpredictable Policy Windows: Institutional and Exogenous Correlates of Canadian Federal Agenda Setting. *Canadian Journal of Political Science* 31 (3): 495-524.

Howlett, M. 2009. Process Sequencing Policy Dynamics. Beyond Homeostasis and Path Dependency. *Journal of Public Policy 29 (3): 241-262.*

Jones, M.D., Peterson, H.L., Pierce, J.J., Herweg, N., Bernal, A., Raney, H.L., and Zahariadis, N. 2016. A River Runs Through It – A Multiple Streams Meta Review. *Policy Studies Journal* 44(1): 13-36.

Kay, A. 2005. A Critique of the Use of Path Dependency in Policy Studies. *Public Administration* 83 (3): 553-571.

Keeler, J. T. S. 1993. Opening the Window for Reform Mandates, Crises, and Extraordinary Policy-Making. *Comparative Political Studies* 25 (4): 433-486.

Kingdon, J. W. 1995. *Agendas, Alternatives and Public Policies.* New York: Longman.

Laffan, B. 1997. *The Finances of the European Union.* London: Palgrave Macmillan

Laffan, B. 2000. The big budgetary bargains: from negotiation to authority. *Journal of European Public Policy* 7 (5): 725-743.

Laffan, B., and Lindner, J. 2014. *The Budget. Who gets what, when and how?* In *Policy making in the European Union*, Eds. Wallace, H., Pollack, M.A., and Young, A.R., 220-242. Oxford: Oxford UP.

Le Cacheux, J. 2007. Funding the EU Budget with a Genuine Own Resource: The Case for a European Tax. *Notre Europe Studies* 57. Paris.

Prime Minister's Office. 2010. *A letter from Prime Minister David Cameron and other European leaders to the President of the European Commission on 18 December 2010.* https://www.gov.uk/government/news/letter-to-president-of-european-commission; 2 September 2016.

Lindblom, C. E. 1959. The Science of "Muddling Through". *Public Administration* 19 (2): 79-88.

Lindner, J. 2006. *Conflict and Change in EU Budgetary Politics.* Abingdon: Routledge.

Lindner, J., and Rittberger, B. 2003. The Creation, Interpretation and Contestation of Institutions – Revising Historical Institutionalism. *Journal of Common Market Studies* 41 (3): 445-473.

Neheider, S., and Santos, I. 2011. Refraiming the EU-Budget Decision-Making Process. *Journal of Common Market Studies* 49 (3): 631-651.

Mahoney, J., and Thelen, K. 2010. A Theory of Gradual Institutional Change. In *Explaining Institutional Change. Ambiguity, Agency, and Power,* Eds. Mahoney, J., and Thelen, K., 1-37. Cambridge: Cambridge UP.

Olsen, J. P. 2009. Change and continuity: an institutional approach to institutions of democratic government. *European Political Science Review* 1 (1): 3-32.

Pierson, P. 1996. The Path to European Integration. A Historical Institutionalist Analysis. *Comparative Political Studies* 29 (2): 123-163.

Pierson, P. 2004. *Politics in Time. History. Institutions, and Social Analysis.* Princeton/Oxford: Princeton UP.

Pollack, M. A. 1996. The New Institutionalism and EC Governance: The Promise and Limits of Institutional Analysis. *Governance* 9 (4): 492-458.

Pollack, M A. 2004. *The New Institutionalism and European Integration*. In *European Integration Theory,* Eds. Wiener, A., and Diez, T., 138-156. Oxford: Oxford UP.

Princen, S., and Rhinard, M. 2006. Crashing and creeping: agenda-setting dynamics in the European Union. *Journal of European Public Policy* 13 (7): 1119-1132.

Rubio, Eulalia. 2011. *The "added value" in EU budgetary debates: one concept, four meanings.* Notre Europe Policy Brief no. 2. Paris: Notre Europe.

Rüb, F. W. 2009. Multiple-Streams-Ansatz: Grundlagen, Probleme und Kritik. In *Lehrbuch der Politikfeldanalyse 2.0.,* Eds. Schubert, K., and Bandelow, N. C., 348-375. München: Oldenbourg.

Sapir, A. 2003. *An Agenda for a Growing Europe. Making the EU Economic System deliver.* Brussels: Report of an independent high-level Study Group established on the Initiative of the President of the European Commission (Sapir-Report).

Schild, J. 2008. How to shift the EU's spending priorities? The multi-annual financial framework 2007-2013 in perspective. *Journal of European Public Policy* 15 (4): 531-549.

Schüssel, W. Europe's Finances - The old system at its limits. *Spotlight Europe* No. 2007-08.

Spohr, F. 2016. Explaining Path Dependency and Deviation by Combining Multiple Streams Framework and Historical Institutionalism: A Comparative Analysis of German and Swedish Labor Market Policies. *Journal of Comparative Policy Analysis* 18 (3): 257-272.

Streeck, W., and Thelen, K. 2005. Introduction: Institutional Change in Advanced Political Economies. In *Beyond Continuity. Institutional Change in Advanced Political Economies*, Eds., Streeck, W., and Thelen, K., 1-39. Oxford: Oxford UP.

Tarschys, D. 2005. The Enigma of European Added Value: Setting Priorities for the European Union. *SIEPS Studies Report* 4/2005, Stockholm.

Tarschys, D. (Ed.). 2011. The EU Budget. What should go in? What should go out? *SIEPS-Report* 3/2011, Stockholm: Swedish Institute for European Policy Studies.

Thelen, K. 1999. Historical Institutionalism in Comparative Politics. *Annual Review of Political Science* 2: 369-404.

Tsebelis, G., and Chang, E.C.C. 2004. Veto Players and the Structure of Budgets in Advanced Industrialized Countries. *European Journal of Political Research* 43 (3): 449-476.

Zahariadis, N. 2003. *Ambiguity and Choice in Public Policy: Political Manipulation in Democratic Societies.* Washington, DC: *Georgetown UP.*

Zahariadis, N. 2008. Ambiguity and choice in European public policy. *Journal of European Public Policy* 15 (4): 514-530.

Zohlnhöfer, R., Herweg, N., and Rüb, F. 2015. Theoretically refining the multiple streams framework: An introduction. *European Journal of Political Research* 54 (3): 412-418.

Zohlnhöfer, R. 2016. Putting together the Pieces of the Puzzle: Explaining German Labor Market Reforms with a Modified Multiple-Streams Approach. *Policy Studies Journal* 44 (1): 83-107.

The First Multiannual Financial Framework under the Lisbon Treaty: The Dynamics in the European Parliament from the Perspective of an Insider

Anne Vitrey[1]

This article describes the negotiations that led to the conclusion of the 2014-2020 Multiannual Financial Framework (MFF), the first one concluded under the provisions of the Lisbon Treaty (Council Regulation No 1311/2013, see Council of the European Union 2013). The article tries to highlight the impact of the new Treaty rules on the procedure to adopt the MFF, as seen through the eyes of a practitioner who had the opportunity to follow closely the different phases of the negotiations.

Benedetto (2016) and others demonstrated that the changes in the annual procedure, introduced by the Treaty, have reinforced the position of one arm of the budgetary authority, traditionally the Council, whose objective is to maintain the annual budget at the lowest level. As a result of the new Treaty, the European Parliament (EP) has full legislative co-decision (ordinary procedure) but its role in budgetary negotiations has changed.

Where does the balance of power lie in the procedure leading up to the adoption of the MFF? How does the new codification of the MFF differ under the Treaty of Lisbon? Through the story of the 2014-2020 negotiations, this article will try to highlight the main new elements versus the previous situation.

It is useful to recall that each negotiation, starting with the one in 1988 (Delors I), has been influenced by the economic and political situation at the time. In a nutshell, the first two financial perspectives (1988-1993 and 1993-1999) substantially increased the resources for European policies. The third programming period, Agenda 2000 (2000-2006), represented a substantial status quo, while the 2007-2013 and 2014-2020 frameworks were negotiated in quite a difficult economic climate, with a restrictive approach by the net contributors to the budget. The six major net contributors, in both MFF negotiations, set the scene, announcing their common positions to limit the payments appropriations for the whole period at one percent of EU Gross National Income (GNI). The result of both negotiations was a reduction, in real terms, in the resources allocated to European policies.

Even though its influence on the outcome of the negotiations, in terms of concrete increased amounts allocated, is not easily measurable, the EP played a major role in framing new mechanisms within the MFF. From the point of view of internal organisation, as in the last two procedures, the EP created special committees[2] to influence the Commission proposal ahead of the negotiations (European Parliament 2005). These special committees, composed of Members the Committee on Budgets as well as Members from different specialized committees were useful in establishing the initial EP negotiating position and subsequently creating a reference throughout the negotiating process. Three elements emerged from the experience of the 2014-2020 procedure:

- The European Council going beyond its legal prerogatives, with very detailed decisions;
- The difficulty for the EP to change the figures decided by the European Council;
- The ability of the EP to link this procedure with other elements, i.e. a sufficient level of payments in the annual procedure, and other mechanisms providing more flexibility.

This article shows that, in terms of influence, the EP contributed much more than just with a simple consent procedure. In conclusion, the objective of this article is not to offer a scientific or a legal overview of the negotiations from the respective Institutions in this important procedure, but rather to describe the facts. This will allow others, should they so wish, to provide a more in-depth academic analysis of the role of the Institutions following the entry into force of the Lisbon Treaty.

Changes brought by the Treaty of Lisbon

Before the Lisbon Treaty came into force in December 2010, the MFF – previously known as Financial Perspective – existed in the form of a table annexed to an Interinstitutional Agreement (IIA). The table reflected the agreement reached between the EP, the Council and the Commission on a seven-year "perspective" with ceilings for the financing of EU policies organised under "headings". The text of the IIA contained rules to ensure budgetary discipline and sound financial management to improve the functioning of the annual budgetary procedure and cooperation between the institutions on budgetary matters (European Parliament et al. 2006).

These (soft law) rules existed in parallel to those in the Treaty (primary law). Over the last decades, the IIA increasingly substituted to the provisions of the Treaty, which had remained unchanged since the 70s and were often inadequate *vis-à-vis* the institutional development that had occurred since then.

For the first time since 1975[3], the Treaty of Lisbon substantially modifies the budgetary rules of the EU and introduces a specific title dedicated to financial provisions (Title II, Art. 310-325). It refers to the MFF (Art. 312). The main modifications introduced by the Treaty on the Functioning of the European Union (TFEU) and relating to the MFF are the following:

- The legislator decided that the provisions laying down the MFF should be enshrined in hard law and that the IIA was no longer sufficient. The MFF becomes a regulation and the IIA remains as an accompanying document (soft law), mainly describing the steps and provisions of the annual and multiannual procedures.
- The Treaty imposes binding ceilings, which can only be changed with a modification of the MFF regulation. With regard to the new legal form of the MFF, a Council Regulation for the MFF as introduced by the Treaty (TFEU) is a rigid instrument that requires a complex procedure in the event of modification. In other words, the revision of ceilings requires unanimity in the Council.
- "The annual budgets of the Union shall comply with the Multiannual Financial Framework". This provision creates a new rigidity for the annual budgets since they cannot diverge from the ceilings established by the MFF and, therefore, cannot easily adjust to new priorities. This new rigidity has contributed to the failure to agree on a joint text in Conciliation during the annual procedures of 2011, 2013 and 2015.
- As always when budgetary issues are involved, the obligation of results is a main objective. The budget must be adopted to allow for actions and policies to be implemented. In its article 312.5, the legislator calls for the three institutions: the EP, the Council and the Commission to cooperate and actively facilitate the adoption of the MFF. In other words, the role of the negotiators to adopt the MFF is recognised. This article has been interpreted as a step towards the EP playing a positive role in the negotiations. One can observe that no reference is made to the European Council.
- Apart from the "Delors I package" (1988-1993) which was the first multiannual programming and whose duration was decided for a period of five years, the subsequent ones always covered a seven-year pe-

riod. The Treaty opens up the possibility of returning to a shorter period of "at least five years" (Art. 312(1) TFEU). The duration of the MFF has been a subject of diverging views between the Institutions; while both the Commission and the Council support the idea of a longer programming which guarantees budgetary stability, the EP is in favour of a shorter period (five years) which could better match the Commission's and EP's mandates for democratic purposes. However, even within the EP, the "cohesion countries" are reluctant to shorten the period. In its assessment of the 2007-2013 IIA, the Barroso-II Commission had suggested a 5+5 period with a review after five years.

Point 30 of the IIA of 17 May 2006 on budgetary discipline and sound financial management, which used to be the sole legal instrument before the entry into force of the Treaty of Lisbon, states that before 1 July 2011, the Commission will present proposals for a new MFF.

Two comments can be made at this stage about transition and duration. First, when the IIA was adopted in 2005, the Treaty of Lisbon did not exist and the legislator had the duty to ensure the continuity of the multiannual programming of related instruments beyond the expiry of the current IIA. Second, the Commission strongly insisted on keeping a long period of preparation and negotiation for a new MFF (18 months) which meant that internally, the Directorates-General established their priorities twelve or more months in advance.

Institutional steps: Overview

Commission proposals

The European Commission presented proposals for the 2014-2020 MFF on 29 June 2011 (European Commission 2011a, 2011b); they were later adjusted in July 2012 to take on board the latest macroeconomic factors and the impact of enlargement to Croatia (European Commission 2012).

The main contents of the Commission proposals were definitely more realistic than in 2001. For the 2007-2013 MFF, the Barroso-I Commission had been unable to select priorities and had piled up the traditional European policies i.e. mainly the Common Agricultural Policy (CAP), Structural Funds and the new Growth, Jobs and Competitiveness related policies. The level of commitment appropriations (CA) amounted to 1.08 percent of EU GNI after inflation and included Croatia. The level of payment appropriations (PA) was set at the symbolic level of one percent of EU GNI.

It is interesting to note that the Commission has taken over the idea, initiated by the EP in its position on the 2007-2013 MFF, to provide for the financing of the so-called Special Instruments (Emergency Aid Reserve, European Union Solidarity Fund, Flexibility Instrument, European Globalisation Adjustment Fund) beyond the MFF ceilings. This time, the Commission also proposed to leave the large scale programmes (Galileo, Global Monitoring for Environment and Security, International Thermonuclear Experimental Reactor) outside the ceilings. The other main highlights of the proposal were:

- A significant increase for Competitiveness, Growth, Job Creation (heading 1a);
- A slight increase for Cohesion (heading 1b);
- A stabilisation of CAP (heading 2);
- An increased amount to cover the challenges of migration and civil protection in heading 3;
- A moderate increase to cover the external policies (development) in the world in heading 4.

The EDF was maintained outside of the MFF.

Council position

The Council started an intensive examination of the Commission proposals under the Danish Presidency (1st semester of 2012) followed by the Cyprus Presidency (2nd semester of that same year). The negotiations with the EP, and in view of a final deal, only began after the European Council had reached an agreement (in February 2013) conducted by the Irish and Lithuanian Presidencies. Despite the institutional continuity imposed on the rotating Presidencies, the system can only weaken the Council in its negotiating position, the main decision-making role being exerted by the European Council.

Both the Danish and Cypriot Presidencies worked under the "negotiating box" method which consisted of analysing the figures, heading by heading and programme by programme, to try to build a consensus within national delegations, only "closing" the boxes and indicating an amount at a very late stage. In this way, the Council prepared the European Council decision.

Given that the decision on the MFF is dealt by the European Council, and according to the internal rules of the Council, the responsibility for the negotiations lies with the General Affairs Council (GAC) and not with the Economic and Financial Affairs Council (ECOFIN).

Among the priorities and "red lines" established by the Council, the following "blocks" appeared very early in the process: Poland and other eastern countries refused to reduce the overall level of expenditure proposed by the Commission. The UK, Sweden and Finland imposed a reduction of 100 billion on the level of payments and Germany asked for a capping of commitments at the level of 960 billion, including large-scale projects.

It was once again clear that the Council, particularly in this context, acted more as a coordinating body and was unable to provide an overall guidance, or impose a decision. This role was played by the European Council, which also explains the limitations imposed on the Commission and on the EP.

Preparation within the EP

Facing such a clear imbalance of power in these negotiations, in 2005 and again in 2010, the EP looked for a way to impose its role and to expose its priorities at an early stage of the process. Whether the contents of the EP's requests formulated in its resolutions was reflected in the final outcome, has to be evaluated beyond this article. However, from an institutional point of view, it was seen as necessary, on the one hand, to show support for the Commission proposals and to express different views and priorities to those of the Members States, on the other.

As for the previous MFF, the EP decided to set up a special committee, SURE, in September 2010, with a wide-ranging mandate, which can be summarised as follows:

- Define political priorities after 2013;
- Evaluate the necessary financial resources;
- Define the duration of the next MFF;
- Propose a new structure to better reflect the EU main areas of activity;
- Propose orientations for an indicative allocation of resources;
- Define a link between resources and spending.

After one year of intensive work and of internal and external consultations, a strong majority (+468, -134, o54) adopted the report as a political message by the EP on 8 June 2011 (European Parliament 2011), three weeks before the presentation of the Commission proposal. The resolution was an early positioning with a view to influencing the forthcoming MFF proposals, rather than a negotiating position since it was adopted *before* the Commission proposals whereas for the previous MFF (2007-2013), the EP had adopted its resolution *after* the Commission proposals and *before* the decision by the European Council.

The EP (SURE) resolution expressed an ambitious goal in terms of amounts, i.e. ceilings of the previous year (2013 level) plus five percent, reaching a 1.11 percent of EU GNI, with an exception for CAP and Cohesion, which were to remain at the 2013 levels. It produced a wide-ranging analysis of EU policies across headings (176 paragraphs) including a proposal for a new structure for the next MFF with three headings only: Europe 2020, Global Europe, and Administration. It requested a duration of five years from 2020 onwards to match the institutional cycle with a longer programming for CAP, Cohesion and TENs after a transitional period of seven years until 2020.

The role of the European Council

The 2014-2020 MFF was on the agenda of the European Council three times. On 13 November 2012, the so-called Herman Van Rompuy Compromise No 1 proposed to reduce the CAP by 20 billion and Cohesion by 70 billion compared to the previous MFF, with an overall amount of 973,1 billion of payments for seven years. The "Friends of Cohesion" group of countries vetoed this compromise. On 22-23 November 2012, in the so-called Herman Van Rompuy Compromise No 2, the proposal was revised to reduce CAP by 10 billion and Cohesion by 50 billion compared to the previous MFF, with an overall amount of 971,8 billion of payments for seven years. This time the "Friends of Better Spending" group of countries vetoed the compromise. It was not until 7-8 February 2013 that the European Council reached a deal by unanimity on a level of 960,4 billion in commitments and 908,4 billion in payments (European Council 2013).

The "big bargaining" between national delegations had been organised with the main aim of reaching a zero sum game at the end. As in 2006, a number of "gifts" were distributed to facilitate the agreement[4] for each one and to make the overall low figures acceptable to all.

The European Council bargaining capacities in the MFF negotiations are probably the most sophisticated ones of all, given the magnitude and the sensitivity of the issue. A number of analyses have been made on this which go beyond the scope of this article.

Outcome

Ten months after the European Council reached an agreement, the Institutions concluded a deal on the 2014-2020 MFF in December 2013. The ceilings remained unchanged (Commitment appropriations (CA): 960,4 billion; Payment appropriations (PA): 908,4 billion, see Figure 5.1) from those agreed by the European Council. Neither the Commission nor the Parliament could get closer to their proposals, as shown in Table 5.1 and Table 5.2 below. The reader will find a more detailed analysis in the next section.

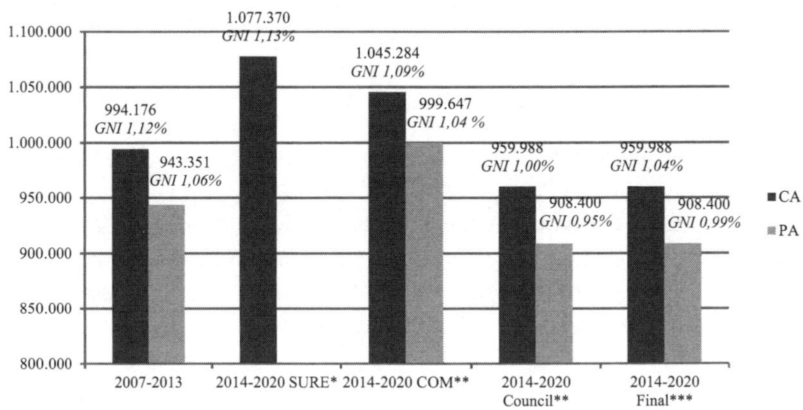

* SURE report calls for at least 5% increase of resources
** excluding Croatia (initial proposal, June 2011)
*** including latest adjustment

Figure 5.1: MFF 2014-2020 total commitment and payment appropriations (in million euro)

The timespan of the negotiations *within* the institutions, notably in the Commission and in the Council, is to be compared with the duration of the negotiations *between* institutions. It took more than two years for the Commission, 18 months for the Council and European Council, and a ten-month process between the agreement at European Council level and the consent given by the EP (February-December 2013).

The rule of unanimity is at the heart of the problems encountered within Council and the prominent role played by the European Council where a "zero sum game approach" is necessary to get a deal were key factors.

Table 5.1: MFF positions and outcomes (in million euro)

Commitment appropriations	2007-2013	2014-2020 SURE 2013 Ceilings*	2014-2020 COM**	2014-2020 European Council **	2014-2020 Final agreement ***
1a. Competitiveness for Growth and Jobs	91,495		164,317	125,614	125,614
1b. Economic, Social and Territorial Cohesion	354,815		338,994	325,149	325,149
2. Sustainable Growth: Natural Resources	420,682		389,972	373,179	373,179
of which market related exp and direct payments	336,686		286,551	277,851	277,851
3. Security and citizenship	12,366		18,809	15,686	15,686
4. Global Europe	56,817		70,000	58,704	58,704
5. Administration	57,082		63,165	61,629	61,629
6. Compensations	920		27	27	27
TOTAL COMMITMENT APPROPRIATIONS	994,176	1,077,370	1,045,284	959,988	959,988
as a percentage of GNI	1.12%	1.13%	1.09%	1.00%	1.04%
TOTAL PAYMENT APPROPRIATIONS	943,351		999,647	908,400	908,400
as a percentage of GNI	1.06%		1.04%	0.95%	0.99%

*The SURE report calls for "at least a 5% increase of resources". A specific breakdown between the headings is not given but the SURE report calls for the funding in headings 1b and 2 to be "at least maintained" and calls for enhanced funding in headings 1a, 3 and 4.
**Excluding Croatia (initial proposal, June 201)
***Including latest adjustment

Table 5.2: Main contents of the MFF 2014-2020 deal

Proposal for a Global Deal	Consent Deal
Ceilings unchanged (CA: 960 bn, PA: 908,4 bn)	An end to the structural deficit of payments (RALs, outstanding commitments, 11,2 billion)
Flexibility increased compared to the previous MFF - Global margin for payments for an amount of 4,5 bn over the period - Global margin for commitments for growth and employment (youth) - Contingency margin (up to 0.03% of EU GNI) in case of unforeseen circumstances (amounts shall be fully offset in current or future financial years) - Special flexibility to tackle youth unemployment and strengthen research (front-loading) - Flexibility instrument (471 million may be used up to year N+3)	More flexibility (see column 1) A compulsory mid-term review/revision accompanied by a legislative proposal (as appropriate)
Special instruments to be mobilised over and above the ceiling (EP's interpretation) "It must be highlighted, however, that some ambiguity remains in the MFF regulation about whether financing beyond the ceilings concerns only commitments or both commitments and payments. The Council interpretation differs from that of the Commission and the EP, for whom both commitments and payments should be "fresh money" i.e. financed beyond the ceiling of the respective category. Since 2014, each time these instruments were mobilised, Council wanted to impose an offsetting of the amounts. Clarification of this issue is still an EP requirement for the review/revision." (European Parliament 2016).	The creation of a High Level Working Group mandated to recommend a reform of the system of own resources Recalling of the principle of unity of the budget

The Negotiations: an unbalanced game

The wide internal consultation, at both technical and political levels, to align the financial programming with the political priorities over seven years created a heavy and lengthy process within the European Commission. This was without counting the reform of the financial rules (revision of the Financial Regulations and simplification) which was often worked on in parallel. Due to these administrative, legal and political requirements, the length of the negotiating phase was reduced and lacked an interactive dynamic.

Article 312(5) TFEU allows for new possibilities in the decision making process: throughout the procedure leading to the adoption of the financial framework, the EP, the Council and the Commission shall take any measure necessary to facilitate its adoption.

Point 11 of the European Council conclusions from 7-8 February 2013 recalls the "intensive contacts" with the EP and invites the Presidency "to rapidly take forward discussions" (European Council 2013).

For the first time, a delegation from the EP (the Chairman of the Committee on Budgets and Rapporteurs) was invited to attend the briefing and debriefing meetings of the GAC during the Danish and Cypriot Presidencies. This initiative facilitated information sharing between the Council and the EP but no more. In fact, the Treaty provision of Art. 312(5) TFEU remains to be exploited further.

After the deal reached at the level of Member States, two levels of negotiations were held in parallel:

- At a budgetary level, mainly focusing on the level of payments, flexibilities and the mid-term review/revision;
- At a legislative level, roughly 60 related legal acts (almost all under the ordinary legislative procedure) were negotiated in alignment with the MFF overall decision.

The conclusions of the European Council were very detailed and always contained a significant number of legislative elements that should have been decided under the co-decision procedure between the Council and the EP. The prerogatives granted by the Treaty to the EP under the ordinary legislative procedure, as well as its right to amend on equal footing with the Council, were, therefore, hindered.

This occurred in clear contradiction to the Treaties and notably Art. 15(1) which stipulates that the European Council does not exercise legislative functions. Instead, the conclusions of the European Council became negotiating instructions for the Council and often indicated their "red lines".

In the given context, there was little room for manoeuvre left for the EP in its capacity as budgetary and legislative authority. However, since there could be no MFF without Parliament's consent, the EP used this power to the full. The committees and political groups were organised into a Contact Group, chaired by the President of the EP himself, and managed to maintain unity within the EP and apply constant pressure on the Council with a number of requests, which became *sine qua non* conditions to giving its consent.

Before being able to give its consent, the EP voted a set of resolutions (adopted by huge majorities) in response to the ongoing negotiations and reiterated the EP's "red lines" (European Parliament 2012, 2013a, 2013b, 2013c).

In its resolution of 23 October 2012 (votes +537, -126, o19), the EP "[i]nsists on a qualitative approach to the MFF Regulation and related multiannual programmes negotiations; stresses that they are to be considered as a package, and reaffirms the principle that 'nothing is agreed until everything is agreed'" (European Parliament 2012).

In its resolution of 13 March 2013 (votes +506, -161, o23), the Parliament reacted to the deal reached by the European Council as follows (European Parliament 2013a):

> Takes note of the European Council's conclusions on the MFF, which represent no more than a political agreement between Heads of State and Government; *rejects this agreement in its current form*, as it does not reflect the priorities and concerns expressed by Parliament – notably in its resolution of 23 October 2012 – and *disregards Parliament's role and competences as set out in the Treaty of Lisbon*; considers that this agreement, which will bind the Union for the next seven years, cannot be accepted *without the fulfilment of certain essential conditions.*

The four main conditions laid down by the EP were:

- Putting an end to the structural deficit of payments in the EU budget, amounting to 23,4 billion of unpaid bills which the Parliament had constantly deplored as reaching a critical level and against the provisions of the Treaty (Art. 310 and 323 TFEU);
- A maximum overall flexibility to compensate for the low ceilings;
- A comprehensive and compulsory mid-term review/revision, accompanied by legislative proposals "as appropriate";
- The creation of a High Level Working Group mandated to recommend a reform of the system of own resources, at the origin of the "purely accounting vision of the EU budget on behalf of Member States bargaining their national interests and maximising their returns".

Finally, the reduction of the "deficit" was cut by half (+11,2 billion euro in payments up to the 2013 ceiling) to be paid in two instalments before EP consent. The EP gave its consent to the 2014-2020 MFF, having considered that the above conditions had been fulfilled, and voted by a huge majority (votes +539, -126, o19) on 19 November 2013 (European Parliament 2013c).

Final considerations

The first MFF negotiated under the provisions of the Treaty of Lisbon faced political and institutional considerations:

- The efforts of fiscal consolidation, pursued by Member States, did not allow for an ambitious multiannual budget for the EU;
- The added value and leverage effect of the EU budget, which is predominantly an investment budget and has a potential role in strengthening economic governance and stimulating national actions for growth, competitiveness and employment, were disregarded;
- The current system of Own Resources and National contributions based on GNI as the main resource (75 percent), which favours a logic of fair returns and bargaining among Member States instead of a logic of European added value (net balances, "gifts", zero sum game), must be reformed;
- The Council continued to follow a top down approach (capping commitments and payments with an overall figure) while the EP looked for a bottom up process based on an assessment of needs;
- No selection of common or positive or negative priorities could be achieved in a real negotiation;
- The unanimity rule, which imposed an agreement based on the lowest common denominator to avoid the veto of a single Member State, should be reviewed (use of the *passerelle* clause of Art. 48(7) of the Treaty on European Union, TEU);
- The facilitation measures provided by Art. 312(5) TFEU need to be properly implemented;
- The European Council should not act as legislator and thus hinder the EP's co-decision prerogatives.

The EP adopted a resolution on 15 April 2014 entitled "Negotiations on the MFF 2014-2020: lessons to be learned and the way forward" which gathered a number of considerations based on past experience as reported below (European Parliament 2014).

The EP was the first institution to present its vision on the 2014-2020 MFF with the SURE Committee report. The resolution deplores the bargaining power of Member States whose first objective is to secure their national interests and maximise their returns, instead of being driven by the logic of the European added value. Parliament regrets that no meaningful negotiations were held with the Council, despite the openness made by Art. 312(5) TFEU. Parliament also deplores that the conclusions of the European Council are to be seen as negotiating instructions for the Council and contained significant legislative elements that should have been decided under the ordinary legislative procedure.

As always throughout European history, it takes time for the changes brought about by a new Treaty to be smoothly integrated. The Treaty of Lisbon changed the budgetary landscape of the EU significantly. No changes of such importance had been made since 1975. For 35 years, the multiannual planning of the EU budget had been developed on a soft law basis (IAAs, Financial Perspectives) led by an obligation of results and keeping the original institutional balance.

The changes brought about by the Treaty of Lisbon introduce a new rigidity through a codification of the MFF, of which the annual budgets become a simple slice or adjustment.

Three annual procedures failed to agree on a joint text during the budgetary Conciliation (in 2011, 2013 and 2015). Based on this and the first negotiations of the first post-Lisbon MFF, it seems that the EP considers that its role as a full representative of the budgetary authority as granted by the Treaty of Brussels, has been diminished - to the benefit of the other branch (Council) in annual budgetary procedures and to the benefit of Member States (European Council and Council) in multiannual negotiations. Nevertheless, in a less favourable institutional, political and economic context, the EP obtained a degree of success notably by imposing new flexibility mechanisms (between headings, within headings, across the period and even beyond the ceilings), despite the Council's resistance to impose the principle of offsetting almost every time.

The EP also obtained a mid-term review/revision. The Commission has just presented its proposals (on 14 September 2016) for a substantial mid-term review/revision. Although it is impossible to evaluate the magnitude and impact of this new exercise, it should be noted that it did take place, which is another success for the EP.

To compensate for the low ceilings that were not challenged, the EP obtained an additional amount of 11,2 billion of payments thus avoiding the risk of shortages or a slowing down effect in the implementation of policies. The EP used its power of consent not to delay the adoption of the MFF, but to get the fulfilment of its conditions (see Table 5.2) which, at first, were not well received by the Council and Member States, but finally they delivered.

Finally yet importantly, the EP, amongst the conditions set out to provide its consent, called for, and obtained, the creation of a High Level Group (chaired by Mario Monti). This was because it appeared increasingly obvious that the role of Member States and the importance of the returns expected from the EU budget had their origin in the current system of Own Resources, mainly financed by national contributions (GNI). Within this new institutional context, the EP continues to fight to preserve the original balance based on a dual budgetary authority and is likely to go on doing so in the future.

Notes

1 Director for Budgetary Affairs, European Parliament. The content of this document is the sole responsibility of the author and any opinions expressed therein do not necessarily represent the official position of the European Parliament.

2 For example, the Special Committee on Policy Challenges and Budgetary Resources for a Sustainable European Union after 2013 (SURE).

3 The Treaty of Brussels (1975) significantly increased the budgetary powers granted to the EP.

4 An overall amount of 17,730 million euro was distributed to 26 countries.

References

Benedetto, G. 2016. Power, money and reversion points. The European Union's annual budgets since 2010. *Journal of European Public Policy* Early View: doi 10.1080/13501763.2016.1154589.

Council of the European Union. 2013. Council Regulation (EU, Euratom) No 1311/2013 of 2 December 2013 laying down the multiannual financial framework for the years 2014-2020. *Official Journal of the European Union* L347: 884-892.

European Commission. 2011a. *A Budget for Europe 2020*. COM(2011) 500 final.

European Commission. 2011b. *A Budget for Europe 2020 – Part II: Policy Fiches*. COM(2011) 500 final.

European Commission. 2012. *Amended proposal for a COUNCIL REGULATION laying down the multiannual financial framework for the years 2014-2020*. COM(2012) 388 final.

European Council. 2013. *European Council Conclusions – Multiannual Financial Framework*. EUCO 37/13.

European Parliament. 2005. *Report on Policy Challenges and Budgetary Means of the enlarged Union 2007-2013 (FINP)*. PE 353.270.

European Parliament. 2011. *European Parliament resolution of 8 June 2011 on Investing in the future: a new Multiannual Financial Framework (MFF) for a competitive, sustainable and inclusive Europe*. P7_TA(2011)0266.

European Parliament. 2012. *Multiannual financial framework for the years 2014-2020. European Parliament resolution of 23 October 2012 in the interests of achieving a positive outcome of the Multiannual Financial Framework 2014-2020 approval procedure*. P7_TA(2012)0360.

European Parliament. 2013a. *European Parliament resolution of 13 March 2013 on the European Council conclusions of 7/8 February concerning the Multiannual Financial Framework*. P7_TA(2013)0078.

European Parliament. 2013b. *European Parliament resolution of 3 July 2013 on the political agreement on the Multiannual Financial Framework 2014-2020*. P7_TA(2013)0304.

European Parliament. 2013c. *European Parliament legislative resolution of 19 November 2013 on the draft Council regulation laying down the multiannual financial framework for the years 2014–2020 (11791/2013 – C7-0238/2013 – 2011/0177(APP))*. P7_TA(2013)0455.

European Parliament. 2014. *European Parliament resolution of 15 April 2014 on negotiations on the MFF 2014-2020: lessons to be learned and the way forward*. P7-TA(2014)0378.

European Parliament. 2016. *European Parliament resolution of 6 July 2016 on the preparation of the post-electoral revision of the MFF 2014-2020: Parliament's input ahead of the Commission's proposal*. P8_TA(2016)0309.

European Parliament, Council of the European Union, and European Commission. 2006. Interinstitutional Agreement between the European Parliament, the Council, and the Commission on budgetary discipline and sound financial management. *Official Journal of the European* Union C139: 1-17.

What Multi-level Parliamentary System? Parliamentary Discourses in EU Budgetary Negotiations (MFF 2014-2020)

Linn Selle

Introduction

Negotiations over the EU budget are most often perceived as classical domains of fierce intergovernmental bargaining between EU member states in the (European) Council (Hagemann 2012; Neheider/Santos 2011). At the same time, budgetary questions are also classical domains of parliamentary institutions. The authority to decide on the budget was the first independent parliamentary power. Moreover, it has always been also perceived as a 'crown jewel' among parliamentary functions. In EU budgetary matters, the academic interest to this parliamentary influence has been mostly directed to the European Parliament (EP) as it is directly included in the budgetary negotiations (see i.a. Benedetto 2015). However, in the EU multi-level budgetary system both the EP and national parliaments perform a functional role in the budgetary process. This split function can be labelled as a "divided parliamentary budget authority", since the revenue and expenditure lines of the overarching budgetary instrument, the Multiannual Financial Framework (MFF), are divided in terms of parliamentary legitimation between national and supranational parliamentary bodies. Therefore, the parliamentary dimension of EU budgetary involvement needs to be considered as a joint endeavour of both national and EU parliaments in the EU multi-level system.

The following analysis takes the parliamentary communicative function as point of departure for the analysis of the performance of the EU parliamentary budget authority from a multi-level perspective.[1] In analysing the parliamentary debate surrounding the MFF 2014-2020, this chapter will look at the precise discursive practices in the German Bundestag and the EP in light of the heuristic of a multi-level parliamentary field (Crum/Fossum 2012; Crum/Fossum 2009). Communication is an overarching and prime parliamentary function. It relates parliamentary actors towards their electorate and the public sphere, as well as connects parliamentary actors among each other. Therefore, the parliamentary debate is mapped with the help of tools from discourse network analysis.

The empirical findings suggest that parliamentary actors dispose of similar views on what are the most important issues to be debated in the budgetary process. However, different channels of representation exist in the budgetary debate that diverge at the level of the policy and the politics of the parliamentary debate. While the overarching political priorities expressed by parliamentary actors (policy) follow joint party-political cleavages opposing national and supranational party groups, the overall budgetary discourse is largely centred on institutional-structural questions such as the own resources or the size of the EU budget (politics). National and European parliamentary levels dispose of different orientations that originate in their respective perception of the EU budgetary architecture and the attribution of parliamentary power therein.

The EU budget from a parliamentary perspective

Parliaments can be regarded as the prime instances of creating and upholding legitimacy within a political system. They are directly accountable to their voters and represent the shortest link between the political system and the citizens. In terms of their communicative function, parliamentary representatives need to explain and justify the political decisions taken. By the nature of their office they are accountable to their voters and therefore need to be responsive to them.

The parliamentary powers of accountability and responsiveness are rooted in the authority of parliamentary actors to decide on the financing of the government. One of the very first independent parliamentary powers was the authority to decide on taxes, and to give a parliamentary consent to the governmental budget in order to have a direct connection between the financing of the executive and the will of the people. Budgetary research thus often stresses the parliamentary component within budgetary decision-making (Lienert 2013; Müller-Osten 2007; Oppenheimer 1985; Wehner 2010). This is further underlined by the institutional importance attached to budgetary institutions inside parliamentary bodies. Budget committees figure among the most prestigious and senior committees inside parliament and the general debates of the budget rank among the most widely perceived plenary debates. Budget deliberations should be understood as the condensation of political priorities (Wildavsky 1988, p. 2). Given the fact that nearly all major political priorities of a government need to be financially represented in the budget, the parliamentary deliberation on those priorities is of particular importance, as it represents the opportunity of an overarching debate on governmental priorities that is widely perceived in public. As parliaments contribute to this public debate and the communication of the overarching priorities to be achieved by the means of the budget, they contribute to the overall legitimacy of a political system.

The parliamentary component of the EU budgetary system developed in an incremental way without disposing of a clear path of parliamentary involvement. While at the beginning of European integration, budgetary questions were solely legitimated through national parliaments, in the 1970s, with the establishment of the EP came in the 1970s, the institution gained the prerogative of co-budget authority, along with the Council in matters related to the expenditure side of the budget (Becker 2014a, p. 32; Bache et al. 2011, p. 298). The Lisbon Treaty has established that the budgetary process be validated through both the EP and national parliaments.

The EU's MFF is the most important budgetary agreement in the European Union, as it sets the binding guidelines of budgetary expenditure which has to be followed by the EU's annual budgets (for this argument see also: Patz/Goetz 2015; Goetz/Patz 2016). Within the EU budgetary procedures governing the negotiations of the seven-year multiannual budget, national parliaments remain in charge to legitimize the EU's Own Resources Decision (Art. 311 of the Treaty on the Functioning of the European Union, TFEU) which covers the revenue strand of the EU budget. The EP formally gives its assent and thus parliamentary legitimacy to the expenditure strand of the EU budget, namely the Regulation on the Multiannual Financial Framework (MFFR, Art. 312 TFEU). Therefore, parliamentary institutions on the national and supranational level play a function role in the EU budgetary process. They have to be regarded together in respect to the broader inclusion of parliamentary actors in the negotiations on the MFF.[2]

The EU budget negotiations are characterized by multiple dimensions that also have an impact on the parliamentary budget authority. The EU budget certainly disposes of a *financial dimension* which relates to the allocation of funds to specific political programmes and the decision on the overall level of revenue through the respective budgetary institutions. These purely financial questions, which are equally at the heart of national budgetary politics, however, are superposed at EU level through a political and by an institutional-bargaining dimension. The *political dimension* represents the overall struggle of all representative actors involved in budgetary negotiations to use and define EU budgetary deals in terms of their broader focuses in EU politics. The EU budget touches most EU policy areas and funding programmes and stands for the structure and the independence of the Union as a political system. This is an important dimension that horizontally crosses all major budgetary areas and also serves as an indicator of the state of EU integration. The *institutional-bargaining dimension*, finally, is directed to the inter-institutional power game that is reflected in budgetary politics. The EU budget can therefore be described as the "mother" of European package deals. It is thus also a major tool for the political actors involved to strengthen their political position inside the EU's institutional triangle. This institutional-bargaining dimension takes place both within and between the institutions participating in budgetary negotiations.

Parliamentary communication in the EU multi-level parliamentary field

The functional linkage between parliamentary actors as it is the case in EU budgetary matters has also gained traction in the analysis of the EU representative system in the past years. As the EU multi-level political system is not based on one clear strand of parliamentary legitimation, it has been argued that both parliamentary levels should be regarded holistically in order to assess the overall parliamentary legitimacy of the European Union (Abels/Eppler 2011; Maurer 2012).[3] In this respect, next to the individual position of parliamentary actors in the European Union, the linkages between parliamentary levels became a focus of research in a quest for new channels of parliamentary representation and legitimacy in the EU.

Neither the EP alone, due to its still feeble legitimacy and visibility among its electorate, nor national parliaments are able to fully perform their parliamentary functions in the EU political process, because of their primarily national allocation of tasks. It has thus been argued that both national and supranational strands of parliamentary legitimation should be looked at jointly as two constituting channels of parliamentary representation. This idea has been further substantiated by the heuristic of a "multi-level parliamentary field" (see i.a. Crum/Fossum 2009; Crum/Fossum 2013; Herranz-Surrallés 2014). It may serve as a toolkit to assess the position and the perceptions of parliamentary actors in the EU multi-level system and the cooperation between parliamentary levels in light of reinforcing parliamentary representation in the European Union more generally.

The framework therefore addresses overarching questions on how parliamentary democracy might be achieved without focusing exclusively on either the EP or on national parliaments. Different to multi-level political systems in federal states like Germany, the European Union is "more disaggregated than a fully-fledged EU-federal representative system would have been" (Crum/Fossum 2009, p. 261). These "overlapping [and partly contradicting, LS] authority claims" (Herranz-Surrallés 2014, p. 971) of parliamentary actors address both conflict and cooperation between parliamentary levels (see. i.a. Schulz/Broich 2013; Kreilinger 2014; Hefftler/Gattermann 2015).

Taking into account the interconnectedness of parliamentary institutions in the EU policy process is particularly important in budgetary politics, as both parliamentary levels are formally embedded in the EU budgetary procedure. In the EU budgetary process, parliamentary actors on the EU and national level perform a "divided budget authority". As both parliamentary institutions dispose of a functional position inside the EU's budgetary process, it follows that their formal-legal embeddedness in the revenue and expenditure strand of budgetary politics goes beyond a mere "participation" of national parliaments within EU politics and underlines the need to consider parliamentary positions more holistically within the framework of a broader multi-level parliamentary field.

From parliamentary research it can be learned that parliaments play an important role in contributing to the overall legitimacy of a political system and that they ideal-typically create dense links between the political system and the society and electorate they represent. In this respect, parliaments' main vehicle for legitimacy certainly is their overarching *communicative function* (Patzelt 2003, p. 25). As parliamentary actors seek to form channels of interaction and communication within the political system and between parliamentarians and their electorate, they seek to circulate interests, to allocate resources and, overall, to legitimate the political system (Patzelt 1993, p. 48). Parliaments need to explain and justify the positions taken towards their electorate and to the general public to a greater extent than executive actors.

In this context, the parliamentary debate occupies a prominent position among the parliamentary communicative tools and disposes of multiple aims within the political process. It reflects the broader structure of society within the parliamentary assembly in the deliberation of policies, it communicates the representative's position towards the public sphere, towards the electorate and the media as intermediary institution, and it explains and justifies the political positions take, to show the electorate that their interests are well represented inside parliament (Eriksen/Fossum 2011; Neyer 2014; Deschouwer et al. 2014, p. 1). In this respect, the parliamentary communication of policies serves as a justification to the citizens and applies to all public political speeches even if most of those debates are not widely followed by the electorate or reported by the media. In this respect, tracing the overarching debates and discursive characteristics of representative democracy in the EU not only puts an emphasis on the processes of public opinion formation but also on the structure of the intermediate public sphere (Buzogàny 2013, p. 20). Therefore, the analysis of the parliamentary debate, the claims used and the coalitions formed in the deliberation of the EU budget aims at a better understanding of the orientation of parliamentary actors among themselves in the performance of their communicative function in order to gain a clearer view of the positions and perceptions of parliamentary actors within the EU multi-level system in EU budgetary policies.

The parliamentary communicative function is an important overarching function to display to the electorate that "something is done" and to differentiate between the political positions present inside parliament: "Without debates allowing the electorate to identify competing leaders and policy agendas it is difficult for them to assess the performance of the government and to hold it accountable" (Auel/Raunio 2012, p. 47–48). Therefore, parliamentary debates may serve as an important vehicle to assess the empirical state of the multi-level parliamentary field and the respective parliamentary interests associated with budgetary politics in the European Union. The empirical analysis therefore aims at better understanding the structure of the budgetary debate that is being constructed by parliamentary actors at both governmental levels in the EU budgetary process. Through the structure of political claims, the main interests and focuses of the parliamentary work can be assessed and compared between parliamentary levels and political parties therefore serving as a proxy for the EU budgetary process from a parliamentary perspective.

While the EP is an obvious choice for studying parliamentary debates on the supranational level, on the national parliamentary level the German Bundestag has been chosen as a case. The Bundestag is an active and pro-European parliamentary institution in the European Union (Hefftler/Gattermann 2015). Also its budgetary function is a strongly anchored within the Bundestag's internal proceedings, a fact that has also been underlined during the euro crisis and has been the source of particularly heatedly debate inside the German parliament. From this follows that the Bundestag may be regarded as being a most-likely case for becoming involved in the EU budgetary debate. It has to be equally noted that the findings from this case cannot be transferred to other national parliaments due to starkly diverging institutional and cultural structures of parliamentary inclusion in the EU multi-level system (Auel et al. 2015).

In order to properly assess the structural characteristics of the budgetary debate, data collection proceeded along the following lines. All public plenary debates that fell into the analytic period of the debate on the MFF 2014-2020 between the first Commission draft and the final conclusion of the MFF legislative packages were gathered.[4] Within this time frame there were a totality of 24 debates within the EP, the German Bundestag, the General Affairs Council and European Council statements.[5] From these debates, those claims being used most often by parliamentary actors were coded deductively with the help of the Discourse Network Analyzer (DNA) (Leifeld 2011; Leifeld 2013; Leifeld/Haunss 2012). This rather new analytical toolkit is a combination of social network analysis and content analysis and aims at tracing, analysing and illustrating the major positions and major cleavages of a specific discourse or political debate in relational approach. Coming from the methodological tools of network analysis, the DNA connects specific claims with the actors supporting or rejecting these arguments. This enables not only the display of the major claims used within the budgetary debate but also allows us to show how arguments were linked among parliamentary actors in the structure of an approval or rejection of claims.

The parliamentary debate on the MFF 2014-2020

The negotiations on the MFF 2014-2020 were, for the first time, conducted after the new rules of the Lisbon Treaty. Negotiations took place between June 2011 and November 2013.[6] While the EP debated its position towards the MFF inside the temporary SURE[7]-committee already before the European Commission presented a first draft budget in June 2011, the German Bundestag only formally embarked on its budgetary deliberations when the Commission proposals were forwarded to parliament through the formal information mechanisms constituted by the Treaty of Lisbon. In the following, the analysis will only focus on the formulation phase of the budgetary negotiations after the European Commission formally proposed the first draft budget.

The temporal structure of the parliamentary debate first of all underlines the assessment that parliamentary actors are embedded at different time periods of the EU policy cycle (Maurer 2012), reflecting their divergent embeddedness in the EU budgetary process. The German Bundestag has been particularly active during the first part of the formulation phase at the time when the Council was debating on a position towards the Commission drafts, while the EP was particularly active during the last phase when it was formally included in the negotiations after the European Council came up with a joint position. Despite this embeddedness at different points of the formulation phase, it can be conceded that the parliamentary debate itself was largely focused on similar claims that were uttered by parliamentary actors on the national and supranational parliamentary level (see Figure 6.1).

The claims that have been used most frequently by parliamentary actors were related to the size of the budgetary framework, the political priorities attached to the budget and questions surrounding the MFF's revenue strand, the own resources system. Other claims were made regarding the unity of the budget, budgetary rebates and regarding the flexibility of the budget. On the German parliamentary level, it can be seen that the government and the conservative majority party was particularly fervent when it came to the size of the budget, while other parliamentary groups in the Bundestag were less straightforward in terms of focusing on one specific claim. The question of budgetary rebates and of the unity of the EU budgetary framework is particularly salient the German parliamentary level.

Inside the EP, the size of the EU budget and the own resources system were the claims the most frequently used. The conservative and liberal party groups (European People's Party, EPP, and Alliance of Liberals and Democrats for Europe, ALDE) particularly stressed the issue of the own resources system, while claims related to the size of the EU budget were mostly put forward by the Socialists & Democrats (S&D), Greens, European Conservatives and Reformists (ECR) and Left party groups. Similar to the German conservatives, the political group of ECR, which did not have its pendant on the German political level at that time, strongly emphasized claims related to the size of the budget.

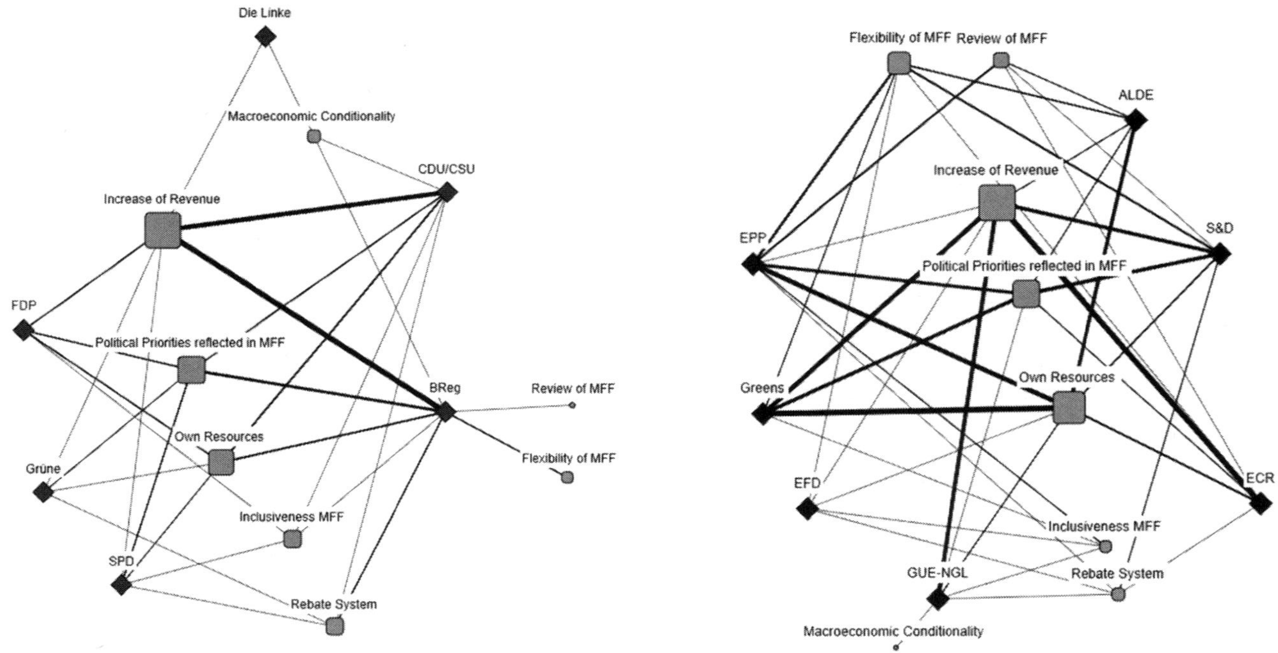

Bundestag

European Parliament

Figure 6.1: Bundestag and European Parliament affiliation network

Despite these nuances in terms of the precise weighing of claims between the respective actors on the national and supranational parliamentary level, an overall shared perception can be stated on what parliamentary actors perceive as the most pressing issues related to EU budgetary negotiations: the budget's size, its revenue system and the political priorities attached to the budget.

So far, however, the distribution of claims uttered in budgetary debates only tells about how often one actors used a particularly claim but it is of even greater importance how parliamentarians situated themselves towards these claims in terms of its approval or rejection. This perspective, which is displayed in Figure 6.2, shows that, despite the overarching similarities in terms of claims uttered, the parliamentary levels dispose of largely diverging views on their respective positioning towards these claims.

Inside the EP, all major political groups favoured an increase of the EU budget. Only the ALDE group takes a conflicting position on the matter. In the German Bundestag, however, the governmental majority party groups clearly speak out against an increase of the budget's size, while the opposition parties do not take a clear position on the matter, as they make claims both in favour and against an increase of the EU budget. Inside the European Parliament, the justifications for a larger budget ranges from the increased tasks the EU had to execute with the Treaty of Lisbon, to the nature of the budget as being an investment budget whose funds flow back to the member states and the economic situation on the continent:

> "First of all we need adequate financing for the job we have to do, jobs for young people. (…) Therefore, we need an adequate budget", S&D, Hannes Swoboda, (European Parliament 2013).

In this respect, the EP party groups mostly perceive an increased EU budget as being a reaction to the economic crisis the European Union that has been affecting the EU from 2008. From the position of the EP, an increased budget was supposed to support European growth policies inside the member states.

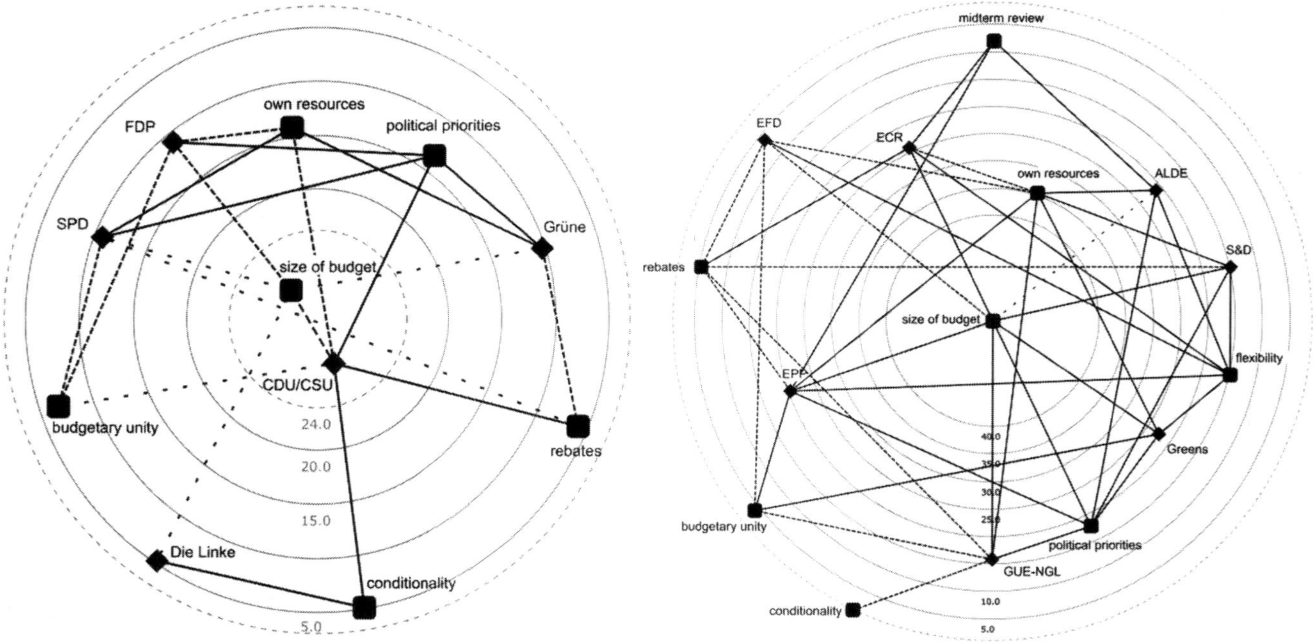

Bundestag

European Parliament

Note: The more claims an actor has uttered, or the more often a concept has been mentioned, the more central it is aligned in the graph. Solid lines stand for approval for the concept, dashed ones for rejection. Dotted lines mean conflicting statements.

Figure 6.2: Approval and rejection of claims in the Bundestag and the European Parliament

By contrast, the parliamentary discourse inside the German Bundestag, disposes of diverging leitmotivs and justifications: the governmental parties take a clear and strong position against any increase of the EU budget. This position is justified, similar to the EP, as a reaction to the economic crisis. However, it takes the opposite stance in arguing that, precisely because of the economic crisis, member states would not be able to spend more into the EU's budget.

> "The budget is deliberated against the background of the biggest debt crisis in the world and in Europe. That's why it is self-evident that we have to cap expenditure and that we simply cannot just spend more", CDU/CSU, Alois Karl (Deutscher Bundestag 2011, p. 17515).[8]

The opposition parties take conflicting positions. They both support the government's argumentation for budgetary cuts while also making the case for more investments.

> "An increase is not a possibility, the burden of the crisis is for many national budgets simply too high. That's why we need to spend EU money more wisely, more targeted and more effectively. We need to create an added value with constant volume", Grüne, Manuel Sarrazin (Deutscher Bundestag 2011, p. 17521).[9]

This discursive structure in terms of the most important claims debated inside the Bundestag and the indecisive claims from the opposition parties reflect the broader discourse in the German public which has been taken root in the public debate after the burst of the US housing bubble in 2008 in putting a strong emphasis on "austerity" and "healthy public finances". This discursive dominance makes it politically impossible to advocate for a budgetary increase – even for the opposition parties in the Bundestag.

Although the parliamentary actors turned out to hold similar perceptions of the priorities the EU budget should tackle (Figure 6.2), the positioning towards these claims was not the same when we look at national and supranational parliamentary actors separately. No overarching common meaning has been established between the two parliamentary levels in terms of the positioning towards the precise budgetary issues. Nevertheless, distinct connections equally become visible, for example the relative silence of the EPP and ALDE groups on the questions of the size of the budget might also be attributed to the broadly skeptical discourse at the level of the member states', as the German government has been particularly vocal in opposing any increase of the EU budget. The conservative government was not the only one to highlight the need for a cut of the EU budget in light of the economic crisis. The budgetary priorities addressed by the parliamentary actors further underline that the formal-legal division of the parliamentary budget authority as it has been elaborated above is not reflected in parliamentary debates. The German Bundestag and the EP both address strands of revenue and expenditure in their deliberations of the budget. Therefore, the "divided budget authority" has not been perceived as such in the public parliamentary debate. Also, on a qualitative level this question has not been taken up in either of the chambers during plenary debates.

Political priorities

Budgetary research frames parliamentary involvement in the budgetary process as debating the overall structure and political direction of the polity in terms of its political priorities. After having taken a more general look at the most important claims that have been debated, in the following, a closer look shall be taken at what the parliamentary actors assign as distinct political priorities in the budgetary debate in terms of the specific policies which should be accomplished by the EU budget.

Measured against the overall number of claims made, the debate on the political priorities occupied a less central position compared to claims related to the institutional structure of the EU budget (see Figure 6.1). In its agenda-setting function, the European Commission aimed at framing the EU budget in light of the Europe 2020 strategy which calls for strengthening the European economies through "smart, sustainable and inclusive growth" by 2020.[10] This focus of the Commission can also be explained in terms of its efforts to link the EU budgetary debate to a bigger integration projects that has been a clear factor of success in past MFF negotiations, for example under the Delors Commission (Shackleton 1990; Laffan 1997). Taking a look at the political priorities highlighted in the parliamentary debates, the Commission's aim to shape the budgetary debate around the Europe 2020 goals – as broad as they are – has been reflected. Nevertheless, the respective focuses differ. The public claims that have been mentioned most often by the parliamentary and governmental actors in the budgetary debate highlight their particular perspective on what the budget should be used for (Table 6.1). The comparison of these claims shows that there is indeed a considerable variation between what the EU budget should tackle most importantly from the perspective of the respective party groups.

Table 6.1: Most important budgetary priorities*

European Commission	Growth, R&D, Infrastructure
German government	Cohesion, Economic Growth, Jobs
CDU	Infrastructure, R&D, Agriculture
EPP	Growth
SPD	Jobs
S&D	Jobs, R&D, Economic Growth
Grüne	Infrastructure, Sustainable Development
Greens	Jobs, Sustainable Development, Cohesion
FDP	Infrastructure, Education, R&D
ALDE	R&D
Die Linke	Structural Funds / Cohesion
GUE-NGL	Structural Funds / Cohesion
ECR	Growth, Infrastructure

* Only those priorities mentioned more than once were added.

The Green party groups on the EU and the German parliamentary level put a particular emphasis on sustainable development and using investments in infrastructure or in research and development (R&D) to further a more sustainable European Union. Both party groups in the Bundestag and the EP have used the common political frame of the "Green New Deal", for their public deliberation on the budgetary negotiations.[11] The social democrats put their discursive focus on the question of jobs and here mainly on youth employment in Europe. Although the S&D party group also strongly highlighted the question of growth policies, the social democratic party groups were united in the discursive quest for creating more employment in the European Union with the help of the EU budget. The left parties (Die Linke in the Bundestag and the European United Left-Nordic Green Left, GUE-NGL, in the EP) equally shared similar claims on the EU budget's priorities. Their main objectives were cohesion policies that would provide for the poorest Europeans and more equal living conditions in the European Union.

The two liberal party groups (the German Free Democratic Party, FDP, and the ALDE party group) mainly supported claims that were related to budgetary expenditure on research and development and on infrastructure policies. In this respect, both groups criticize the ongoing emphasis of budgetary expenditure on agricultural subsidies and regard investment in future technologies as most important priorities for the EU budget. Finally, among conservatives that is the German CDU/CSU and the supranational EPP group, preferences diverge While the German conservatives stressed the importance of agricultural subsidies in the budgetary debate inside the Bundestag, the EPP highlighted the importance of conducting growth policies in order to support investment throughout Europe with the help of the EU budget.

The political priorities being debated by the parliamentary actors therefore underline that, different to the overall priorities in the budgetary debate, similar perceptions existed between the party groups of the same ideological color. In the justification of their political priorities in the parliamentary debate, the parties on the national and supranational levels used similar claims of what the EU budget should support most importantly. Classical party-political cleavages were highlighted instead of underlining differences between the parliamentary levels. Only the conservative group shared less similarities in terms of what is perceived as a political priority for the EU budget. The German conservatives underline agricultural subsidies as a priority while the EPP is more focused on investing in growth policies.

Overall discursive structure

The analysis of the overall discursive structure in the following, looks at the overarching claims and the distinct political priorities together (Figure 6.3). The co-occurrence network enables a mapping of the parliamentary discourse in connecting the respective actors through claims that were shared between them. The more claims were shared between one set of actors, the thicker is the edge connecting them. Communication is relational in being addressed towards the electorate and the public sphere and it also links parliamentary actors among each other. It therefore shows the interconnectedness and embeddedness of parliamentary actors within the budgetary debate.

Overall, it becomes visible that two major coalitions were prevalent in the budgetary debate on the MFF 2014-2020.One reflected the discourse of the national government and majority parties and the other mostly embedded supranational parliamentary actors. The European Commission assumed a brokering position between the two coalitions and national opposition parties were not centrally embedded in the discourse.

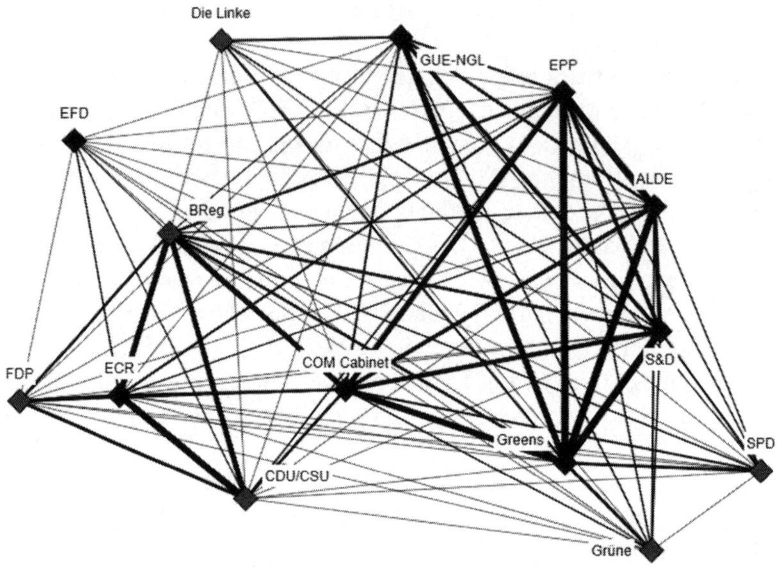

Figure 6.3: Co-occurence network of all budgetary actors

The coalition mostly formed around the German government also comprises of the CDU/CSU, the FDP. The European Council and the Council Presidency were also, though to a lesser extent, embedded in this coalition. It also comprises of the ECR party group, as being a political group on the supranational level, which – similar to the German government – has been a fervent opponent of any increase of the size of the MFF within the parliamentary discourse (although it will be interesting to see to what extent this position changes with the exit of the United Kingdom from the UK and thus from the ECR party groups which will then be dominated by the Polish PiS party). On the supranational level, the major EP party groups, the EPP, S&D, Greens and ALDE formed a densely connected cluster, therefore sharing a multitude of joint arguments in the budgetary debate. The leftist GUE-NGL has been less centrally embedded due to more feeble discursive links to the conservative and liberal party groups. This close linkage between the parliamentary groups underlines the strategy of the EP to stand as one united actor against the interests of the member states in the Council.

The European Commission clearly acted in a discursive brokering position in the budgetary debate. It shared claims with the German government and the ECR group which were mostly related to the size of the EU budget. The European Commission in this respect discursively framed its draft budget, which foresaw no increase of funds but simply an extrapolation of those funds to the 2014-2020 framework, as a statement against an increase of the EU budget. Nevertheless, the Commission has also been densely connected to the supranational parliamentary discourse coalition. The major discursive overlaps in this respect were on the reform of the own resources system which has been equally and strongly supported by the European Commission.

Despite the strong overlaps as what regards the distinct political priorities to be achieved with the EU budget that have been elaborated above (Table 6.1), the transnational party-political links in the overall budgetary debate remain rather weak. The genuine political priorities had limited impact in the overall budgetary debate that was largely dominated by institutional and structural questions inside parliamentary bodies. However, it can be asserted that the German opposition parties dispose of most shared claims between their respective party groups: While the Greens share most representative claims with their respective sister party group, same is true for the Left party groups and the social democrats (which, however, also share many statements with the Greens). While CDU/CSU and FDP party groups dispose of strong transnational links, the same does not apply with their respective sister parties on the EU level but with the ECR party group due to the strong focus of the party groups on the budget's size which has not been reiterated by party groups in the EP.

The most dominant conflict structure or most visible overlap between political positions was between the territorial levels – the German government standing against the positions of the major party groups that were organized in the EP. Genuine political priorities were not strong enough to distinctly shape the budgetary debate in the parliamentary bodies in Germany and in the EP. The two discourse coalitions emerging in the budgetary debate not only used diverging claims in their shaping of the budgetary debate but they also disposed of two inherently diverging discursive frames and orientations in the justification of their position of budgetary policies. While the first coalition – dominated by the German government and the ECR group in the EP – strongly rejected the increase of the EU budget or the reform the own resources system, the second coalition – mostly dominated by the major EP parliamentary groups – was in favour of these proposals. Behind these two positions stood a bigger perspective. The German-led coalition justified their position towards the EU budget as a financial reaction to the economic and political context, whereas the second coalition framed the EU budget as a tool to exit this very crisis. This further underlines the broader divergences on what position the EU budget should have in the financial and political architecture of the European Union in view of parliamentary bodies in the European Union, therefore reflecting the political dimension of the EU budgetary debate superseding the purely financial deliberations.

Conclusion

The communicative function of parliamentary actors takes a prime position in any representative democracy and aims not only at linking parliamentary actors with their electorate and the public sphere but also relates parliamentary actors and their positions among each other. The analysis of parliamentary debates in the MFF 2014-2020 negotiations have shown that parliamentary actors on the national and supranational parliamentary level dispose of similar perceptions of what were the most important issues to be tackled with the EU budget. Also, these did not reflect the formal division of the budgetary process between the national and supranational parliamentary level in terms of a "divided budget authority". The representative actors embedded in the budgetary discourse related to similar claims, such as the size of the budget, the own resources system and political priorities to be tackled with the EU budget. Therefore, there was a high convergence on which claims were debated and thus regarded as important elements of the budgetary debate. The parliamentary debate equally tackled not only the clear-cut financial questions and political priorities of the political system such as national budgetary processes are most dominantly about but also the institutional-bargaining position and the political *finalité* of the EU which is exemplified throughout the EU budgetary architecture.

In the structure of the budgetary debate, two paths of parliamentary representation became visible. These two paths of parliamentary representation, however, are different to what has been claimed with respect to the multi-level parliamentary field where two channels of parliamentary representation were said to exist between national parliaments and the EP. In the case of budgetary policies, these should not necessarily be drawn between parliamentary institutions on the national and supranational level but rather between the policy and polity level of the budgetary process that were addressed by parliamentarians. While parliamentary actors have been linked through party-political lines in the question of what political priorities should be addressed with the EU budget – which is the classical policy dimension of the budgetary debate, stark differences existed between the political parties and a convergence of views along the national-supranational level became visible with respect to the polity level of budgetary deliberations, namely the institutional and structural questions related to the EU budget.

The party-political interests were most broadly related to the question of what the EU budget should accomplish in terms of political priorities. In these questions, the party-political cleavages brought together national and supranational party groups. While the social democrats demanded more employment to be created with the EU budget, the Greens demanded a "green New Deal" to be financed with the MFF. These party-political overlaps also became indirectly visible for example in the position of the EPP group regarding the size of the budget. While the EPP formally supported the general claim of the EP to increase the EU budget's size, the EPP in the public debates on the EU budget did not explicitly mentioned this issue – reflecting the deeply conflicting positions on this issue within the party group which represented many conservative governments in the European Union. Same was true for the liberal EP party group which faced similar constraints inside the EU member states therefore underlining the linkage between the national and supranational governmental level through parties.

With regard to the institutional and structural aspects of the EU budget, however, no common meaning was established between the national and supranational parliamentary levels. Although joint meanings were established in terms of the political priorities of the budget, the institutional bargaining positions lied with the respective institutional self-interests of the respective national and supranational parliamentary institutions. While the EP broadly favoured an increase of the size of the EU budget and a reform of the own resources system in order to enable a more stable and independent financing of the European Union, the parties in the German Bundestag – both in the majority and the opposition party groups – were more cautious or even strictly against both proposals, as the perception was to restrict spending in order to help member states coming out of the economic crisis with a reform of the own resources system was viewed like a restriction of the Bundestag's sovereignty in budgetary matters.

In classical budgetary research, budgetary debates are primarily perceived as aiming at an overarching deliberation of the political priorities of a given system and a general debate on the government's performance and priorities. In the case of the EU budgetary debate, however, the impact of the EU's multi-level political system on a multitude of institutional conflicts arising from the budgetary process have to be considered as being more prevalent than a genuine deliberation of the political direction and priorities of the European Union for itself. They therefore underline the distinct structure of the EU's political system where institutional-bargaining aspects of the budgetary debate are more salient compared to the classical political cleavages along which debates are structured in national political systems.

From the perspective of a multi-level parliamentary field, it has already been argued that neither the EP nor national parliaments can fulfill all parliamentary tasks in the EU multi-level system. The channels of parliamentary representation in the European Union, however, should not only focus on the antagonism between national parliaments and the European Parliament but also take a closer look at the structure of parliamentary orientations and interests, as it has been done with regard to the EU budgetary process. Both national parliaments and the EP dispose of distinct party-political and territorial-institutional interests that bind parliamentary institutions together while at the same time pulling them apart. On the one hand parliamentary institutions are connected through party-political linkages binding party groups together. These party-political linkages result from the anchorage of Members of European Parliament (MEPs) within the respective national parties and close connections between national and supranational career patterns (Beauvallet/Michon 2012; Corbett et al. 2011); hence creating a common political perception between national and European MPs. At the same time, however, parliamentary actors equally relate to distinct territorial interests. National parliaments – also due to the close links between parliamentary majority and the government in parliamentary political systems – are generally prone to support their government's action inside the (European) Council (Abels 2013; Auel et al. 2015; Calliess/Beichelt 2015, p. 30). The EP equally disposes of rather strong territorial interests at the supranational level, as it has perpetually sought to strengthen its own position inside the European political architecture and that of the EU-level at large compared to the national sphere of influence (Bache et al. 2011; Hix et al. 2007; Rittberger 2005).

These two strands of parliamentary representation inside the EU multi-level system explain both the similarities and the divergences that were observed in the analysis of budgetary debates in the German Bundestag and the EP. Due to the high political importance and the still unresolved question on the institutional anchorage of the EU budget that still shifts between a programming and a redistributive budget, unresolved institutional questions were more prevalent than shared party-political cleavages. This permits the reverse conclusion that if the overarching institutional quarrels surrounding the EU budget would be resolved at one point, this would lay the ground for a more pronounced joint oversight and parliamentary debate from national and supranational parliamentary on the political priorities to be achieved with the EU budget. This potential reorientation of the budgetary debate on policies and not so much on the politics-aspects of the budget may indeed be projected to a far-away future. However, the distinct similarities between parliamentary groups in terms of political cleavages highlight the need to focus more on those political priorities to be achieved with the EU budget from parliamentary actors.

Notes

1 The empirical research of this work is based on the PhD research of the author which has been formally submitted to the European University Viadrina, Frankfurt/Oder in November 2016.

2 Due to reasons for simplicity, in the following using the term MFF will comprise both revenue and expenditure strands of the EU budget – the MFF Regulation and the Own Resources Decision which are closely linked temporally and politically, but dispose of diverging decision-making processes.

3 It has even been argued to include sub-national parliaments in this analysis Abels/Eppler (2015).

4 Representing the period between 29 June 2011 and 19 November 2013. The agenda-setting and the implementation phase of the EU budgetary process have been deliberately not included as the focus of research was on the formal policy formulation.

5 The European Parliament conducted more debates on the MFF and the multitude of implementing regulations. For this research, those debates have been chosen were an overarching horizontal debate on the MFF in general were conducted.

6 For a more detailed account of the legal system and procedures of negotiations see Benedetto (2012); Becker (2014b).

7 The SURE Committee was the “Special committee on the policy challenges and budgetary resources for a sustainable European Union after 2013” which worked from June 2010 to June 2011.

8 Own translation.

9 Own translation.

10 The precise policy areas, the strategy wants to contribute to, are: employment; research & development; education (university, tertiary, and lifelong learning); fighting social exclusion; and climate change and green technologies, http://ec.europa.eu/europe2020/europe-2020-in-a-nutshell/targets/index_en.htm, accessed 11 September 2015.

11 This claim has been equally used in other political debates by the Greens, such as on the reaction to the Eurocrisis and the subsequent debate on how to trigger economic growth in the European Union.

References

Abels, G., and Eppler, A. (Eds.). 2011. *Auf dem Weg zum Mehrebenenparlamentarismus? Funktionen von Parlamenten im politischen System der EU*. Baden-Baden: Nomos.

Abels, G., and Eppler, A. (Eds.). 2015. *Subnational Parliaments in an EU Multi-level Parliamentary System: Taking Stock of the Post-Lisbon Era*. Innsbruck: Studien-Verlag.

Abels, G. 2013. Parlamentarische Kontrolle im Mehrebenensystem der EU - ein unmögliches Unterfangen? In *Parlamentarische Kontrolle und Europäische Union*, Eds. Eberbach-Born, B., Kropp, S., Stuchlik, A., and Zeh, W., 79-104. Baden-Baden: Nomos.

Auel, K., Rozenberg, O. and Tacea, A. 2015. To Scrutinise or Not to Scrutinise? Explaining Variation in EU-Related Activities in National Parliaments. *West European Politics* 38: 282-304.

Auel, K., and Raunio, T. 2012. Debating the State of the Union? Comparing Parliamentary Debates on EU Issues in Finland, France, Germany and the United Kingdom. *National Parliaments, Electorates and EU Affairs,* 47–78. Wien.

Bache, I., George, S., and Bulmer, S. 2011. *Politics in the European Union.* Oxford: Oxford University Press.

Beauvallet, W., and Michon, S. 2012. Faire carrière au Parlement européen. Activation des dispositions et socialisation institutionelle. In *Le champ de l'Eurocratie. Une sociologie politique du personnel de l'UE*, Ed. Georgakakis, D., 13-43. Paris: Economica.

Becker, P. 2014a. *Das Finanz- und Haushaltssystem der Europäischen Union. Grundlagen und Reformen aus deutscher Perspektive*. Wiesbaden: Springer VS.

Becker, P. 2014b. Haushaltspolitik. In *Jahrbuch der Europäischen Integration 2014*, Eds. Weidenfeld, W., and Wessels, W., 209-212. Baden-Baden: Nomos.

Benedetto, G. 2012. Budget Reform and the Lisbon Treaty. In *European Union Budget Reform. Institutions, Policy and Economic Crisis*, Eds.. Benedetto, G., and Milio, S., 40-58. Basingstoke: Palgrave Macmillan.

Benedetto, G. 2015. The Balance of Power over the EU Budget. European Expenditure sinde the Lisbon Treaty. *European Policy Analysis* 15. Stockholm: SIEPS.

Buzogàny, A. 2013. Learning from the best? Interparliamentary networks and the parliamentary scrutiny of EU decision-making. In *Practices of inter-parliamentary coordination in international politics. The European Union and beyond*, Eds. Crum, B. and Fossum, J.E., 17-32. Colchester: ECPR Press.

Calliess, C., and Beichelt, T. 2015. *Die Europäisierung des Parlaments. Die europapolitische Rolle von Bundestag und Bundesrat.* Gütersloh: Verlag Bertelsmann Stiftung.

Corbett, R., Jacobs, F. and Shackleton, M. 2011. *The European Parliament.* London: John Harper.

Crum, B., and Fossum, J. E. 2009. The Multilevel Parliamentary Field: a framework for theorizing representative democracy in the EU. *European Political Science Review* 1(2): 249-271.

Crum, B., and Fossum, J. E.. 2012. A Democratic Backbone for International Organizations: The Multilevel Parliamentary Field. In *Multilayered representation in the European Union. Parliaments, courts and the public sphere*, Eds. Evas, T., Liebert, U. and Lord, C., 91-105. Baden-Baden: Nomos.

Crum, B., and Fossum, J. E. (Eds.). 2013. *Practices of inter-parliamentary coordination in international politics. The European Union and beyond.* Colchester: ECPR Press.

Deschouwer, K., Depauw, S. and André, A. 2014. Representing the People in Parliaments. In *Representing the People. A Survey among Members of Statewide and Substate Parliaments*, Eds. Deschouwer, K. and Depauw, S. 1-18. Oxford: Oxford University Press.

Deutscher Bundestag. 2011. 146. Sitzung. 01.12.2011 *17513.* Berlin.

Eriksen, E.O., and Fossum, J. E. 2011. Representation through Deliberation: The European Case. *Arena Working Paper* 5. Oslo.

European Parliament. 2013. *Plenary Debate. Preparations for the European Council meeting* (7-8 February 2013). Strasbourg.

Goetz, K.H., and Patz, R. 2016. Pressured budgets and the European Commission: towards a more centralised EU budget administration? Journal of European Public Policy 23: 1038-1056.

Hagemann, S. 2012. Negotiations of the European Union Budget. How Decision Processes Constrain Policy Ambitions. In *European Union Budget Reform. Institutions, Policy and Economic Crisis*, Eds. Benedetto, G., and Milio, S., 23-39. Basingstoke: Palgrave Macmillan.

Hefftler, C., and Gattermann, K. 2015. Interparliamentary Cooperation in the European Union: Patterns, Problems and Potential. In *The Palgrave Handbook of National Parliaments in the European Union*, Eds. Hefftler, C., Neuhold, C., Rozenberg, Olivier, and Julie Smith, 94-115. Basingstoke: Palgrave Macmillan.

Herranz-Surrallés, A. 2014. The EU's Multilevel Parliamentary (Battle)Field: Interparliamentary Cooperation and Conflict in Foreign and Security Policy. *West European Politics* 37: 957-975.

Hix, S., Noury, A., and Roland, G. 2007. *Democratic politics in the European Parliament.* Cambridge, New York: Cambridge University Press.

Kreilinger, V. 2014. Possibilities for Upgrading Inter-parliamentary Cooperation after the 2014 European Elections. *The Polish Quarterly of International Affairs:* 57-67.

Laffan, B. 1997. *The Finances of the European Union.* Basingstoke: Macmillan.

Leifeld, P, and Haunss, S. 2012. Political discourse networks and the conflict over software patents in Europe. *European Journal of Political Research* 51: 382-409.

Leifeld, P. 2011. *Discourse Networks and German Pension Politics.* Dissertation. Konstanz.

Leifeld, P. 2013. Reconceptualizing Major Policy Change in the Advocacy Coalition Framework. A Discourse Network Analysis of German Pension Politics. *Policy Studies Journal* 41: 169-198.

Lienert, I. 2013. Role of the Legislature in Budget Processes. In *The International Handbook of Public Financial Management*, Eds. Allen, R., Hemming, R., and Potter, B.H., 116–136. London: Palgrave Macmillan.

Maurer, A. 2012. *Parlamente in der EU.* Wien/Wien: UTB; Facultas Universitätsverlag.

Müller-Osten, A. 2007. *Der öffentliche Haushalt als Institution parlamentarischer Kontrolle. Theoriegeschichtliche Grundlegung - interaktionsökonomische Analyse.* Marburg: Metropolis-Verl.

Neheider, S, and Santos, I. 2011. Reframing the EU Budget Decision-Making Process. *Journal of Common Market Studies* 49: 631-651.

Neyer, J. 2014. Justified Multi-level Parliamentarism. Situating National Parliaments in the European Polity. *Journal of Legislative Studies* 20: 125-138.

Oppenheimer, B E. 1985. Legislative Influence on Policy and Budgets. In *Handbook of Legislative Research*, Eds. Loewenberg, G., Patterson, S. C., and Jewell, M. E., 621-668. New York: Harvard University Press.

Patz, R, and Goetz, K.H. 2015. From politicised Budgeting to Political Budgets in the EU? *Paper prepared for the International Conference on Public Policy*, Milan. Munich.

Patzelt, W. J. 1993. *Abgeordnete und Repräsentation. Amtsverständnis und Wahlkreisarbeit.* Passau: Rothe.

Patzelt, W. J. 2003. Parlamente und ihre Funktionen. In *Parlamente und ihre Funktionen : institutionelle Mechanismen und institutionelles Lernen im Vergleich*, Ed. Patzelt, W.J., 13-49. Wiesbaden: Westdt. Verl.

Rittberger, B. 2005. *Building Europe's Parliament. Democratic Representation beyond the Nation-State.* Oxford: Oxford University Press.

Schulz, F, and Broich, M. 2013. Die Zusammenarbeit zwischen MdB und MdEP - Ansichten aus dem Maschinenraum. In *Parlamentarische Kontrolle und Europäische Union*, Eds. Eberbach-Born, B., Kropp, S., Stuchlik, A., and Zeh, W., 131-150. Baden-Baden: Nomos.

Shackleton, M. 1990. *Financing the European Community.* London: Primer.

Wehner, J. 2010. *Legislatures and the Budget Process: The Myth of Fiscal Control.* New York: Palgrave Macmillan.

Wildavsky, A. 1988. *The new politics of the budgetary process.* Glenview, Ill.: Scott, Foresman.

Assessing the European Parliament's Power of the Purse: Rights, Capabilities, and Strategies

Michael W. Bauer and Stefan Becker

The European Parliament (EP) appears to be on an "unrelenting rise" (Dinan 2014). Each treaty revision after the establishment of the European Communities in 1967 brought more powers to the EP; and since it became the single directly elected institution on the European Union (EU) level in 1979, its empowerment accelerated. The Lisbon Treaty, that went into force at the end of 2009, further strengthened the EP by making co-decision the standard legislative procedure, expanding the need for parliamentary consent for international agreements, and strengthening its role in selecting the Commission president. At the same time, members of the EP (MEPs) have repeatedly shown that they are willing and able to translate these formal empowerments into actual influence (recently, Kohler 2014; Hix/Høyland 2013; Hobolt 2014). For all the evidence of parliamentary empowerment, there seems to be an important exception to its unrelenting rise—the EU budget. While Benedetto (2012, 2013) analyzes the respective Lisbon Treaty reforms and argues that the EP has lost budgetary clout, the outcomes of recent negotiations hardly read as parliamentary success stories. Does the budget thus represent an exception to the trajectory of ever more EP empowerment, and will the future of EU budget politics be characterized by an enduring Council, i.e., member state, dominance?

We seek to provide an answer by assessing several determinants of the EP's powers of the purse. Focusing on its influence on spending, we first differentiate between figures and procedure to evaluate outcomes of budget negotiations after the Lisbon treaty. With reference to prominent literature on EU policy-making and EP influence, we then assess the relevance of three parliamentary capabilities—internal preference homogeneity, organizational capacities, situational factors —and four strategies—rule interpretation, coalition building, issue linkage, and application of normative pressure—for these outcomes. Against the backdrop of the EP's formal budgetary rights after the Lisbon Treaty, we gauge the importance of these factors in a case study of the parallel negotiations on the Multiannual Financial Framework (MFF) 2014-2020 and the 2014 budget. The analysis builds on official documents and interviews with relevant MEPs, as well as budget officials in the EP Secretariat-General, the Council secretariat, and the Commission.[1]

We show that formal rights alone—while central—hardly determine the EP's power of the purse; as in other policy areas, the EP's actual ability to influence outcomes is more volatile than an exclusive focus on treaty provisions suggests. In recent negotiations, a crisis-ridden political environment, increasing internal preference heterogeneity, and few coalition-building opportunities kept the EP from achieving better results in terms of budget figures. They did not, however, constrain the EP in pursuing greater budgetary flexibility. Furthermore, the EP already sought to link budgetary issues and enhance its organizational capacities to improve its bargaining position. So even if there is little chance that its formal status in budgetary matters will be advanced—and the EP itself can do little in terms of rule interpretation and application of normative pressure towards this end—its weak position is subject to change. The EU budget is, therefore, an exception to the general trajectory of ever-greater EP empowerment. However, its weaker, formal standing should not be overestimated. A less critical environment, more internal heterogeneity, realistic coalition building opportunities, or more organizational capacities could all lead to more parliamentary influence in budgetary matters.

EP influence on the budget: Evidence from budget negotiations

Budget negotiations revolve around figures (how much to spend) and procedure (how to spend). The figures attract most public attention, and budgetary battles on the EU level also revolve heavily around this theme. Traditionally, there has been a clear and stable difference between institutional preferences—the EP is eager to increase spending, while the Council is more status quo oriented (Lindner 2006). Procedural questions receive less attention, but they are also important because budget flexibility may grant the involved actors opportunities to alter the budget after it has been passed (Wehner 2006, p. 31-38). In this regard, the Council favors a more rigid and stable budget, while the EP advocates more flexible spending. MFF and annual budget negotiations since 2008 show that the EP's power of the purse differs in these two dimensions.

In terms of figures, the MFF is the crucial budgetary agreement, laying the foundation by setting ceilings for EU spending in seven-year periods. The agreement for the years 2014–2020 can be considered a defeat for the

EP. The firm stand of net payer governments in the Council, especially the UK, Germany, the Netherlands, and Sweden, kept the size of the multiannual budget (in terms of commitment appropriations) at roughly one percent of the EU's Gross National Income (GNI). This figure is 3.5 percent lower than in the previous MFF, and is thereby far from the EP's position—voiced in a resolution in 2011 (P7_TA(2011)0266)—that it was a five percent increase, at least. EP President Schulz accordingly called the figures "far from perfect."[2] While there is a difference between strategic positioning and actual preferences, a nominal decrease in spending is remarkable, and can be considered a blow for the traditionally pro-spending EP.

The figures of annual budgets between 2008 and 2015 add to the impression that the EP lost budgetary clout. Figure 7.1 shows the respective budget concessions of the Council and the EP, measured by the difference between their original positions and the eventually adopted budget in terms of payment appropriations. While the EP has always made more concessions than the Council, the adopted budgets from 2011 and after hardly differ from the original Council positions—with the 2014 budget as an outlier. Again, strategic positioning and actual preferences may differ, but a trend of decreasing parliamentary influence suggests itself.

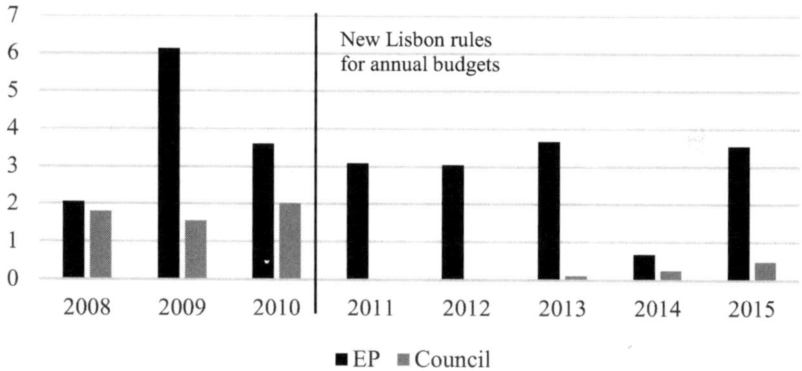

Figure 7.1: Council and EP concessions in annual budgets 2008-2015

Note: Figures represent the payment appropriation deviation of the adopted budget from the original positions (as adopted in first readings) in percent: EP figures are negative (i.e., the final budget is smaller than demanded), Council figures are positive (i.e., the final budget is bigger than demanded).
Source: EP BUDG committee, Balance of Activities Reports 2009 and 2014; EP and Council 2015.

In terms of procedural issues, the most important decisions are again made during MFF negotiations. They predominantly relate to options for transferring funds between years and/or headings, as well as the establishment of financing facilities outside the agreed spending ceilings. In these matters, the EP was arguably more influential. The MFF from 2014 to 2020 compromises features of many of the parliamentary demands, including options to bring forward expenditure in specific areas (e.g., youth employment and research), the continuation and establishment of special funds that run outside the MFF ceilings (e.g., the Globalisation Adjustment Fund), and a revision clause for the MFF that requires the Commission to consider and possibly propose revisions in a midterm evaluation.

The outcomes of budget negotiations thus paint a mixed, but overall bleak picture of the EP's power of the purse. It was able to realize its preferences in terms of procedure, but it was weak in influencing budget figures. The following analysis shows how these outcomes came about. It considers EP rights, capabilities and strategies.

Rights: The EP in the budgetary system after the Lisbon Treaty

The EU's budgetary system is divided into four areas: the own resources system for revenues, multiannual financial planning, annual budgeting, as well as implementation and discharge. This system comprises the full extent of possible EP rights: being consulted in matters of revenue, giving consent to multiannual planning, "co-deciding" annual budgets, and independently granting discharge after the implementation of the budget. As our analysis focuses on spending, we only discuss the rules for the MFF and annual budgets.[3]

In this regard, the Lisbon Treaty brought three major reforms. First, the MFF was upgraded from an interinstitutional agreement (IIA) to hard law. The procedure of MFF decision-making remains broadly the same: the Council decides unanimously after obtaining the consent of the EP (Article 312 Treaty on the Functioning of the European Union, TFEU), which leaves parliamentarians with veto power; however, the effects of upgrading the MFF to hard law are significant, as it strongly constrains annual budgeting.[4] As a result, the new MFF rules are widely considered to be a decrease of parliamentary influence, because the EP is no longer able to threaten the Council with terminating the agreement, and thus loses a bargaining chip in annual budget negotiations (see Pollack 2008; Lindner 2006, p. 87). The threat of renouncing the MFF was not just a theoretical possibility—it was a frequent, if sometimes implicit, argument in budget negotiations before the Lisbon Treaty (Interviews #1, #9).

Second, the Lisbon Treaty eliminated the distinction between compulsory and non-compulsory spending categories, putting the EP on equal, formal footing in all sections of the annual budget. What first appears to be an empowerment of the EP (especially its stronger involvement in agricultural spending) is actually an overall decrease of influence, as Parliament loses power in the area of non-compulsory spending. This category gained importance over the years, and now amounts to roughly 60 percent of the EU budget. The loss of the EP's last unilateral say in this area is thus significant. While the EP's spending inclination was already curbed by maximum rates of increase and bargaining considerations (i.e., using non-compulsory spending as leverage to control compulsory spending), this reform effectively weakens the EP's ability to shape the annual budget (Interview #1).

Third, the fallback option in the event that budget negotiations fail, the provisional twelfths mechanism, was reformed.[5] The EP is now able to "co-decide" in all policy areas in monthly budgets, but only to the extent that it can block increases or impose decreases (Benedetto 2012, p. 50). Before, it was able to vote for increases in non-compulsory spending. This reform renders it difficult for the EP to threaten the Council with letting the negotiations fail, as no agreement means no unwanted increases from the Council's perspective.

Overall, then, the Lisbon Treaty reforms on the spending side of the budget system are to the disadvantage of the EP. As the implementation of these rules coincides with disappointing budget outcomes from a parliamentary perspective, the verdict seems clear; the Lisbon Treaty effectively weakened the EP's power of the purse. Influence over policy outcomes is, however, contingent on more than formal rights. The next section shows how EP capabilities also affected recent budget negotiations.

Capabilities: The EP's core strengths in budgetary bargaining

Institutional capabilities are necessary to translate formal rights into actual influence. Following the prominent literature on the EP's role in EU policy-making (Farrell/Héritier 2003; Hix/Høyland 2013; Shackleton 2006; Thomson/Hosli 2006), there are three dominant factors: internal preference homogeneity, organizational capacities, and situational factors.

Internal preference homogeneity

When collective actors are bargaining, internal preference homogeneity is crucial, as splits can be exploited by others (e.g. Scharpf 2000). In the EU, member states in the Council and political groups in the EP frequently struggle to reconcile preferences in order to come up with a common position. In particular, the EP's ability to present a "unified front against the Council and the Commission" (Hix/Høyland 2011, p. 60) is far from assured. Traditionally, no political group is close to having a majority, and legislative coalitions are more fluid than in national legislatures. Thus intra-institutional bargaining is intense (Shackleton 2006, p. 122).[6] Coordination and cooperation problems are further aggravated by the second-order character of EP elections, and the easier access to small parties with little experience (Reif/Schmitt 1980; Hix/Høyland 2013).

Table 7.1: EP final votes on budgets (budget years 2009-2015)

				Votes	
EP term	Budget procedure	Budget year	For	Against	Abstention
8	New	2015	60%	34%	6%
7	New	2014	74%	24%	2%
7	New	2013	74%	24%	2%
7	New	2012	75%	21%	4%
7	New	2011	76%	21%	3%
7	Old	2010	84%	14%	2%
6	Old	2009	90%	5.5%	4.5%

Source: votewatch.eu (accessed 6 July 2015)

In budgetary matters, the EP was able to build a "unified front" among its various party groups for a long time (Lindner 2006). However, as it matured, gained further powers, and became more diverse, this ability waned. Pollack (2008, p. 43) draws up a scenario "in which budgetary issues do not unite the EP against a common adversary but increasingly divide MEPs along party-group, committee, or national lines." Indeed, final budget votes in the EP between 2009 and 2015 show a trend of diminishing majorities (Table 7.1). The significant decrease of votes in favor of the budget in just one parliamentary term (2009-2014) is remarkable. Furthermore, the vote on the 2015 budget points towards future challenges, with only 60 percent of the most EU-skeptic EP in history voting in favour. This result is not only due to the influx of more EU-skeptic representatives in the 2014 elections; the percentage of MEPs that voted for the budget resolution is smaller than the number of seats pro-European party groups in the EP have combined.

While instructive, these final votes tell only half the story. Prior intra-institutional preference aggregation is even more important because it determines the EP's bargaining strength. In this regard, our data support Pollack's scenario: MEPs' preferences toward the budget are indeed becoming more heterogeneous. While there has always been a plethora of requests—the Budget Committee frequently receives up to 3,000 amendment proposals (Interview #1)—previously there was a tendency to eventually pull together when negotiating with the Council. This appears to be changing. As one interviewee (#5) succinctly remarks, "personal" or "party-political" agendas are increasingly at play in budgetary politics.

Decreasing internal preference homogeneity can also be observed in the MFF negotiations. Again, the final EP votes suggest a relatively strong unity. In the end, 79 percent of MEPs voted for and 18 percent against the compromise, with three percent abstaining. However, the EP was far from presenting a unified front against the Council during the negotiations. In the beginning it was able to convince the Council that it would use its veto power if need be. As time passed, however, it was not able to uphold a credible threat, and its broad majority was disintegrating. In February 2013, for instance, when the European Council came up with a more concrete position (EUCO 37/13), the liberal group in the EP was quick to assert that it would not seek to challenge the overall figures. That made it difficult for others to push for a bigger budget, as it would make them look profligate. This had a "huge effect" on the negotiations (Interview #4), as it set the scene for the upcoming debates.

Nevertheless, serious considerations in the EP remained concerning letting the negotiations break down. This was a sentiment strongest among more generalist and budgetary MEPs (Interviews #5, #6, #7). At the same time, however, many other MEPs were concerned about the spending programs of their interest. Therefore, they put pressure on the negotiators to reach a compromise, even if it meant settling for lower spending than desirable, in order to ensure that these programs ran smoothly. In addition to these internal disputes, there was also pressure from national capitals. EP President Schulz even considered making the MFF vote secret to shield MEPs from external interference.[7] In particular, parties in national governments used the upcoming EP elections as leverage, as party lists had to be drawn up and candidates selected. As a result, there were effectively two camps in the EP, one dedicated to pushing for more funds, the other arguing for austerity in the EU budget (Interview #4). While such a split is not surprising, their *balance* certainly is. During the MFF negotiations, the EP thus lost a credible veto threat and its bargaining position was weakened due to heterogeneous internal preferences.

What was less contentious within the EP, and therefore a focus in the advanced stages of the MFF negotiations, were procedural matters. The EP delegation put emphasis on the fact that the figures were unmovable. "The Council is dictating the figures. And we are dictating the flexibility," as one interviewee (#6) summarized the strategy in the later stages of negotiation. The procedural outcomes were considered a success, not least because in times of low spending ceilings, "The strength attached to how the budgetary machinery functions [turns out] to be quite important," as one Commission official (#11) put it, acknowledging the EP's assertiveness in these matters. Indeed, the eventual outcome was a much more flexible MFF than the Commission originally called for.

The 2016 EP thus featured political groups and single parliamentarians pursuing diverging spending agendas. Pressures through national party channels were increasing. This internal heterogeneity works to the detriment of the overall institutional agenda, traditionally focused on increasing the budget. Procedural matters, on the other hand, were less contested in the EP, which allowed budget negotiators to pursue a more assertive strategy.

Organizational capacities

Bargaining strength also relies on expertise, and capacities for information processing and analysis are particularly important in parliamentary settings (Krehbiel 1991). In this regard, the EP competes with the expertise of both the Commission and the Council. It has already been shown that a lack of organizational capacities and technical expertise can constrain the EP in co-decision (Thomson/Hosli 2006). Differentials in expertise may also influence conduct in negotiations, as actors with limited resources are sometimes keen to spend as little of those resources as possible on a subject (Farrell/Héritier 2003, p. 583).

It goes without saying that budgeting is a prime example of complex issues requiring plenty of expertise (Wildavsky 1986, p. 10). The actors have to summarize past revenues and expenditures, forecast future economic conditions and fiscal outcomes, and estimate costs and consequences of new programmatic initiatives. Indeed, many important legislative conflicts are resolved on the basis of numbers derived from mathematical models that require specialized knowledge (e.g., Khimm 2011). Institutions with stronger budgetary capacities can influence negotiations through control of information. In the national setting, this is usually the executive branch (e.g., Wehner 2006).

On the EU level, Parliament also faces institutions with high expertise in budgetary matters. The Commission employs a specialized career staff and has a whole directorate-general dedicated to budget issues, and the Council can make use of expertise from 28 national governments. Both institutions thus have an informational advantage over Parliament in budgetary issues. In the EP, the Budget Committee is supported by the secretariat, where the Directorate for Budgetary Affairs employs around 50 people. This includes, however, assistants with clerical tasks (Interview #7), and the directorate is also responsible for supporting the Budgetary Control Committee. Furthermore, the number of political group staff dedicated to the budget—the second important contributor to the EP's overall expertise (Dobbels 2013, p. 202)—is also relatively small; one of the two largest groups employed four budget advisors in the last legislative period (Interview #5), the overall number of staffers directly dedicated to the budget is thus likely not higher than fifteen. Including the *specialized* MEPs and their assistants, parliamentary resources are, therefore, rather small compared to the Council and the Commission.

The relevance of this asymmetry in organizational capacity becomes evident in the 2014 budget negotiations. Generally, the budget procedure in the EU is strictly timed and highly routinized. For all the routine, however, even the experts in the EP face obstacles in processing the relevant information. In a short period of time, the budget secretariat staff is mostly occupied with "procedure," "consolidating texts and amendments," and thus it does not have any time to "reflect" on the Commission figures (Interview #1). As a result, MEPs, especially those in policy committees, have hardly any opportunity to create substantiated claims based on independent analysis. Instead, they have to resort to Commission proposals as their points of departure for the negotiation. Around 95 percent of all adopted budget lines are identical to the Commission proposal, one interviewee (#4) estimates. Most of this can be attributed to the incremental nature of budgeting (Citi 2013) and the Commission's experience in submitting acceptable proposals. Yet, in certain cases, the EP's inability to scrutinize the Commission figures in detail can also be considered an additional reason.

It could be expected that the MFF negotiations, ongoing for more than two years, provide more opportunities for analytical exercises by the EP—and also more urgency, given the importance of this agreement. Yet normal parliamentary work goes on, and there are numerous policies to be decided, not least the 65 multiannual programs needed to accompany the MFF. In the last negotiation cycle, the whole MFF package, including "details in structural funds, in agriculture policy, about the national envelopes, about compensations, about the levels of co-financing and other ideas" was simply "too much for everybody," as one EP interviewee (#6) stated. In particular, the parliamentary delegation considered itself lacking important budgetary expertise in negotiations, and Commission and Council officials also noticed that EP representatives entered budget talks less well-prepared (Interviews #10, #11). This asymmetry has not only *hard* impacts when it comes to arguing over figures, but also *soft* consequences when expertise can be considered an important source of an actor's authority. When Council or Commission delegates are "not convinced" about their parliamentary counterpart's knowledge, as happened in budget talks (Interview #10), this influences the conduct of negotiations.

Some MEPs recognized this and started pushing for stronger organizational capacities in budgetary matters. As of January 2014, the EP has a new research service. One unit with around 20 administrators is dedicated to institutional, legal and budgetary matters. Yet given that they work on broad portfolios in addition to budgetary matters, this staff number is small compared to the 250 employees of the U.S. Congressional Budget Office, which served as a role model for some MEPs and administrators (Interviews #4, #5, #6).

Therefore, the EP has insufficient organizational capacities to process all relevant budgetary information to substantiate its own positions and effectively counter Council or Commission claims. More expertise would not solve political conflicts inside the EP, but it would inform the debate and could make for a more assertive negotiation strategy. Organizational capacities are, however, much more relevant for budget figures than for procedural issues. The analysis of innumerable budget lines requires more capacities than designing flexibility instruments—more so as institutional templates are already available. Therefore, the lack of capacities hardly affects bargaining strength in procedural questions.

Situational factors

The political environment shapes bargaining power, but often situational factors affect actors to different degrees. In the EU, member state governments in the Council are accountable to their citizens via their national political systems, while MEPs are directly accountable to voters. In theory, this should make the EP more sensitive to situational factors in the political environment. Practically, however, its members face little pressure from the electorate as EU elections are still diffuse, second-order national elections (Reif/Schmitt 1980; Farrell/Héritier 2003, p. 583; Hix/Høyland 2013). This is typically considered a bargaining strength for the supranational parliament.

In budget negotiations since 2009, however, this remoteness was reduced. One the one hand, the political environment was overshadowed by the enduring financial and economic crisis. National governments took great pains to consolidate their finances, including large budget cuts, sometimes under heavy pressure from Brussels. On the other hand, European integration, in general, is increasingly politicized and subject to fierce criticism. The EU institutions face a growing "constraining dissensus" (Hooghe/Marks 2008, p. 5). EU-skeptic parties on the rise in many member states proved quite successful in the 2014 EP elections. Even mainstream parties increasingly issue complaints about "Brussels" being too powerful and interventionist.

As a result, more attention is also paid to EU finances, and the MFF 2014-2020 negotiations were in the spotlight like never before. The increased attention was not only felt in the Council, where disputes between net payers and net receivers became fiercer (Interview #9, #10), but also in the EP. After all, demanding more funds and redistribution is a delicate task in times of national fiscal crises. It is perhaps no coincidence that in 2012 the EP Bureau established a Directorate for Impact Assessment and European Added Value that, among other things, draft reports on the cost of "Non-Europe" and the benefits of existing policies. Inter alia, these endeavors are to substantiate claims for a larger budget. However, these efforts proved futile during the MFF 2014-2020 negotiations, which were permeated by the crisis and austerity considerations (Interviews #5, #9). Pressures from national parties were also crucial in this regard (Interviews #4); there was close to no room for MEPs to maneuver, due to the crisis.

Apart from economic considerations, MEPs were also concerned about negative effects on the overall integration project. Regarding the MFF negotiations, one interviewee (#5) from the EP stated, "The situation, the political pressure of the present economic crisis has been so intense that it was basically impossible for the Parliament [...] to block a deal. [...] The political effects of a budget crisis on top of the economic crisis for the moment meant that the main political parties of the Parliament decided not to use the veto power." Legitimacy concerns were a major factor for the empowerment of the EP (Rittberger 2003), and they still form a strong basis for its influence, as it can invoke its status as the single directly elected institution on the EU level. Indeed, the EP was the most trusted EU institution involved in legislative policy-making in 2013, even if it had also suffered a loss of trust since the onset of the crisis (Eurobarometer 79 2013). MEPs are cautious to further risk this important asset with overly confrontational strategies.

In contrast, the crisis bolstered arguments for more budget flexibility. The high level of uncertainty as to where resources would be most needed in the next years supported earlier EP claims. Especially the continued, and even increased, use of specialized funds and the MFF midterm review can be partly attributed to EP invoking the crisis. In terms of figures, however, the crisis was a strong constraint for the EP's bargaining strength, and the MFF can without a doubt be considered an austerity budget.

Strategies: The EP's pathways of influence in budgetary bargaining

In general, the EP can do more than follow formal procedures. It can employ various strategies to maximize its influence. The literature on EU policy-making and the EP (Kaeding/Selck 2005; Pollack 2008; Thomson et al. 2004; Rittberger 2003, 2012, 2014) puts forward four major pathways: rule interpretation, coalition building, issue linkage, and application of normative pressure.

Rule interpretation

If there is a legal basis, the EP may seek to transform the bargaining game instead of playing it. As Rittberger (2014, p. 1177) states, "incompleteness of the formal treaty rules is at the centre of the EP's attempts to exercise discretion and engage in the interpretation of the rules to obtain a more favourable allocation of decision-making powers." The most recent instance of this strategy would be the (eventually prevailing) EP interpretation of the Lisbon Treaty rules for selecting the Commission president; having one of the EP election's *Spitzenkandidaten* at the top of the Commission is considered "an important victory in the inter-institutional battle for power" (Hobolt 2014, p. 1537).

In budgetary matters too, the EP used to interpret rules to its advantage. It was particularly engaged in defining what constitutes non-compulsory expenditure and the calculation of the maximum rates of increase (Lindner 2006). These opportunities have now vanished. Budget management has grown into a sophisticated and dense field. The IIAs had already eliminated most of the room for interpretation (see also De Feo 2017), and with the Lisbon Treaty, the rules for budgetary politics seem to be finally settled. The EP is thus confined to playing the given game.

Coalition building

One strategy to maximize influence within the given rules is coalition building. In the EU, the most prominent case is the alliance of the EP and the Commission in advocating supranational solutions. For a long time, these two institutions have favored and jointly pursued policies much more integrationist than the median government in the Council (e.g., Kaeding/Selck 2005; Thomson et al. 2004). However, cracks have appeared in this alliance. The Commission is seen to be in general decline, preoccupied with managing tasks or moving towards the Council (Bauer/Becker 2014; Kassim et al. 2013, p. 131-133).

The Commission used to be a reliable partner for the EP in budgetary matters. For a long time, it "generally did not play the role of honest broker, but rather demonstrated a set of policy preferences close to that of the Parliament," Pollack argued in 2008 (p. 24). After 2005 however, this period appeared to be over. The Commission's draft budgets between 2006 and 2010 were rather defensive from a supranational perspective. The EP position deviated from the budget draft much more significantly than the Council position; it appears that the Commission was tilted towards the preferences of national governments. Following that, Commission drafts and EP positions have almost aligned, and the Commission's MFF proposal was also in line with the EP position. However, the Commission proved rather passive as the moderator of budget negotiations; EP representatives have been disappointed with recent Commission performances. In their opinion, the Commission was overly defensive, mainly focused on getting some kind of agreement and thus avoiding gridlock. It is described as "no longer as strong as it used to be," and "too weak" (Interviews #5, #6). Perhaps unsurprisingly, Commission officials, also see their institution as in the middle, sometimes with the Council, other times siding with the EP (Interviews #11, #12).

The Commission has a second role in budget procedures that is relevant to EP influence. It serves as the central provider of relevant information. In the past, with its ties much closer, the EP depended comfortably on the Commission documents and analysis, and this move usually played out in favour of the parliamentarians. While they still rely on the Commission, MEPs have become skeptical of the quality of information. In their view, the Commission fails to provide "the figures they should" (Interview #5). Even though its estimates are "usually accepted" (Interview #2), a creeping sense of mistrust in budgetary matters is noticeable.

In terms of budget procedures, however, the Commission was broadly in line with the EP, although its initial proposals for flexibility were less ambitious than the parliamentary position. Commission President Barroso underlined this position shortly after the Council set out its position on the MFF in 2013, when he said the envisaged framework would only have a chance to work with the "proper level of flexibility."[8] The Commission subsequently sought to facilitate agreements in this area, and it successfully cooperated with the EP. It has to be said, however, that the Council was more indifferent in terms of procedure than it was in terms of figures.

Apart from aligning with the Commission, the EP can also seek to exploit disagreement in the Council.[9] However, as of 2016, there was no critical mass of member state governments it could form a coalition with. In the case of the MFF, the Council was split between the so-called "Friends of Better Spending", net payers advocating austerity, and the "Friends of Cohesion Policy", net recipients calling for more spending. The latter group modestly sided with EP demands. Yet given the unanimity requirement and the economic situation at the time, the balance of power between these two groups in the Council was far from even. The net payers had hardly any trouble realizing their preferences. Most in the EP are (unsurprisingly) annoyed with the status quo orientation of MFF decision-making, which is why it called for the use of qualified majority voting in the future (Resolution 2014/2005(INI)). But with (net payer) member states yielding power, this is a rather remote possibility.

With the exception of procedure, the EP is mostly left to its own devices when fighting for budgetary influence. While the Commission puts forth rather ambitious proposals, it does not follow through, acting rather passively during negotiations. Furthermore, from the EP's point of view, it fails to be a reliable provider of authoritative information.

Issue linkage

Strategies of issue linkage are ubiquitous in the EU, and the budget is no exception. An example is the EP extracting concessions in "compulsory spending" by offering modesty in "non-compulsory" spending (Enderlein et al. 2005). In a similar vein, when its legislative powers were more limited, the EP used its budget powers to influence policy-making, often by putting funds on hold until its demands were fulfilled (Pollack 2008, p. 24). Both strategies are now outdated, but with many separate decisions on revenues, expenditure, and implementation, the fragmentation of the EU budgetary system still provides several issue linkage opportunities. Indeed, the EP pursued two such strategies in the 2013 negotiations.

The first was aimed at the EU's revenues through the own resources system. Much to the dismay of parliamentarians, the Lisbon Treaty hardly affected the revenue system, and they consequently sought to gain influence by linking it to other budgetary issues. The EP's initial rejection of the 2011 budget was motivated by this concern (Benedetto 2012, 40). Then, in 2013, the EP put the issue back on the agenda during the MFF negotiations by threatening to use its veto power. As one interviewee (#1) stated, the MFF opened up "a small window" in the battle for reforming the own resources system (see also the relevant resolution, EP 2013a). Afterwards, the Council was open to discussing reform options. The first tangible result was the creation of a high-level group on own resources, made up of several members appointed by the EP, the Commission and the Council, and chaired by the former Italian prime minister and EU Commissioner, Mario Monti (EP 2014).

The second incidence of issue linkage concerned the question of unpaid bills from previous years (see also D'Alfonso/Sapała 2017). After the problem had been on the agenda for a while, and governments in the Council dodged more ambitious amending budgets, the EP again used the MFF negotiations to put pressure on the Council. Budget Committee Chair Alain Lamassoure stated that there would be no parliamentary consent to the MFF unless there was an agreement on the matter of unpaid bills (EP 2013). Again, the Council was accommodating. In this case, the EP's assertiveness helped to provide more funds for outstanding payments.

Its general willingness to link issues begs the question of how the EP uses its strongest power, the right to grant discharge, to influence other budgetary matters (see also Cipriani 2017). Interestingly, there is a paradox of power. The fact that a refusal of discharge can bring a Commission downfall renders the threat to use this "atomic bomb" (Interview #4) for ordinary policy-making purposes very implausible. Still, the discharge procedure provides an opportunity to put forward or reiterate budgetary claims, but this has yet to be realized. One reason is the way the Budget Control Committee works; many MEPs feel its conduct has been too specialized and too occupied with financial management. Instead, many wish that the committee would place more emphasis on scrutinizing the added value of EU spending, thereby generating insights that can be used for future budget negotiations. Since the Lisbon Treaty, the EP and the Council receive evaluation reports from the Commission in addition to the purely formal "budgetary statements" indicating that the EU funds have been used appropriately. This information has potential for "forward-looking" budgeting (Interview #1), and the results could then be used in the hearing of Commission candidates. For this to happen however, coordination between the budget-making and budget-controlling actors has to improve.

Overall, the EP is willing to strengthen its overall budgetary influence by linking different issues. The issue of outstanding payments can be considered the most tangible EP success yet; it remains to be seen whether its efforts regarding the own resources system will yield substantial results.

Application of normative pressure

The final pathway the EP has to maximize influence is the application of normative pressure. Bargaining dynamics between the Council and the EP are not solely based on material factors and strategies. In fact, the history of the EP receiving more power with every treaty change is commonly explained by ideational or normative arguments (Rittberger 2003). By the writing of this, the supranational parliament continues to emphasize legitimacy gaps to expand its involvement. One example is its criticism of the process and outcome of the predominantly intergovernmental management of the financial and economic crisis (Rittberger 2014). However, in terms of the budget, it is precisely because the EP is on equal formal footing with the Council in the annual procedure that such normative arguments are futile. But regarding the MFF and the revenue system such arguments could still be effective. From the EP's perspective, the EU budget is still representation without taxation, and the reinvigorated debate on the own resources system features normative arguments akin to claims for the legislative empowerment of the EP. Yet there is a strong possibility that the conflict between net payers and net receivers will overshadow any EP demands. Also, in times of crisis and decreasing budgets, the urgency of such normative questions is weak.

Conclusion

Since its first direct election, the powers of the EP have increased in all fields of parliamentary activities from legislation, to controlling the Commission, to selecting political personnel. However, budgetary power appears to be an exception to this general trend. The Lisbon Treaty reforms constitute—for the first time in the history of European integration—a step back from parliamentary empowerment. The crucial question is how significant these changes really are. Based on the literature on general EP influence in policy-making, we sought to assess the EP's power of the purse with an analytical framework combining rights, capabilities, and strategies.

Our empirical insights lend support to a more complex interpretation of the EP's recent budgetary defeats. We agree that the EP's budgetary rights have been curbed, and there is little remedy for this disenfranchisement by way of rule interpretation or application of normative pressure. We have, however, shown that the outcomes of recent budget negotiations are also driven by other factors. Above all, the crisis-ridden political environment, increasing internal preference heterogeneity, and few coalition-building opportunities limited the EP's bargaining power, at least in terms of budget figures. All of these factors, however, do not remain constant. For example, the next MFF negotiations could take place in a more stable political environment, with a more assertive Commission, a Council that is less firm without the UK, and a new EP that is again pro-integration. Also, the EP is already willing to link different budgetary issues to improve its bargaining position, as can be seen in the cases of own resources and unpaid bills. It is also enhancing its organizational capacities to increase its budgetary expertise. Its power of the purse is thus more flexible—or less doomed—than its budgetary rights after the Lisbon Treaty and recent budgets would suggest.

By distinguishing between figures (how much to spend) and procedure (how to spend it) as objects of budgetary negotiations, we have also shown that the EP was not as unsuccessful as it may have seemed. Its negotiators have understood the current predicament and switched from fighting for higher figures to fighting for greater flexibility. Such procedural questions are, in the short-term, less important than overall figures; however, in the medium and long-term, they represent opportunities to reshape EU spending to some extent. Even if the current constellation of factors remains, the EP could still put an emphasis on procedure and establish "veto points" in order to wield more influence later (Immergut 1992).

In sum, the budget is an anomaly in the overall trajectory of EP empowerment, but a better understanding of budgetary politics is needed to make authoritative claims about the EP's power of the purse. We have shown that some factors generally considered for EP influence in policymaking are highly relevant for budgetary negotiations, while others are not. Our case study only provides a snapshot that delivers a subtle ranking order for the significance of these factors. Future research, especially of the qualitative kind that is missing in budgetary politics, could yield a clearer picture of parliamentary influence.

Notes

1 In total, twelve semi-structured interviews were conducted on 10 and 11 July 2013, in Brussels. In addition, the interviewees answered a questionnaire with closed and open questions.

2 "Parliament gives final approval to EU long-term budget", Euractiv.com, 20 November 2013, Available at http://www.euractiv.com/priorities/eu-budget-gets-massive-approval-news-531817 (6 July 2015).

3 More comprehensive accounts of the post-Lisbon budgetary system and the role of the EP can be found in Lindner 2006; Benedetto and Høyland 2007; Giuriato 2009; Corbett et al. 2011; Hix and Høyland 2011; Benedetto 2012; Benedetto 2013; Benedetto and Milio 2012 and Becker 2014.

4 EU budget deficits are forbidden by treaty law (Art. 310 TFEU). The own resources system broadly defines spending, but there is some room for maneuver. Before the negotiations on the latest MFF for the period 2014–20 began, it was theoretically possible to generate and spend up to 1.23 percent of the EU's GNI (Council Decision 2007/436/EC, Council decision 2010/196).

5 "A sum equivalent to not more than one twelfth of the budget appropriations for the preceding financial year may be spent each month in respect of any chapter of the budget" (Article 315 TFEU).

6 It goes without saying that, in general, the same applies to the Council (e.g., Kaeding and Selck 2005), and even the commission is not as monolithic as it was long portrayed (recently Hartlapp, Metz & Rauh 2014).

7 "Parliament to use secret ballot in vote on EU budget", Euractiv.com, 8 February 2013, Available at http://www.euractiv.com/priorities/ parliament-hold-secret-vote-eu-b-news-517661 (6 July 2015).

8 Speech by President Barroso on the outcome of the European Council meeting on the Multiannual Financial Framework of 7-8 February 2013 (European Parliament Open Conference of Presidents), SPEECH/13/130.

9 The Commission and the Council are the two options of relevance here, as the complexity and technical density of budgetary politics make it a unlikely case for policy activism in wider civil society.

References

Bauer, M.W., and Becker, S. 2014. The Unexpected Winner of the Crisis: The European Commission's Strengthened Role in Economic Governance. *Journal of European Integration* 36(3): 213–229.

Becker, P. 2014. *Das Finanz- und Haushaltssystem der Europäischen Union. Grundlagen und Reformen aus deutscher Perspektive*. Wiesbaden: Springer VS.

Benedetto, G. 2012. Budget Reform and the Lisbon Treaty. In *European Union Budget Reform. Institutions, Policy and Economic Crisis*, Eds. Benedetto, G. and Milio, S., 40-58. London: Palgrave Macmillan.

Benedetto, G. 2013. The EU Budget after Lisbon: Rigidity and Reduced Spending? *Journal of Public Policy* 33(3): 345-369.

Benedetto, G., and Høyland, B. 2007. The EU Annual Budgetary Procedure: The Existing Rules and Proposed Reforms of the Convention and Intergovernmental Conference 2002-04. *Journal of Common Market Studies* 45(3): 565-587.

Benedetto, G., and Milio, S. (Eds.). 2012. *European Union Budget Reform. Institutions, Policy and Economic Crisis*. London: Palgrave Macmillan.

Cipriani, G. 2017. The EU Budget, the Accountability Gap and a Possible Way forward. In *The New Politics of the European Union Budget*, Eds. Becker, S., Bauer, M.W., and De Feo A., 225-258. Baden-Baden: Nomos Verlag.

Citi, M. 2013. EU budgetary dynamics: incremental or punctuated equilibrium? *Journal of European Public Policy* 20(8): 1157-1173.

Corbett, R., Jacobs, F., and Shackleton, M. 2011. *The European Parliament*. London: John Harper.

Crombez, C., and Høyland, B. 2012. The Budgetary Procedure in the European Union and the Implications of the Treaty of Lisbon. *FEB Research Report N*o. MSI 1227 Belgium: Katholieke Universiteit Leuven, Department of Managerial Economics, Strategy and Innovation.

D'Alfonso, A., and Sapała, M. 2017. Abnormal Payment Backlog as a New Problem in the Implementation of the EU Budget. In *The New Politics of the European Union Budget,* Eds. Becker, S., Bauer, M.W., and De Feo A., 195-224. Baden-Baden: Nomos Verlag.

De Feo, A. 2017. The European Budget: Motor or Brake of the European Integration? A Walk through 40 Years of Budgetary Decisions. In *The New Politics of the European Union Budget*, Eds. Becker, S., Bauer, M.W., and De Feo A., 33-82. Baden-Baden: Nomos Verlag.

Dobbels, M. 2013. *The European Parliament – A Giant with Feet of Clay?* Maastricht: University of Maastricht.

Enderlein, H., Lindner, J., Calvo-Gonzalez, O., Ritter, R. 2005. *The EU Budget. How much scope for institutional reform?* European Central Bank, Occasional Paper, 27.

European Commission. 2013. *Standard Eurobarometer 80.*

European Parliament. 2007. Resolution of 29 March 2007 on the Future of the European Union's Own Resources. *P6_TA(2007)0098.* 29 March.

European Parliament. 2010. Resolution of 25 November 2010 on the Ongoing Negotiations on the 2011 Budget. *P7_TA(2010)0433.* 25 November.

European Parliament. 2013a. Resolution of 3 July 2013 on the Political Agreement on the Multiannual Financial Framework 2014–2020'. *P7_TA(2013)0304.* 3 July.

European Parliament. 2013b. *Social Report 2012.* Brussels: European Parliament, Directorate-General for Personnel.

European Parliament. 2013c. *Parliamentary Democracy in Action. Summary.* Brussels: Cabinet of Secretary-General.

European Parliament. 2014. *High-level Group on EU "Own Resources" Launched by EU Institutions' Three Presidents.* Press release, 25 February.

Farrell, H., and Héritier, A. 2003. Formal and Informal Institutions under Codecision: Continuous Constitution-Building in Europe. *Governance* 16(4): 577-600.

Giuriato, L. 2009. Reforming the EU Budgetary Procedure: Is Codecision a Step Forward? *CESifo Economic Studies* 55(1): 57-93.

Hix, S., and Høyland, B. 2011. *The Political System of the European Union.* London: Palgrave Macmillan.

Hobolt, S.B. 2014. A vote for the President? The role of Spitzenkandidaten in the 2014 European Parliament elections. *Journal of European Public Policy* 21(10): 1528-1540.

Hooghe, L., and Marks, G. 2008. A Postfunctionalist Theory of European Integration: From Permissive Consensus to Constraining Dissensus. *British Journal of Political Science* 39 (1): 1–23.

Immergut, E. M. 1992. *Health politics: interests and institutions in Western Europe.* Cambridge: Cambridge UP.

Kassim, H., Peterson, J., Bauer, M. W., Connolly, S., Dehousse, R. Hooghe, L., and Thompson, L. 2013. *The European Commission of the Twenty-First Century.* Oxford: Oxford University Press.

Kaeding, M., and Selck, T. J. 2005. Mapping out Political Europe: Coalition Patterns in EU Decision-Making. *International Political Science Review* 26(3): 271-290.

Khimm, S. 2011. Why Does Anyone Trust the CBO? *Washington Post – Wonkblog.* http://www.washingtonpost.com/blogs/wonkblog/post/why-does-anyone-trust-the-cbo/2011/07/27/gIQARUVfeI_blog.html; 6 September 2016.

Kohler, M. 2014. European Governance and the European Parliament: From Talking Shop to Legislative Powerhouse. *Journal of Common Market Studies* 52(3): 600-615.

Krehbiel, K. 1991. *Information and Legislative Organization.* Ann Arbor: University of Michigan Press.

Lindner, J. 2006. *Conflict and Change in EU Budgetary Politics.* New York: Routledge.

Pollack, Mark A. 2008. *Member-State Principals, Supranational Agents, and The EU Budgetary Process, 1970–2008.* http://dx.doi.org/10.2139/ssrn.1119108.

Reif, K. and Schmitt, H. 1980. Nine second-order national elections: A conceptual framework for the analysis of European election results. *European Journal of Political Research* 8(1): 3-44.

Rittberger, B. 2003. The Creation and Empowerment of the European Parliament. *Journal of Common Market Studies* 41(2): 203-225.

Rittberger, B. 2012. Institutionalizing Representative Democracy in the European Union: The Case of the European Parliament. *Journal of Common Market Studies* 50(S1): 18-37.

Rittberger, B. 2014. Integration without Representation? The European Parliament and the Reform of Economic Governance in the EU. *Journal of Common Market Studies* 52(5): 1174-1183.

Scharpf, F. W. 2000. *Interaktionsformen: Akteurzentrierter Institutionalismus in der Politikforschung*. Opladen: Leske + Budrich.

Shackleton, M. 2006. The European Parliament. In *The Institutions of the European Union*, Eds. Peterson, J., and Shackleton, M., 104-124. Oxford: Oxford UP.

Shackleton, M. 2011. The European Parliament: The Major Winner of the Lisbon Treaty? *Maastricht Monnet Paper Series* No. 4/2011. Maastricht: Maastricht University.

Thomson, R., and Hosli, M. 2006. Who Has Power in the EU? The Commission, Council and Parliament in Legislative Decision-making. *Journal of Common Market Studies* 44(2): 391-417.

Thomson, R., Boerefijn, J., and Stokman, F.N. 2004. Actor Alignments in European Union Decision Making. *European Journal of Political Research* 43: 237-261.

Wehner, J. 2006. Assessing the Power of the Purse: An Index of Legislative Budget Institutions. *Political Studies* 54(4): 767-785.

Wildavsky, A. 1986. *Budgeting. A Comparative Theory of Budgetary Processes.* 2nd ed. New Brunswick, NJ: Transaction Publishers.

List of interviews

1. Official from the European Parliament, 10 July 2013
2. Member of the European Parliament, 10 July 2013
3. Member of the European Parliament, 10 July 2013
4. Official of the European Parliament, 10 July 2013
5. Member of the European Parliament, 10 July 2013
6. Member of the European Parliament, 11 July 2013
7. Official of the European Parliament, 11 July 2013
8. Official of the Council of the European Union, 10 July 2013

9. Official of the Council of the European Union, 11 July 2013
10. Official of the Council of the European Union, 11 July 2013
11. Official of the European Commission, 10 July 2013
12. Official of the European Commission, 11 July 2013

Abnormal Payments Backlog as a New Problem in the Implementation of the EU Budget[1]

Alessandro D'Alfonso and Magdalena Sapała

Introduction

The backlog of unpaid claims at year-end has been one of the most hotly debated issues during budgetary negotiations in recent years. In the second half of the 2007-2013 financial period, following years of sluggish absorption of the amounts committed to EU programmes, the flow of payment claims submitted by Member States and other recipients of EU funds accelerated. The demand for payments exceeded the level of appropriations authorised by the budgetary authority. Consequently, the backlog of payments piled up and reached a peak in 2014, when it was estimated at approximately 26 billion euro (corresponding to roughly 19 percent of the payment appropriations authorised in the annual budget). The situation began to improve over the course of 2015 and early 2016, thanks to a number of factors, including interinstitutional initiatives. However, as the main drivers of the problem persist, there are concerns that the abnormal backlog may re-emerge.

The issue has proven complex and contentious, both as an element of the financial management system and as a topic of political debate. Whilst it may appear to be merely a technical accounting matter, it can be linked directly to the EU's system of "own resources", the flexibility of the Multiannual Financial Framework (MFF), and more broadly to the political dimension of the EU's finances. Moreover, the issue may have negative and far-reaching consequences for beneficiaries of EU funding, as well as for the implementation and effectiveness of EU policies, to say nothing of the potential damage to the EU's reputation at home and abroad.

This paper considers the elements of the payments backlog, how it evolved between 2011 and 2016, and its main drivers and consequences. Moreover, it gives an overview of what has been done thus far to remedy the situation. The analysis leads to some conclusions on other measures that could be taken to avoid similar problems in future.

The paper shows that the problem of an abnormal payments backlog in the EU budget has been driven by different factors. Some of them have a more general character and are linked to the dynamics of the interinstitutional negotiations on the MFF and annual budgets. The other group of drivers is related to EU cohesion policy. Specific aspects of this policy, and changes introduced to its rules in particular, contributed to the growth of the year-end backlog of payments.[2]

Context

Many different features of the EU's financial provisions have exacerbated the problem of unpaid claims at year-end confronting the EU in recent years. These involve both institutional and technical aspects, including the following:

- The *principle of equilibrium* (Article 310(1) Treaty on the Functioning of the European Union, TFEU), which prevents the EU from borrowing money to finance its budget;[3]
- *Asymmetry in the budgetary powers* of the European Parliament (EP) and the Council depending on the matter at hand (annual budget vs. multi-year financial planning; expenditure vs. revenue), which may sharpen the differences in perspective of the two arms of the budgetary authority (Patterson 2011);
- The *financing system of the EU*, which significantly relies on own resources perceived as national contributions that Member States wish to see minimised;
- The *differentiated appropriations* (commitments and payments) characterising many categories of spending in the annual EU budget,[4] which lead to outstanding commitments (or RAL, its French acronym)[5] and an EU budget liability in the short and medium term;[6]
- The *involvement of a range of players in the implementation of the EU budget* (in particular, Member States manage 80 percent of it under shared management), which implies that the quality of the forecasts of payment needs prepared by the European Commission also depends on the accuracy of Member State forecasts in key spending areas; and
- The *various annual spending caps* on the EU budget (such as the overall ceilings for commitments and payments as well as the commitment ceilings for individual spending areas in the MFF), which may limit the capacity of the EU budgetary system to respond to unforeseen circumstances.

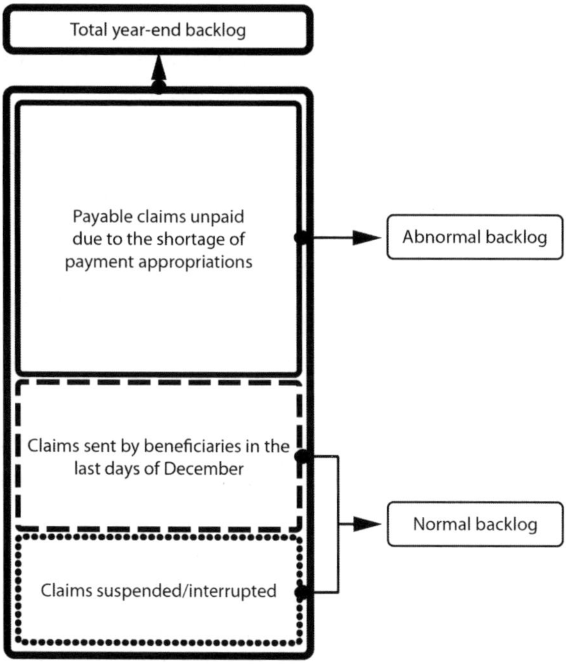

Figure 8.1: The components of the year-end backlog

Source: D'Alfonso/Sapała 2015

Against this backdrop, the payments backlog at year-end is a snapshot of the payment situation of the EU budget at a specific point in time. This snapshot provides an overview of the payable claims that beneficiaries of EU funding have sent during a given year but are still outstanding on 31 December. Within the payments backlog at year-end (see Figure 8.1), the European Commission (2015b) identifies two possible components:

- The *normal backlog*: claims sent by beneficiaries in the final days of December (too late to be processed by year-end), as well as those suspended by the European Commission pending checks or the provision of missing information;
- The *abnormal backlog*: claims that cannot be paid by the European Commission because the relevant budget line does not have a sufficient level of payment appropriations authorised by the EU's budgetary authority.

On the basis of this classification, the existence of a payments backlog at year-end is not *per se* a worrying signal. However, it becomes a negative feature if it is not limited to its "structural" component (the normal backlog), its composition deteriorates and the size of the abnormal backlog grows over time.

Since the reference date for the abnormal backlog is 31 December, the phenomenon is not related to possible cash flow constraints that the EU may experience in the first months of the year due to the timing of own resources payments from Member States and the prohibition on borrowing money. However, as the following year's budget will be partially used to cover these unpaid claims, a snowball effect in the abnormal backlog may create or worsen cash flow constraints in the first months of the new financial year.

Abnormal payments backlog: a recent phenomenon

The development of a significant level of unpaid payment claims at year-end due to insufficient payment appropriations authorised by the budgetary authority for the year in question appears to be a relatively recent phenomenon in the implementation of the EU budget. Since the authorised level of payment appropriations is one factor in the emergence of an abnormal backlog, a short overview of some relevant budgetary negotiations and decisions in recent years, identifying three phases, may help to understand how the phenomenon has evolved (D'Alfonso/Sapała 2015).

2011 budget: the appearance of the abnormal backlog

The issue of the abnormal payments backlog at year-end became significant at the implementation stage of the 2011 budget, the first to be negotiated under the new budgetary procedure with a single reading introduced by the Treaty of Lisbon. Under the new rules, the EP no longer has the final say over certain parts of the budget (what used to be called "non-compulsory expenditure"), but on the other hand gained equal status with the Council on the entire budget. Some analysts deem this development to reduce, in practice, Parliament's strength in this area (Benedetto 2013).

Figure 8.2 shows the development of the abnormal backlog in cohesion spending – the area where, due to its features, the bulk of the issue in absolute terms is to be found. While there was a six billion euro backlog in cohesion spending at the end of 2010, this was related to the late arrival of claims, interruptions and suspensions and, hence, could be classified as normal backlog. At the end of 2011, the backlog increased to 10.7 billion euro, with almost half of this amount (some five billion euro) due to a lack of payment appropriations.

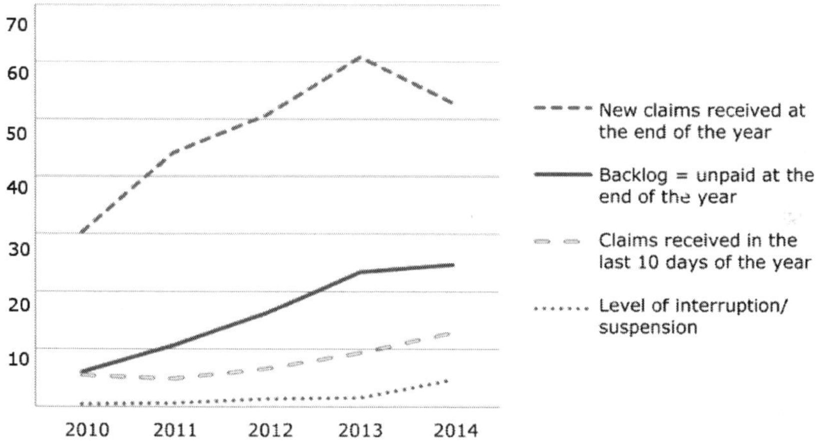

Figure 8.2: Payment claims and backlog in Subheading 1b (Economic, Social and Territorial Cohesion) in billion euro

Source: European Commission 2015b

When observing the annual negotiations between the EP and the Council that had led to the establishment of the 2011 budget, a new pattern appears to emerge in the first years governed by the new rules. Under the old provisions in their respective readings, the Council cut the payment appropriations put forward by the Commission, while the EP significantly increased them, already expressing concern about the level of payments and the increasing gap between commitments and payments. Table 1 shows that the final agreements for the 2007-2010 budgets set payment appropriations at a level between the Council's positions and the Commission's proposals (in one case slightly above the latter).

Table 8.1: Payment appropriations in 2007-2016 EU budgets (in billion euro)

	Commission proposal	Council's initial position	EP's initial position	Voted budget
2007	116.3	114.6	122.0	115.5
2008	121.5	119.4	124.2	120.3
2009	116.7	114.9	124.5	116.1
2010	122.3	120.5	127.5	122.9
2011	130.1	126.5	130.5	126.5
2012	132.7	129.1	133.1	129.1
2013	137.9	132.7	137.9	132.8
2014	136.1	135.0	136.1	135.5
2015	142.1	140.0	146.4	141.2
2016	143.5	142.1	146.5	143.9

Source: Own compilation based on data from the European Parliament Legislative Observatory.

Following the failure of the conciliation procedure for the 2011 budget, the EP and the Council eventually agreed to set payment appropriations at 126.5 billion euro, in line with the Council's position. The initial Commission proposal was cut by more than 3.6 billion euro. With implementation of ongoing programmes reaching full speed, the Commission had estimated that payment needs would require a 5.9 percent increase in payment appropriations in comparison with 2010. Similarly, the EP's reading included a six percent increase in payment appropriations. The Council's reading for payment appropriations, which eventually prevailed, raised them by only 2.9 percent from 2010. In a joint declaration, the two arms of the budgetary authority committed to acting swiftly to tackle any payment shortages that should arise (European Parliament 2010).

In 2012, the European Commission's Financial Report drew attention to the five billion euro abnormal backlog at the end of 2011, noting that a very high level of payment claims sent by Member States towards the end of the year could not be met because authorised payment appropriations were not sufficient. In his foreword to the report, Janusz Lewandowski, Commissioner for Financial Programming and Budget at the time, expressed concern over the growing gap between authorised commitments and payments, warning of the risk of a repeat in 2012 (European Commission 2012).

2012-2014 budgets: the peak of the "payment crisis"

Figure 8.2 confirms that the situation deteriorated in subsequent years, with an increasing gap between the total backlog on the one hand, and claims that arrived late or were interrupted or suspended on the other. The budgetary negotiations, decisions and implementation patterns relating to the 2012, 2013 and 2014 budgets share a number of similar features:

- The budgets adopted in the annual procedure set the payment appropriations at exactly (or close to) the amount called for by the Council in its reading. Against a backdrop of fiscal consolidation in the Member States, the Council systematically cut the amount estimated by the Commission in its initial proposal as necessary to cover payments.
- Pressure on payment appropriations regularly emerged before the end of the year. Whilst the bulk of payment shortages was in cohesion spending, expenditure in other policy areas began to be affected as well (e.g. under the Erasmus and research programmes).
- Each year (and as was already the case in 2011), the Commission tabled draft amending budgets (DABs) to cover shortages in the current budget, calling for increases in payment appropriations of: nine billion euro in October 2012 (COM(2012) 632); 11.2 billion euro in March 2013 (COM(2013) 183); and 4.7 billion euro in May 2014 (COM(2014) 329).
- Discussions between the EP and the Council on DABs meant to fix shortfalls in payments for the current budget proved to be difficult, and played a significant role in the annual procedure for the following budget. In 2013, the abnormal payments backlog also featured in the intense negotiations on the 2014-2020 MFF. In its July 2013 resolution on the political agreement on the new MFF, the EP set a number of conditions to be fulfilled before giving its final consent to the MFF agreed by the European Council. These conditions included the approval by the Council of amending budgets to cover the 11,2 billion euro payment shortfall identified by the Commission in full. Furthermore, the EP stressed that it would not adopt the 2014 budget until the same condition was fulfilled.
- A "snowball effect" became apparent, since outstanding payment claims from the previous year's budget contributed to worsening the payments outlook for the current budget early on.

A number of measures supported by the EP and the Commission, such as the mobilisation of the Contingency Margin in 2014, helped to contain the payments backlog. This kept increasing, however, and reached an estimated peak of some 26 billion euro at the end of 2014, when the tight ceilings of the new MFF added a new source of pressure on payment appropriations. At least half of the 24.7 billion euro backlog in cohesion spending was classified as abnormal.

2015-2016 budgets: phasing out of the abnormal backlog

In its reading of the 2015 draft budget, the Council again adopted a position to reduce payment appropriations in comparison with Commission estimates.[7] The EP, which has consistently criticised the Council's approach to payment appropriations, tried to tackle the growing backlog by promoting the use of higher revenue from fines against companies breaching competition law, and by supporting maximum use of the flexibility instruments provided for in the MFF.

In December 2014, the EP and the Council reached an agreement on the 2015 budget and the amendments to the 2014 budget. For the first time under the new procedure, the compromise set payment appropriations at an amount closer to the initial Commission proposal than to the Council's position. The deal included measures to address the payment backlog, such as: extra payment appropriations for 2014; the establishment of a payment plan to reduce the backlog, with a particular focus on that related to cohesion policy; and close inter-institutional monitoring of payment implementation and forecasts, with at least three joint meetings on the topic at key stages of the annual budgetary procedure (Spring, July and October).

In March 2015, the Commission submitted to the EP and the Council "Elements for a payment plan to bring the EU budget back onto a sustainable track". In the document, the year-end backlog for 2007-2013 cohesion spending was estimated to decrease from 24.7 billion euro in 2014 to 20 billion euro in 2015, at least half of which would remain abnormal backlog, as for the preceding three years. The Commission expected to be able to phase out the abnormal backlog of cohesion spending by the end of 2016. As regards other spending areas, the total backlog was much smaller in size, totalling some 1.8 billion euro at the end of 2014. However, the Commission said that the reduction in payment ceilings under the MFF had also contributed to problems with payment claims across the other headings of the budget.

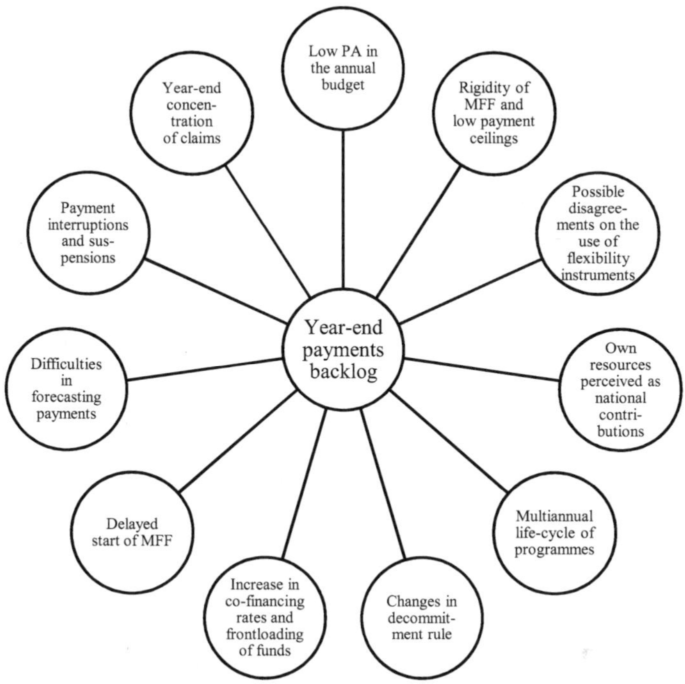

Figure 8.3: The main drivers contributing to the year-end payments backlog
Source: Authors' own chart

The 2016 budgetary procedure produced a new result under the Lisbon rules, with agreed payment appropriations for the first time higher than those initially proposed by the Commission. In its active monitoring of budget implementation note of March 2016, the Commission confirmed the objective of reducing the backlog in cohesion to the "normal level" of two billion euro by the end of the year, and reported that it was shrinking faster than planned (8.2 billion euro at the end of 2015) due to a mix of factors, such as significantly fewer claims being submitted by the Member States in 2015, and a topping up of payment appropriations for 2007-2013 programmes due to a slow start to the new ones (European Commission 2016a).

Main drivers of the payments backlog at year-end

The chief drivers of the abnormal backlog can be inferred from its development since 2011. In addition, it is worth exploring specific drivers in the area of cohesion spending, since this accounts for the bulk of the backlog (roughly 95 percent at the peak of the payments crisis in 2014). Both aspects are analysed below and recapitulated in Figure 8.3.

General drivers

Firstly, following the entry into force of the new budgetary procedure, for five consecutive years *payment appropriations in the annual budge*t have been authorised at a level lower (and significantly lower in 2011-2013) than that estimated necessary by the European Commission on the basis of legal obligations subscribed to by the EU. This appears to be linked to the Council's approach in budgetary negotiations, with Member States often facing fiscal consolidation at national level in times of crisis and aiming to minimise their contributions to the EU budget.

Secondly, in 2014 a new element of pressure was introduced by the *payment ceilings in the new MFF*, which was also negotiated against the backdrop of the economic crisis. The resources available for the EU budget have shrunk in comparison to 2007-2013, with the total ceiling for payments decreasing by 34.4 billion euro (-3.7 percent) in constant prices (Council of the European Union 2013). Annual payment ceilings for 2014-2020 are consistently lower than those set for each financial year of the preceding programming period except 2009 (Georgieva 2015). However, payment appropriations for 2014-2020 need to cover part of the commitments from the previous period due to the multiannual implementation of programmes, and due to the development of the abnormal backlog. This additional pressure on payment appropriations proved to be particularly significant in 2014, when the payment ceiling was 8.4 billion euro lower than the final payments for 2013.

At the time of the negotiations on the 2014-2020 MFF, the conditions set by the EP (2013) to give its consent to the reduced ceilings established by the European Council included the strengthening of the *flexibility provisions in the MFF*, with a view to ensuring full use of the agreed resources. However, the use of flexibility tools (as well as the adoption of amending budgets) can prove difficult and require time. For example, the Commission called for the mobilisation of the Contingency Margin in

May 2014, but the Council agreed to the proposal only at the end of the year.

Finally, another element contributing to upward (but also downward, for example in 2015) changes in the backlog is the need for the Commission to *forecast payment needs for complex programmes*, which are implemented by Member States over several years. This is particularly the case for cohesion spending, where the Commission is responsible for overall estimates, but needs to rely on Member State forecasts, which can differ from actual budget implementation.

Specific drivers in the area of cohesion policy

The main goal of cohesion policy is to strengthen economic, social and territorial cohesion. It is implemented through different funds, currently referred to as the European Structural and Investment Funds (ESI Funds), and represents roughly one third of the EU budget (Sapała 2015).[8] The ESI Funds are an important contribution to public investment in the Member States. Their role in this respect has increased since the economic crisis significantly limited public investment, especially at local and regional levels (European Commission 2015d).

The budgetary and regulatory framework of cohesion policy is considered very complex (Bachtler/Mendez 2007; Bachtler et al. 2013; Krieger-Boden 2016). The policy implementation cycle is multiannual (with the funds implementation processes overlapping with the following programming periods) and based on many detailed rules. The funds are subject to shared management, i.e. they are managed jointly by the Commission and the Member States, and their implementation involves a multitude of stakeholders at different administrative levels.

The issue of the payments backlog shows that any disturbances in this complex system, not only delays but also acceleration of the implementation process, may have serious consequences for the financial management of the policy. Based on multiannual strategic documents, cohesion policy is implemented through thousands of individual projects at national, regional and local level. Many of these, especially large infrastructure investments, are implemented over several years. This means that the funds are committed in the year they are appropriated and paid gradually over the following years as implementation progresses. In other words, there is a delay between decisions on commitments and the moment when corresponding payments are made. This phenomenon, known as RAL, is characteristic of the cohesion policy cycle and, to some extent, expected and "normal". However, prolonging the conclusion of legal commitments and stretching the delay between commitments and payments entails implementation delays and may seriously upset the payments plan.

In order to minimise RAL, provisions applicable to the cohesion funds provide for an automatic de-commitment rule, known as the N+2 and N+3, under which the funds committed in a given year (N) have to be covered by payment claims within a certain number of years or else are lost to the programme and de-committed.[9] The rule aims to strengthen financial discipline and encourage proactive management of individual projects by the Member States and beneficiaries of the funds. Its impact on spending between 2000 and 2006 has been assessed as positive (Bachtler/Ferry 2015). However, in some Member States, after 2007, the consequences of the financial crisis began to translate into serious problems with absorption of the cohesion funds, and the threat of de-commitment became more serious. In these circumstances, as part of the European Recovery Plan, the rule was relaxed and the de-commitment deadlines were lengthened (Regulation (EU) No 539/2010). As a consequence, the first de-commitments for the 2007-2013 programming period were made in 2011 instead of 2009 (European Commission 2015c). Moreover, between 2010 and 2013, in order to alleviate the pressure on national financial resources in the countries most affected by the crisis, the co-financing rates and pre-financing levels were increased.[10]

This shows how the cohesion funds turned out to be a useful tool to mitigate the consequences of the economic crisis (Smail 2010). At the same time, however, the changes introduced have exacerbated the payments backlog. Although these decisions were well-founded and aimed at improving the Member States' absorption capacity, they inevitably hampered financial planning by weakening financial predictability. The smooth implementation of these changes required considerable budgetary flexibility and availability of relevant financial resources in terms of payment appropriations in a given year. This was difficult to achieve with a rigid MFF and low annual payment ceilings.

Another driver of the payments backlog is a delayed start to implementation of financial periods. The problem recurs with each financial period and is a repercussion of difficult and prolonged negotiations on financial envelopes between the Member States. The fund-specific regulations can be adopted only once a decision on the financial framework is taken. Consequently, a delay in financial decisions triggers a series of delays in the policy cycle, including adoption of operational programmes, organisation of first competitions for projects and disbursement of pre-payments. A slow start to programme implementation results in a low level of payments in the first three years and a peak in payment requests submitted in the later years, as well as a prolonging of the payments cycle for years beyond the duration of that particular programming period.[11]

Another factor hindering the financial management of cohesion funds is the limitations of medium and long-term forecasts of the amount of payment claims. Commission estimates are essentially based on Member States' forecasts. Since they are usually overvalued (14 percent on average in 2011-2015), the Commission reduces them accordingly when proposing the following year's budget (European Commission 2015b, 2015c). As experience shows, the Commission's prudent figures are cut further in the Council's position during interinstitutional negotiations on the annual budget. Thus, the discrepancy between the level of payment appropriations adopted in the annual budget and actual needs increases.

The remaining drivers for the growth of a payment backlog are perceived by the European Commission as components of the normal backlog (Figure 8.1). One of them consists of claims suspended and interrupted in cases of serious irregularities or deficiencies in implementation. An interruption period may last up to six months for 2007-2013 funds, and this period may be extended to nine months for funds in 2014-2020.

Another component of the normal backlog consists of claims unpaid due to their being submitted at the very end of the year, i.e. too late to be processed and reimbursed. Although the Member States are asked to send their payment claims regularly three times per year, in line with Article 87 of Regulation (EC) No 1083/2006, the tendency has been to submit the bulk of the claims at the end of December (as much as 35 percent of the annual total) (European Commission 2015b). Although the forecast pattern in the distribution of claims during 2016 is different for the first time – 96 percent of the payable claims are predicted to be sent in the first part of the year (European Commission 2016a) – this phenomenon may increase in the coming years under the growing pressure of the automatic de-commitment rule.

To summarise, there are many reasons why cohesion policy is especially prone to financial management difficulties. Still, for many years the level of outstanding commitments was efficiently controlled and the payments backlog was considered "normal". In recent years however, in addition to the regular pitfalls of financial management, the additional, crucial driver of insufficient payment appropriations being authorised in the budget has come into play. This combination has seriously destabilised the payments cycle.

Implications of the abnormal payments backlog

The implications of payment appropriation shortages are both short- and long-term. Some are only potential and may become hazardous if the abnormal payments backlog increases and recurs, while others are already visible and quantifiable. To a greater or lesser extent, they impede the achievement of EU goals and may contribute to the deterioration of the EU's reputation among European citizens, as well as abroad (Figure 8.4).

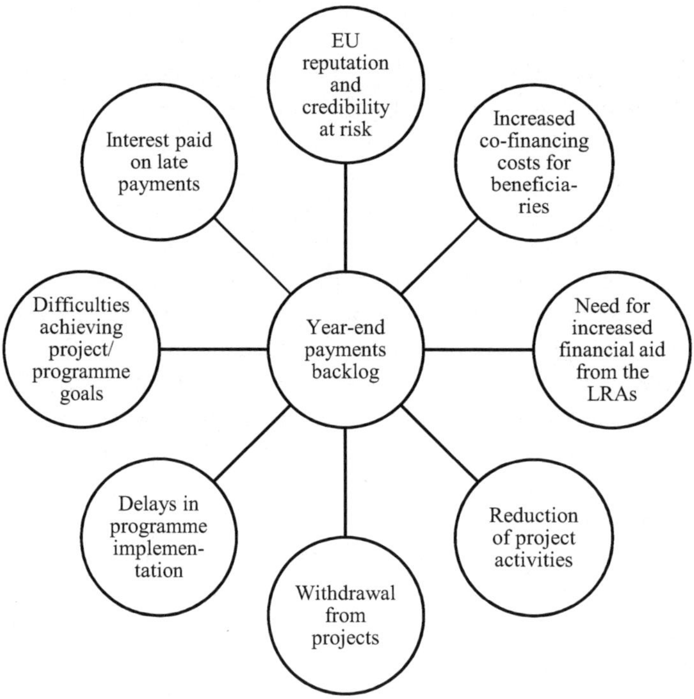

Figure 8.4: The main implications of the year-end payment backlog
Source: Authors' own chart

EU reputation and credibility

If no resources are available to pay obligations, an organisation loses credibility (Berman 1997; Slemrod 2001). Whilst the damage should not be overestimated, the fact that the EU finds itself in a situation where it cannot meet part of its obligations, even if only temporarily, is certainly not without significance for its reputation. Some beneficiaries have had to wait longer than expected for transfers from the EU budget, contracts have been signed later than expected, and calls for projects have been cancelled or postponed.[12] On a more general level, the problem of the payments backlog may serve as an argument in criticism of the EU for inconsistency in its decisions. The same EU that imposes strict fiscal rules on Member States is not capable of seamlessly managing its own budget. Therefore, as the then Commission President Barroso remarked, the lack of relevant resources to cover commitments, "is not just a technical or purely budgetary exercise: it is a question of the credibility of the political decisions taken by the European Council" (Barroso 2014).

The payments crisis has significantly impeded the already difficult interinstitutional negotiations on annual budgets in recent years (D'Alfonso 2014a). In 2011 and 2013, due to prolonged disputes over the lack of resources for payments, agreement within the prescribed deadlines proved impossible, and the Commission was forced to prepare a new draft budget. Similarly, the problem undid a compromise during negotiations on the 2015 budget. In fact, from 2011 until the peak of the crisis, annual negotiations between budgetary authorities increasingly focused on remedies for the payment backlog, rather than on the following year's budget itself.

Member States' budgetary negotiations may attract media interest, but they do not improve the EU's reputation. Communication with citizens is focused on who gets what and who is the winner or loser, rather than on a common concern for priorities and the successful functioning of the EU (Sapała 2013). The payments backlog was thus presented in the media in sensational fashion: "Union's coffers will run dry" (Europolitics 2013), "the pile of unpaid bills" (Nielsen 2014) and "there is no cash in the EU budget" (Wyborcza 2013). The impression given is that EU finances are mismanaged and that the European Commission asks for more money than was agreed.

Other stakeholders may also add to the reputational issue, including national parliaments. For example, in July 2014, the Chair of the European Union Committee of the UK House of Lords asked the Financial Secretary of the UK Treasury whether the problem of payment shortages in the 2014 budget had not been anticipated by any institutions and, if so, whether this constituted an indictment of the Commission, the Council, the EP and the budgetary process as a whole (House of Lords 2014).

Interest paid on late payments

The consequence of late payments that is most easily quantified is the interest incurred in accordance with Article 92 of the Financial Regulation 966/2012. However, the interest is applicable only to the programmes directly managed by the European Commission, thus excluding most of the payments from the cohesion and structural funds.[13] Therefore, the bulk of the backlog is not reflected in the figures presented by the Commission. Despite this fact, and the measures taken to alleviate the negative effects of payment shortages, the amount of interest paid as a penalty for delayed payments increased five times between 2013 (653,392 euro) and 2014 (3 million euro). The total value of the interest paid from 2008 to 2015 amounts to approximately 10.58 million euro, and half of this was in the last two years (European Commission 2015b, 2016a). The largest share of the interest paid came under Heading 4: "Global Europe", and Subheading 1a: "Competitiveness for growth and jobs". It should be noted, however, that along with a decrease in the backlog during the course of the year 2015, the late interest payments have also fallen to about two million euro. Still, this is much higher than ever before 2014 (European Commission 2016a).

Implications for cohesion policy

Half of the 24.7 billion euro backlog in cohesion spending in 2014 was linked to the lack of payment appropriations that were authorised. In practice, this means that part of the duly submitted payment claims from the Member States could not be paid because authorised payment appropriations on the relevant budget line were exhausted.

When the backlog of unpaid bills increases, the question of the impact on project implementation and individual beneficiaries arises. Since the payments backlog mainly exists under Subheading 1b: "Economic, Social and Territorial Cohesion", it might be expected that the negative consequences would be evident to the beneficiaries of ESI Funds. Yet, to date, official documents give little quantified evidence of a detrimental impact on programmes on the ground. In addition, contrary to directly managed spending, the cohesion policy legal framework does not provide for interest on late payments. Although relevant articles of the ESI Funds Regulation oblige the Commission to make payments within certain deadlines after registering a payment claim, these provisions remain explicitly conditional on the availability of funding (Regulation 1083/2006, Regulation 1303/2013).

Another difficulty in detecting the impact on cohesion policy results from the fact that under shared management, payment transfers flow from the Commission to national accounts, and not directly to the beneficiaries. Some Member States encourage the implementation of the projects and pay pre-financing from their national budgets even before they receive the transfer from the Commission. Thus, the detrimental impact of the delays may be to a large extent absorbed by the national treasuries.

In countries where national treasures do not pre-finance EU projects, the beneficiaries are responsible for financing their projects without any preliminary support and are reimbursed only after submission of the relevant documents. In this situation, for individual beneficiaries such as local and regional authorities (LRAs), small and medium-sized enterprises (SMEs), NGOs and research institutes, any delay in transfers from the EU budget increases their risk of losing investment on co-financed projects and incurring higher financing costs. Consequences may include a reduction in activities, withdrawal from the projects, or short-term loans. Beneficiaries may request extra support from their local authorities, who may in turn have to take loans to bridge the financing gap. This may lead to serious financial and organisational problems. Examples of such a problem were observed in the INTERREG Northern Periphery Programme 2007-2013 (cooperation between Finland, Ireland, Sweden and the United Kingdom), where some project partners, including SMEs in the fishing sector, suffered financially due to late payments.[14] On a larger scale, implementation of operational programmes and delivery of expected results may be delayed, reducing the impact of cohesion policy programmes. Thus, on the one hand, cohesion policy rules and instruments are increasingly reworked to remedy the consequences of the economic crisis, whilst on the other, their initial goals are side tracked and policy effectiveness is limited.

Implications for other EU policies

The payment appropriations shortfall also affected other areas of expenditure, in particular under Subheading 1a: "Competitiveness for Growth and Jobs"; Heading 4: "Global Europe"; and Heading 3: "Security and Citizenship".[15] With the exception of Asylum, Migration, Borders and Security funds, which are subject to shared management, in these areas the Commission manages the funds directly (through its departments and executive agencies) and indirectly (through entrusted entities, e. g. third countries). These methods of financial implementation allow the Commission more independence and control over, for example, the launch and conclusion of grant procedures and disbursement of funds. Therefore, in these areas of spending the Commission has more legal possibilities to adjust the level of executed payments to the level of available appropriations, and thereby to avoid abnormal backlogs. In practice, the actions taken by the Commission in order to limit the backlog include speeding up actions to recover any undue amounts; limiting idle amounts on fiduciary accounts; reducing pre-financing percentages; making best use of maximum payment deadlines allowed; postponing calls for proposals or tenders and related contracting; and giving higher priority to countries receiving financial assistance (European Commission 2015b).

Even if these mitigating measures help to limit the backlog, in many cases, the positive effect is only temporary and leads to the creation of a "hidden backlog". The moment of disbursement is postponed, but commitments will, eventually, have to be honoured. Thus, in the long term, these measures may result in policy implementation delays and adversely impact on policy goals and the overall performance of the EU in a given field.

Despite the Commission's efforts, the backlog in the headings mentioned above was noticeable and the interest paid on the delayed payments was high, especially in 2014. Implementation of the largest spending programme under Subheading 1a: Horizon 2020 has slowed significantly. In 2014, the level of pre-financing in the programme was reduced from 60 percent to 35 percent, and many calls were postponed to 2015. In September 2014, the EU Commissioner for the budget declared that over 70 projects, amounting to 36 million euro, had been blocked and were incurring interest for late payments (Dominik 2014).

Erasmus+ (formerly known as Erasmus) is another example of a programme under Subheading 1a that has been affected by the shortage of payment appropriations. In 2013 and 2014, the Commission was not able to pay part of the pre-financing to national agencies. Similar constraints were predicted for 2015. In this case the EU's financial problems had an impact on the students themselves – the final beneficiaries of this mobility grant (Hong 2014). The shortfall of payments may lead not only to the reduction of places available for students and the level of grants, but also to the weakening of the programme's reliability and prestige.

Heading 3, which covers the programmes in the field of asylum, migration, borders and security policy, also experienced difficulties. Pre-financing was either reduced or not paid. The consequences of the delayed payments may be especially harmful in the area of humanitarian aid (Heading 4), where the project cycle is very short, lasts from twelve to 18 months, and has a high rate of implementation. Unfortunately, here the abnormal backlog of payments has also had an impact on the implementation of measures (European Commission 2015d, p. 27-28). Since 2013, due to limited payment appropriations, the payments had to be decided based on their priority, on a case by case basis, and the appropriations were transferred to budget lines with the most urgent needs. All the measures were taken with caution and ensuring the continuity of operations. Nevertheless, some projects were delayed, for example humanitarian aid in the Sahel region, in Haiti and the Horn of Africa, as well as in the European Neighbourhood Instrument for Ukraine, Georgia and Moldova (Dominik 2014, European Commission 2015b).

To summarise, the implications of the payment crisis are multiple, visible in most of the spending areas, and affect the beneficiaries on the ground. Moreover, as shown by the interest paid on delays, delays also represent a measurable cost for the EU, while slowing implementation of various EU programmes and hampering the achievement of the EU's goals in certain policies.

Institutional positions and measures to tackle the backlog

The two arms of the budgetary authority: what resources for the EU?

The two arms of the budgetary authority have taken a different approach to the problem of the abnormal backlog in the framework of the budgetary procedure. The EP has called for a sufficient level of payments to be duly appropriated, at least at the level proposed by the Commission on the basis of its estimates of budget implementation. Contrarily, the Council has regularly cut the Commission's proposals in the annual budgetary procedure.

When amending budgets to address shortfalls in payments have been tabled, the Council has often called for proceeding first with redeployments of payment appropriations from other budget lines, even though the Commission has already indicated that all potential redeployments have already been explored and are completely exhausted. Negotiations on amending budgets for the current year have often proven lengthy, becoming an integral part of the negotiations meant to establish the following year's budget.

In a way, the issue of the abnormal backlog can be seen as another aspect of the intensive debate that has informed the difficult negotiations on the 2014-2020 MFF: what level of resources should be available to the EU in order for the Union to effectively carry out the policies it is entrusted with? The Own Resources Decision currently sets the upper limit of payments at 1.23 percent of the Union's GNI, and the annual payment outturn has always been below the own resources ceiling. Despite the EU's expanding to include one additional Member State, the European Council reduced the payment appropriations available in the 2014-2020 MFF in comparison to 2007-2013, both in real terms (34.4 billion euro less in constant prices) and as a percentage of the Union's GNI (from 1.06 percent to 0.95 percent). The EP has always stressed, including most recently during the 2016 budgetary procedure, that EU objectives should be matched with the appropriate resources to achieve them.

When endorsing the political agreement on the 2014-2020 MFF, the EP (2013) acknowledged fiscal consolidation efforts in the Member States, but expressed its concern about the ceilings set by the European Council, saying that these resources may prove insufficient to achieve the EU's objectives and recover from the crisis. The EP underlined the importance of the conditions that it had set to give its consent, including augmented flexibility provisions in the MFF to allow full use of the reduced appropriations (e.g. through the creation of a Global Margin in Payments and a Global Margin in Commitments for the automatic carry-over of unused appropriations from one financial year to the next). Along similar lines, in October 2014, the then Commission President, José Manuel Barroso, stressed that at the time of the MFF agreement it was made clear that the level of the 2014-2020 payment appropriations was the minimum necessary to carry out the agreed policies, and the full use of these resources was only possible by resorting to the flexibility provisions of the MFF. However, the mobilisation of the Contingency Margin in 2014 required lengthy negotiations.

European Commission: active management and mitigating measures

The Commission actively manages the authorised payment appropriations by monitoring budget implementation. If estimates of payment needs for an expenditure item are revised downwards during the year, part of its payment appropriations may be moved to another item, where conversely there is a payments shortfall. These transfers must comply with the rules and conditions set out in Articles 24-29 of the Financial Regulation (principle of specification), which vary depending on the expenditure items involved. Some categories of transfers are decided by the Commission under its own authority, others require transmission to the budgetary authority, either for decision or information.

In recent years, the European Commission's implementation rate of authorised payment appropriations has been at a consistently high level (99 percent in 2015 when extrapolating the data concerning the implementation rate of “assigned revenue”, which follows specific rules). In other words, the European Commission uses the authorised payment appropriations almost entirely and does not appear to keep idle cash resources at year-end.

In 2014, the European Commission used a number of specific mitigating measures to counter the increasing level of the abnormal backlog at year-end in the context of active management of scarce payment appropriations. For many of the programmes directly managed by the Commission (and in some cases as early as 2013), these measures included: reduction of pre-financing, postponement of calls for tenders or proposals and related contracting, and use of maximum payment deadlines allowed. However, the Commission draws attention to the fact that most of these measures are only a short-term fix, since they simply postpone the payment date to following years, thus creating a sort of “hidden backlog”. In addition, some measures may trigger a negative side-effect at operational level such as delays in the implementation of agreed programmes (European Commission 2015b).

The Directorate-General for Budget of the Commission (European Commission 2015a) says that in 2014 the scarce payment appropriations led to some delays in payments and implementation. It adds that a number of Commission departments were confronted with significant managerial and operational challenges, since their payment appropriations were exhausted several months before the end of the year. However, the text concludes that the active management of payment appropriations enabled the

Commission to sufficiently mitigate the financial and reputational impact of the abnormal backlog.

European Court of Auditors (ECA)

In its capacity as the EU's independent external auditor, the ECA has frequently presented its assessments and observations related to the issues of increasing outstanding commitments and shortages of payment appropriations, especially under Subheading 1b (Court of Auditors 2012). In its annual reports, as well as in its special reports on spending in agriculture and cohesion, the Court discussed the issues, usually in a special section, and insisted that the Commission prepare a medium and long-term plan for payment requirements (Court of Auditors 2013, 2014, 2015).

Interinstitutional initiatives

In December 2014, the agreement on the 2014 and 2015 budgets included the establishment of a payment plan to reduce the backlog to a sustainable level, with a particular focus on cohesion policy, and close inter-institutional monitoring of payment implementation and forecasts.

In the "Elements for a payment plan" of March 2015, the European Commission expected to be able to phase out the abnormal backlog of 2007-2013 cohesion spending and to reduce the backlog to a normal level of two billion euro at the end of 2016. The Commission said that its proposal for the following year's budget would include sufficient payment appropriations to achieve this objective and to ensure proper implementation of 2014-2020 programmes across all headings.

In May 2015, the EP, the Council and the Commission agreed on a joint statement on a payment plan for the 2015-16 period as a follow-up to the Commission's document. Among other points, the joint statement includes the EP's and the Council's commitment to provide the 2016 budget with sufficient payment appropriations to reduce the payment backlog for 2007-2013 cohesion programmes at the end of 2016 to the two billion euro forecasted by the Commission. In addition, the two arms of the budgetary authority asked for the Commission to closely monitor the implementation of 2014-2020 programmes and to create an early warning system on payment needs, with a view to avoiding the emergence of similar backlogs in the future. The Commission committed to providing, in the context of the budgetary procedure, rolling forecasts of payments organised by spending category and covering two financial years. Since then, the Commission has been providing the two arms of the budgetary authority with an update on the state of play by means of a new report entitled "Active Monitoring and Forecast of Budget Implementation", which is produced three times a year.

Despite these arrangements, interinstitutional friction over the preparation of the 2016 budget initially emerged, by and large mirroring previous years' positions. In its reading of the draft budget, the Council cut the Commission's estimates for payments by 1.4 billion euro, saying that it took into account budget execution figures in recent years and its forecast of absorption capacities for the future to amend the proposal. The Commission expressed its concern about the reduced appropriations in the Council's position. In its vote on the Council's position, the Parliament reversed all the proposed cuts and further increased commitment and payment appropriations in areas considered of key concern. As regards payment appropriations in particular, the EP underlined the need to comply fully with the agreed payment plan (European Parliament 2015).

The 21-day conciliation procedure between the two arms of the budgetary authority took place against the background of evolving challenges, including the need to mobilise flexibility tools for the financial implications of measures to address the refugee crisis. The procedure resulted in an agreement, which set payment appropriations at a level higher than that initially proposed by the Commission (for the first time under the Lisbon Treaty).

Are additional measures needed in coming years?

While the payment plan appears to be on track to bring the backlog for 2007-2013 cohesion programmes back to a normal level of two billion euro by the end of 2016, the outlook for the following years needs to be further assessed with a view to identifying possible issues. The early warning system that the Commission committed to establishing should contribute to the objective of avoiding the accumulation of abnormal backlog at year-end for 2014-2020 programmes in the years to come.

However, the possibility that new measures will be needed in coming years cannot be ruled out, since the faster-than-planned reduction of the abnormal backlog in 2015 is also due to a slow start to the new programmes. While the Commission does not appear to expect backlog issues for cohesion spending in 2017 (requesting lower payment appropriations in the draft budget than in the 2016 budget), the delays in implementation could lead to a repeat of payment issues during the last years of the MFF and/or in the next programming period. The then President of the ECA notes that in coming years the level of commitments outstanding[16] could prove problematic, in a framework that is going to have broadly stable payment ceilings in real terms for a number of years (Caldeira 2014). Furthermore, these payment ceilings are further reduced due to the fact that the 2014 mobilisation of the Contingency Margin will have to be offset in the last years of the current MFF.

In 2016, useful information should be available to update the forecast of future payment needs. Since the adoption of operational programmes under shared management for 2014-2020 was completed in 2015 (European Commission 2016b), Member States should be able to provide more accurate forecasts of implementation and payment schedules (new figures are due in July 2016), enabling the Commission to update its estimates of payment needs in the coming years. In turn, the exercise could provide valuable information in the context of the MFF review/revision. The debate in EP's committees on the preparation of the revision of the 2014-2020 MFF included points on the issue of the backlog.

Conclusions

Our analysis shows that the problem of the abnormal payments backlog at year-end seen in recent years in the EU budget is multidimensional and driven by different factors. The abnormal backlog has multiple consequences, for both beneficiaries of EU programmes and the Union itself.

While the 2015-2016 payment plan should bring the situation back to a normal level by the end of 2016, the outlook for the following years is yet to be thoroughly assessed. The slow start to new programmes, which contributed to the faster-than-planned reduction of the abnormal backlog in 2015, is not expected to put pressure on cohesion payments in 2017 either, but could contribute to a repeat of backlog issues during the final years of this MFF and/or in the next programming period.

The abnormal year-end backlog is not just a technical matter; it also has a political dimension, since it can be seen as a symptom of the diverging views of different stakeholders on the amount of resources that the Union needs to achieve the policy objectives that it has been set.

The EU's financial provisions strictly cap EU spending. Since the introduction in 1988 of the own resources ceiling (currently at 1.23 percent of the EU's GNI) and of the multiannual financial perspectives (known as MFF), actual spending has always remained below the agreed maximum levels.

On the one hand, the abnormal payments backlog may promote some positive developments, such as improvements to the forecasting of payment needs from all the relevant stakeholders, including both the Commission and the Member States. On the other hand, a shortage of payment appropriations may produce rigidity in a system that already caps expenditure, leading to operational problems, such as those experienced by a number of Commission departments that ran out of resources several months before the end of 2014 (European Commission 2015a). This can in turn hinder the achievement of agreed policy objectives, for instance with partial and/or delayed implementation of programmes.

Cohesion policy, where the bulk of the abnormal backlog has been concentrated in recent years, gives an example of potential contradictions: the European Council supported its full implementation as an investment tool to counter the economic crisis (Council of the European Union 2009), but the payment appropriations that were subsequently authorised were insufficient to honour promptly part of the payment claims when these began arriving at a faster pace. Similarly, the political agreement on the 2014-2020 MFF included the frontloading of appropriations for the Horizon 2020 framework programme for research and innovation. However, mitigating measures to tackle payments shortages, such as the postponement of some calls for proposals (the so-called "hidden backlog"), may have at least partially offset this decision.

In 2016, a number of developments should help to understand how the situation could evolve in subsequent years. The adoption of all the operational programmes for 2014-2020 will enable the Commission to produce more accurate estimates of payment needs after 2016. The Commission is also due to submit a review of the 2014-2020 MFF that could lead to its revision. At the same time, the high-level group chaired by Mario Monti will present its analysis on the financing system of the EU budget, which national parliaments are expected to assess. The Commission will examine whether the outcome of the work justifies new initiatives in the field of own resources, with possible reform of the financing of the EU budget for the period covered by the next MFF.[17]

Notes

1 The content of this document is the sole responsibility of the authors and constitutes a personal opinion.

2 This paper is partly based on the in-depth analysis D'Alfonso, Alessandro. Sapała, Magdalena. 2015. "Payments backlog in recent EU budgets. Lessons learnt and outlook", European Parliamentary Research Service, European Parliament.

3 The only exception concerns building acquisition projects, for which the EU can draw on loans.

4 The existence of differentiated appropriations is typically due to the fact that some activities (e.g. large infrastructure projects) may require multiannual implementation.

5 RAL, which stands for *reste à liquider* (yet to be settled), is the total amount of appropriations that the EU has committed but not yet paid at a certain point in time. Thus, RAL represents an EU budget liability in the short and medium term, with an impact on the level of payment appropriations needed for current and future years. For more details, see D'Alfonso/Sapała 2015, pp. 6-7.

6 The lifecycle of the commitments that make up RAL may differ significantly depending on the category of expenditure and the rules underpinning its implementation: commitments in cohesion policy, for example, usually take much longer to reach completion than those related to humanitarian aid.

7 Procedure files No 2014/2040(BUD) and 2014/2224(BUD) provide an overview of the steps of the 2015 budgetary procedure, respectively for the initial Commission proposal and the new proposal following failure of conciliation.

8 In the financial perspective 2007-2013, cohesion policy covered three funds: the European Regional Development Fund (ERDF), the European Social Fund (ESF) and the Cohesion Fund. In the MFF 2014-2020 cohesion policy is implemented through five funds: ERDF, ESF, the Cohesion Fund, the European Maritime and Fisheries Fund (EMFF), and the European Agricultural Fund for Rural Development (EAFRD). In principle, the problem of a payments backlog concerns the amounts committed under the 2007-2013 MFF, whose implementation has spilt over into the 2014-2020 MFF.

9 The N+2 rule was introduced for the period 2000-2006 (Article 31.2 of Council Regulation (EC) No 1260/99 of 21 June 1999). In 2007-2013 it was stretched to N+3 for Member States with less developed regions (Article 93 of Council Regulation (EC) No 1083/2006 of 11 July 2006). In 2014-2020 the N+3 rule was extended to all Member States (Article 136 of European Parliament and Council Regulation (EU) No 1303/2013 of 17 December 2013).

10 For the legal basis for the increased pre-financing please see: Regulation (EC) No 284/2009, Regulation (EU) No 539/2010). The co-financing rates were increased first for Romania, Latvia, Hungary, Portugal, Greece and Ireland based on Regulation (EU) No 1311/2011) and then for Cyprus, Greece, Ireland and Portugal based on Regulation (EU) No 1297/2013.

11 For example, at the end of 2014, almost one percent of the total allocation for 2000-2006 had not yet been disbursed (European Commission 2015a). Due to a late start to implementation of the 2014-2020 MFF, budget allocations for 2014 were not used and a significant amount had to be transferred to subsequent years by means of a revision of the MFF (Jędrzejewska 2015).

12 Among other areas of expenditure, the reputational damage has been observed, for example, in humanitarian aid (European Commission 2015e).

13 Under Subheading 1b, interest applies only to expenditure on technical assistance at the initiative of the Commission (Article 14 of Regulation (EU) 1083/2006).

14 Information based on a note from the European Commission (DG REGIO) presented to the European Parliament's monitoring group on payments (BUDG Committee) on 30 June 2015. Similar problems were flagged in the study of the Committee of the Regions (Committee of the Regions 2013).

15 Heading 2: "Sustainable Growth: natural resources" has been so far the least affected by the abnormal backlog (European Commission 2015b).

16 At the end of 2013, RAL amounted to 222 billion euro and was likely to continue to increase with annual budgets that usually have higher commitment appropriations than payment appropriations.

17 The manuscript was completed in August 2016.

References

Bachtler, J., and Ferry M. 2015. Conditionalities and the Performance of European Structural Funds: A Principal–Agent Analysis of Control Mechanisms in European Union Cohesion Policy. *Regional Studies* 49(8): 1258-1273.

Bachtler, J., and Mendez, C. 2007. Who Governs EU Cohesion Policy? Deconstructing the Reforms of the Structural Funds. *Journal of Common Market Studies* 45(3).

Bachtler, J, Méndez, C., and Wishlade, F. 2013. *EU cohesion policy and European integration: the dynamics of EU budget and regional policy reform*. Farnham: Ashgate.

Barroso, J. M. 2014. *Letter from President Barroso to the Italian Presidency of the EU Council on the EU budget payment shortages*. Brussels.

Benedetto, G., and Milio, S. (Eds.). 2012. *European Union budget reform. Institutions, Policy and Economic Crisis*. Basingstoke: Palgrave Macmillan.

Benedetto, G. 2013. The EU budget after Lisbon: rigidity and reduced spending? *Journal of Public Policy* 33(3): 345-369.

Berman, E. M. 1997. Dealing with cynical citizens. *Public Administration Review* 57(2).

Caldeira, V. 2014. *Presentation of the Annual Reports 2013* (ECA/14/48).

Committee of the Regions. 2013. *Execution of the annual budget 2007-2013: relevant recommendations for local and regional authorities*. Brussels.

Council of the European Union. 2009. *Presidency conclusions*. (17271/1/08).

Council of the European Union. 2013. *Council adopts the multiannual financial framework 2014-2020*. Press release 15259/1/13 REV 1.

Court of Auditors. 2012. *Annual Report on the implementation of the budget 2011*. 2012/C 344/01.

Court of Auditors. 2013. *Annual Report on the implementation of the budget 2012*. 203/C 331/01.

Court of Auditors. 2014. *Agriculture and cohesion: overview of EU spending 2007-2013.*

Court of Auditors. 2015. *Annual Report on the implementation of the budget 2014.* 2015/C 373/01.

D'Alfonso, A. 2014a. *The bumpy road to the 2015 EU budget.* EPRS European Parliament.

D'Alfonso, A. 2014b. *How the EU budget is financed: The "own resources" system and the debate on its reform.* EPRS European Parliament.

D'Alfonso, A. 2015. *Monti Group's first assessment of EU own resources.* EPRS European Parliament.

D'Alfonso, A., and Sapała, M. 2015. *Payments backlog in recent EU budgets. Lessons learnt and outlook.* EPRS European Parliament.

Dominik, J. 2014. *EU budget: (Not) enough is (not) enough!!!* Press release. 24 September.

European Commission. 2012. *EU budget 2011 – Financial Report.*

European Commission (DG Budget). 2015a. *2014 Annual Activity Report.*

European Commission. 2015b. *Elements for a payment plan to bring the EU budget back onto a sustainable track.*

European Commission. 2015c. *Analysis of the budgetary implementation of the European Structural and Investment Funds in 2014.*

European Commission 2015d. *Investing in jobs and growth - maximising the contribution of European Structural and Investment Funds.* COM(2015) 639 final.

European Commission (DG Humanitarian Aid and Civil Protection). 2015e. *Annual Activity Report 2014.*

European Commission. 2016a. *Active Monitoring and Forecast of Budget Implementation.* 2015 Information note (Info (2016)11).

European Commission (DG Budget). 2016b. *Analysis of the budgetary implementation of the European Structural and Investment Funds in 2015.*

European Parliament, Council of the European Union, and European Commission. 2015. *Joint statement on a payment plan 2015-2016.*

European Parliament. 2010. *Resolution of 15 December 2010 on the draft general budget of the European Union for the financial year 2011, all sections, as modified by the Council.* P7_TA(2010)0475.

European Parliament. 2013. *Resolution of 3 July 2013 on the political agreement on the Multiannual Financial Framework 2014-2020.* P7_TA(2013)0304.

European Parliament. 2015. *Resolution of 28 October 2015 on the Council position on the draft general budget of the European Union for the financial year 2016.* P8_TA(2015)0376..

Europolitics. 2013. *EU budget: Union's coffers will run dry by the end November. 21 October.*

Georgieva, Kristalina. 2015. Presentation on "EU budget focused on results".

Hong, Jose. 2014. Erasmus grant delays blight students' years abroad. *The Guardian* 11 November.

House of Lords. 2014. Lord Boswell (Chairman of the European Union Committee). *The draft EU budget 2015 and draft amending budget 3 (DAB 3) for 2014*, 9 July.

Jędrzejewska, Sidonia. 2015. *Revision of the Multiannual Financial Framework* (Article 19, MFF Regulation). EPRS. European Parliament.

Krieger-Boden, Christiane. 2016. EU cohesion policy, past and present: Sustaining a prospering and fair European Union? *Kiel Working Paper* No. 2037.

Nielsen, N. 2014. Member States owe EU over €320bn. *www.euobserver.com*. 25 November.

Sapała, M. 2013. The European Union Multiannual Financial Framework 2014-2020: how to do more for less. *The Institute for European Studies* Policy Brief.

Sapała, M. 2015. *The European Structural and Investment Funds. How the EU budget is spent*. EPRS European Parliament.

Slemrod, J. 2001. *Trust in public finance*. Paper presented at the conference Public Finances and Public Policy in the New Millennium. Munich. 12-13 January.

Smail, R. 2010. *The response of Cohesion Policy to the economic crisis*. EPAISCOPE 2010/2.

Wyborcza. 2013. Budżet UE. W bieżącym roku brakuje 11,2 mld euro. Będzie korekta. Wyborcza.biz. 27 March.

The EU Budget, the Accountability Gap and a Possible Way Forward

Gabriele Cipriani[1]

The EU fundamentals of the EU budget

The rationale for EU actions is based on the concept of EU added value which encapsulates the notions of "effectiveness", "necessity" and "additionality". For EU spending this means securing "a better deal for citizens than spending at national level" (European Commission 2011, p. 5).[2] However, EU funding is only one among possible options of EU intervention. In fact, EU objectives are mainly pursued through legislative and coordination actions that are often the main drivers for bringing different national laws in line with each other and effecting changes in member countries' basic economic, social and political structures. This is why one should assess beforehand the logical reasoning linking the problem to be addressed, its underlying drivers, the *raison d'être* of EU action, its potential objectives and a range of feasible policy options (including action at national level only).[3] "At the end of this process, policy-makers should know to what extent different policy options would meet their objectives, with what benefits, at what cost, with what implications for different stakeholders, and at what risk of unintended consequences" (European Commission 2015d, p. 24-25).

Member states have set EU finances arrangements in a rather inflexible way through a Multiannual Financial Framework (MFF), a global package where revenue and expenditure go hand in hand. The MFF, negotiated over more than two years,[4] is adopted unanimously by the Council after obtaining the consent of the European Parliament (EP). Even though, the EP has no genuine power of co-decision. This means that what the EU budget should be funding is to a large extent a member states' prerogative.

The MFF sets the overall amount of the resources that can be called over the period (traditionally around one percent of EU Gross National Income, GNI), the maximum amounts that can be spent each year for broad policy areas, the burden sharing among member states and their funds' pre-allocation for the main spending programmes.[5] Thus the EU budget entails a national "imprint", and possibly a regional one in the case of cohesion spending. This is accentuated by the fact that EU policies often give leeway to member states to configure such policies according to national preferences.[6] Furthermore, member states tend to take a restrictive interpretation about what objectives can "be better achieved at Union level" (principle of subsidiarity, Art. 5(3) Treaty on European Union, TEU) and the content and form of Union action deemed "necessary to achieve the objectives of the Treaties" (principle of proportionality, Art 5(4) TEU).[7] Not to mention that the day-to-day management of more than 80 percent of the expenditure (notably for cohesion and agriculture policies) is ensured by national bodies.

This means ultimately that as "a level of government and as a budgetary authority, the EU has very little autonomy compared with that afforded to regional or local governments in multi-level governance systems elsewhere in the world" (Begg et al. 2008, p. 119). Keeping a unitary and self-standing nature of the EU budget is left in principle to the Commission which is responsible for its implementation (Art. 17(1) TEU; Art. 317 Treaty on the Functioning of the European Union, TFEU). Yet, the Commission has made a virtue of necessity refraining from active funds' management, supervising budgetary implementation in a "remote control mode" and making of *ex-post* financial clearance a shortcut for compliance of spending. The Commission's remoteness from the ground field and the fact that the main management functions are carried out by bodies ultimately accountable to their governments has favoured the conditions for a "variable geometry" in managing EU funds. As it will be discussed in the following sections, this context is not without consequences in terms of accountability for EU expenditure.

Accountability, a basic principle of public life

In its essence, accountability is about a relationship of power, involving scrutiny and review by others. Accountability has two interlinked dimensions: "giving an account" (providing information and explanations) and being "held to account" for performance achieved.[8] These two dimensions may be related to the difference between "responsibility" and "accountability". "Responsibility" refers to holding a specific office or duty and it is about working within prescribed tasks, frameworks and standards. "Accountability" is about ensuring that responsibilities are actually carried out and that action is taken where they are not. Therefore, accountability trumps responsibility and is closely associated to "ownership".

Accountability's main purpose is to provide assurance over an activity, to identify timely if something goes wrong and the underlying causes, thus enabling redress through recommendations for future action. In the event of serious misconduct, the accountability process may lead to sanctions for the management, and even to its resignation in case of loss of confidence.

Accountability to Parliament is instrumental in giving legitimacy to public action in the eyes of citizens. To be effective, it requires clarity about the policy objectives to be pursued and the associated outputs, outcomes and impacts desired.

Accountability is not without costs. It requires putting in place systems of oversight, engage in consultations, supplying information to a wide array of constituencies, and assessing claims of malfeasance. Indirect costs may also arise, such as delayed decision making, resistance to policy shifts, introduction of additional levels of clearance (Jenkins 2007, pp. 175-176). Yet, ineffective accountability can cost even more in waste, misuse of power and loss of the government's legitimacy in the eyes of the governed (Auditor General of Canada 2002, p.12).

The EU budget: accountability by whom and for what?

Putting in place for the EU budget the general accountability principles discussed above requires taking account of the EU specific context.

The Treaties provide that the Commission "shall execute the budget and manage programmes" (Art. 17(1) TEU). It shall do so "in cooperation with the Member States", "on its own responsibility" and "having regard to the principles of sound financial management" (Art. 317 TFEU).[9]

In line with the principles of subsidiarity and proportionality, and following a decision of the EU legislature (in general, a co-decision by the EP and the Council), the EU budget is managed in different modes. As a result, there is a variable intensity of EU intervention and degree of decision by the Commission in granting the funds and performing controls at the level of the funds' beneficiaries.

Since the EU has no administration at member state level, the day-to-day management of most EU expenditure is actually "shared" between the Commission and member states' bodies. In such "co-administration" the Commission deals mainly with the financial implementation while member states have primary responsibility for day-to-day management, deciding for example on the beneficiaries of the funds. The rest of the budget is either implemented directly by the Commission, through its own departments or executive agencies, or indirectly (notably through third countries, international organisations, or the European Investment Bank, EIB).

The budgetary implementation is based on a system of checks and balances. In "shared management" arrangements, national bodies must satisfy themselves, by means of controls defined by EU rules, that the funded actions they manage are implemented correctly and effectively throughout the expenditure life cycle. This includes responsibility for investigating irregularities and recovering unduly paid funds. The Commission exercises a supervisory role. It can perform its own controls, including at beneficiary level, and may disallow support from the EU budget. However, the Commission has no hierarchical authority over the thousands of double-hatted national bodies, executing EU tasks while remaining within a national legal framework. [10]

Member states' obligations, resulting ultimately from their general duty to ensuring the application of Union law (principle of sincere cooperation, Art. 4(3) TEU) do not make them accountable at EU level beyond their reporting requirements to the Commission.[11] Parliament has repeatedly pressed member states for taking full responsibility for the EU funds managed by them, through the signature of a "national management declaration" at the highest level certifying that those funds fully comply with EU law (see for example European Parliament 2005, paragraph 21). This stance was however rejected by the Council arguing the need "not to put into question the existing balance between the Commission and the Member States or to compromise responsibility and accountability at the operational level" (Council of Ministers 2005, point 12).[12] Indeed, governments are democratically accountable either to their national parliaments, or to their citizens (Art 10(2) TEU).

In fact, member states' cooperation in the budgetary implementation represents a delegation of tasks. The implementation of the budget as such is not delegated. This means that the Commission remains fully responsible.[13] Such a situation might appear at odds with the legal and political reality (Strasser 1994, p. 203). The Commission would have preferred to set in stone a sharing of responsibilities, at least "when the Member States are responsible for most of the management of funds" (European Commission 2002, p. 6). Yet, each time the Treaty's provisions on the budgetary implementation have been amended (Treaties of Maastricht 1992; Amsterdam 1997; Lisbon 2007) the Commission's ultimate responsibility has been confirmed. This seems the unavoidable consequence of the Commission's overall mission to promote "the general interest of the Union" (Art. 17(1) TEU),[14] acting in full independence, as a counterweight to member states' specific interests.[15] Indeed, the EU budget is in principle a budget for the Union as a whole.

The Commission: an administration *"de mission"* or *"de gestion"*?

The Commission is the EU's executive although not the EU's government. It is a *sui generis* collegial body, with no match elsewhere.[16] Following the Treaty (Art. 17(1) TEU), the Commission's main roles are to propose legislation, to enforce EU law, to supervise the implementation of EU policies, and to execute the budget and manage programmes. Its political legitimacy derives from both the European Council and the EP to whom it is responsible. Rather than directly with citizens, the Commission deals with governments, institutions and national administrations with whom it is intertwined through multiple connections.

To clarify the Commission's nature, it is useful to refer to the concepts of "administration de mission" and "administration de gestion". The *administration de mission* requires the unity of command and the unity of the budget; it is dynamic and bears risks. By contrast, the *administration de gestion* is formalistic, little evolutionary, to some extent inward-looking, and impose the elimination of all risks. While the functions of the *administration de gestion* are neutral, those of the *administration de mission* have an evident political dimension (Pisani 1956, p. 324-325).

Although the Commission has tried to juggle both roles, one taking precedence over the other depending on the systemic and political environment (Schön-Quinlivan 2011, p. 201), there has always been a bias within the Commission in favour of policy formulation as opposed to policy execution (Ludlow 1991, p. 107).

The significant increase of the EU budget appropriations and a corresponding strengthening of the Parliament's budgetary and control powers since the 1970s have triggered a growing pressure for ensuring an error free management of the funds, whose precondition was the improvement of the Commission's budgetary and administrative culture.[17] This trend was accentuated after the resignation of the Santer Commission (March 1999). The subsequent reform process, based on two White papers in particular (European Commission 2000, 2001), was very much inspired by a clear perception that management and monitoring functions "are less highly thought of" by EU officials which prefer "to think rather than to do" (Committee of Independent Experts 1999b, paragraph 8.3), and tend to emphasise "control rather than objectives" (European Commission 2000, part I, p. 8). Hence, the reform's aim was to raise "the level of management skills and create a common management culture across the Commission" (European Commission 2000, part I, p. 12).

More than ten years after the start of the reform, the Commission acknowledges that a "progressive development of a performance culture will take several years to come to full effect, partly because new statistical and other tools need to be developed" (European Court of Auditors 2013, Commission's reply to paragraph 10.1). At the same time, "evidence shows an increasingly bureaucratised administration obsessed with procedures and control" (Schön-Quinlivan 2011, p. 210). Also, reviews indicate that two-thirds of Heads of Unit still seem to prefer a role model as policy innovator and not one as public manager (Bauer/Becker 2013, p. 5). Not to mention a strong opposition to the idea that the Commission should primarily focus on managerial duties (Kassim et al. 2013, p. 133). This shows that taking over managing functions is perceived as inherently looking for difficulties, something that the services do not want to foster due to a risk-averse culture.

The case of the European Fund for Strategic Investments (EFSI) provides an interesting example. To cover potential losses on EFSI operations, this Fund is backed by a EU budget guarantee of up to 16 billion euro (of which eight billion euro will be transferred to a specific fund).[18] Since the EFSI is established within the EIB, the Commission considers that it has no control over EFSI investment decisions.[19] However, the Commission has a majority representation in the Steering Board and, as a member of the EIB Board of Directors, is consulted before EIB approval of each financing and investment operation.[20] This raises the question of potential conflicts of interest currently not addressed by specific procedures (European Investment Bank 2016, pp. 26-27). Most importantly, this situation makes it "difficult to establish for accountability purposes who is ultimately responsible to the EU budgetary and legislative authorities for the performance and risk management of EFSI" (European Cout of Auditors 2016g, paragraph 73).

In line with a role of *administration de gestion*, and as a result of its absence from the ground, the Commission's supervision in shared management arrangements represents fundamentally a "fire alarm" form of oversight reacting to individual warnings, following its own checks and in particular the audits of the European Court of Auditors (ECA). The cornerstone of such strategy is the possibility for the Commission to disallow *ex-post* "expenditure for which disbursements have been made in breach of applicable law" (European Parliament/Council of the European Union

2012, Art. 59(6)b, 60(6)c, 80(4)). The assumption is that thanks to financial clearance all expenditure will ultimately be compliant with applicable rules.[21]

The effectiveness of such approach is however not without raising questions. In the case of multiannual programmes, such as for cohesion and rural development, the final clearance can take place several years after the end of the MFF.[22] Thus, corrective measures may materialise when it is probably too late to cause structural repairing effects. Moreover, the increasing occurrence of disallowances suggests a limited deterrence and effectiveness (European Commission 2016d, Graph 3.2.1, p. 14-15).

The Commission, a dual institution?

The reform process launched in 2000 was driven by the leitmotif of decentralising management functions, in the aim of letting the Commission focus on policy-making.

While acknowledging that "[t]he Commission as a whole has a particular responsibility for managing EU funds, i.e. the taxpayers' money" (European Commission 2000, part I, p. 19), the Prodi Commission indicated a need for more clarity about "who is responsible for policy execution" as a "pre-condition for making the EU system more open and accountable to all European citizens" (European Commission 2001, p. 31). The objective was to embed systematically in financial and sectorial legislation the principle of separation of responsibilities among the different actors involved in the budget implementation. This concerned first the distinction between the Commission's specific management responsibilities and those of the member states as regards establishing and maintaining reliable management and control systems. At the same time, the intention was to strengthen "the Commission's powers to correct irregularities" (European Commission 2004, p. 10). Furthermore, numerous agencies with tasks of a technical, scientific, operational and/or regulatory nature have been established. In particular, six of them have been entrusted with tasks relating to the management of one or more Union programmes.

The Commission stated for itself the principle that "political responsibility lies with each Commissioner and, collectively, with the College, whereas day-to-day management responsibilities rest with the Directors General" (European Commission 2000, part I, p. 7).[23] Hence, as shown by Figure 9.1 below, the College of Commissioners, who is the "Authorising Officer" (AO) for the budgetary implementation (European Parliament/Council of the European Union 2012, Art. 65(1)), delegates its powers and responsibilities to authorising officers by delegation (AOD; in general, the Directors-General who can further sub-delegate their powers to other staff, that is authorising officers by subdelegation, AOSD). AODs have the power to represent the institution. They act under the direct authority of a Commissioner and are fully responsible for the management of the services and for the effective implementation of the guidelines and decisions adopted by the institution (European Commission 2014b, p. 20).

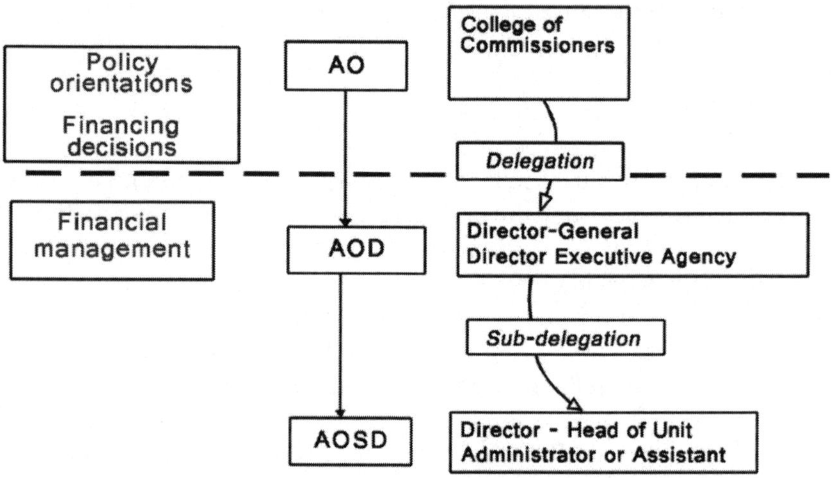

Figure 9.1: Levels of implementation of the EU budget
Source: European Commission, DG Budget

AODs' mission is framed by the College of Commissioners through "financing decisions" based on the MFF. These decisions, authorising the services to implement sectoral programmes, shall specify the objectives pursued, the expected results, the actions to be financed and the amount allocated to each action, as well as the expected implementation timetable. Any element that may be subject to a discretionary margin within the framework of the basic act must be determined in those decisions. "Financing decisions" are implementing acts (Art. 291 TFEU), subject in general to a "comitology" procedure.[24] This represents objectively a limitation to the Commission's autonomy and shows that governments "do not sacrifice their powers absolutely" (Williams 1991, p. 158). Indeed, if the European Union has been designed with very broad objectives, its powers have been demarcated in a very strict manner (Spinelli 1974, p. 276).

AODs cover the entire management process, from determining what needs to be done to achieve the policy objectives set by the institution to managing the activities launched from both an operational and budgetary standpoint. AODs inform and advise their Commissioners on any subjects of relevance that would necessitate specific actions. They report each year to the Commission on the performance of their duties in the form of an activity report.

The above suggests that the Commission "is in fact intrinsically dual, with two levels of action: the College of Commissioners and the services. This ambiguity is a good illustration of the Commission's organisational essence" (Schön-Quinlivan 2011, p. 1; see also Berlin 1987, p. 309). By endorsing the reservations introduced by Commission's Directors-General in their annual activity reports or addressing them specific requests the EP seems to have accepted this duality (European Parliament 2016a, paragraphs 66-69, 197, 281, 315, 318, 330, 371).[25]

The Commission's "political" responsibility, what is it about?

Political responsibility is the requirement for office holders to abandon it when they no longer have the confidence of those to whom they are accountable (Vedel 1974, p. 235). The Commission as a body is accountable to the EP. As in all parliamentary democracies, these relations are centred on Commissioners being "held to account" for their individual responsibilities, as well on "giving an account" by providing all required information in due time and through different means (reports, participation to hearings, response to parliamentary questions).[26]

Concerning the budgetary implementation, the EP and the Council, as budgetary authorities (and, moreover, co-legislators for most EU spending frameworks), are called to draw their conclusions on the management of EU financial resources during the discharge procedure. Usually, each Commissioner is invited before the Parliament's Committee on Budgetary Control to account for his/her spending area. The EP can postpone and even refuse discharge. It can also vote a motion of censure that, if approved, will force the College as a body to resign (Art. 234 TFEU).[27]

The actual scope of Commissioner's political accountability has been an issue surrounding the crisis that led to the resignation of the Santer Commission. At that time, the tendency to evade political responsibility for acts or omissions of the services came under severe criticism. The idea that Commissioners are responsible only for laying down policy while Directors-General implement it was considered untenable both in law and in fact (Committee of Independent Experts 1999a, paragraph 9.3.4, 1999b, paragraph 7.9.1).

While advocating "accountability" as a principle of good governance, (European Commission 2001, p. 10), the reform was "totally silent about the political accountability of the Commission itself" (Verhey 2009, p. 64). This is why Parliament asked the Commission to issue an annual statement of assurance (European Parliament 2011, paragraph 10.II).[28] The Commission has rejected this request considering that this would lead *de facto* to an exoneration of AODs from any responsibility, whereas they are "solely responsible for the execution of their activities" (European Commission 2007, p. 6). In particular, the Commission argues that the apex of its "accountability architecture" is represented by a "synthesis report", based on the assurances and reservations contained in the AODs' annual activity reports, and by which the College takes overall "political responsibility" for the management of the EU budget.[29] This combination is deemed to fulfil "the internal and external accountability objectives", and to be in line with the provisions of Art. 317 TFEU (European Commission 2015h, p. 5, 2016b, p. 10; see also the Commission's reply to European Court of Auditors 2016d, paragraphs V, 21).

This stance seems to diverge from best practices.[30] It gives a narrow interpretation of the concept of the Commission implementing the EU budget "on its own responsibility" (Art. 317 TFEU), limiting such responsibility to the specific tasks of its services, hence excluding *de facto* the budgetary implementation as a whole. Secondly, the requirement for Commissioners to "assume full political responsibility for the work done by the services that report to them" (European Commission 2014b, p. 7) suggests that the College's "political responsibility" is distinct from AODs' responsibilities, whereas its scope remains undefined.[31]

In fact, the co-signing of Directors-General annual activity reports seems the logical consequence of the College's approval, as required by the Treaties (Art. 318 TFEU), of the EU annual accounts (including those of the other institutions and bodies), and of the annual evaluation report on the Union's finances based on the results achieved. The publication of these reports, since 2016, as part of an "Integrated Financial Reporting Package" can only reinforce the need for consistency concerning the College's responsibility.

It has been observed (Van Gerven 2007, p. 13) that assuming "political responsibility" in the synthesis report would add "high value to the discharge procedure" for two main reasons: it would bridge "the distance between policy and implementation" making Commissioners and Directors-General jointly responsible. Also, the Commission would run the risk of being dismissed by the EP following a motion of censure.

One may note in this respect that while AODs are answerable to the College, the synthesis report does not provide a qualitative assessment on the way the "financing decisions", the main "bridge" between policy and implementation, have been executed by the services.[32] In fact, the College's "political responsibility" is basically limited to acknowledging the budgetary implementation by its services. Yet, AODs "are not politically accountable [...] in the sense of explaining and defending decisions that have been taken" (Verhey et al. 2008, p. 309). Only Commissioners are holders of public office.

The risk for the Commission to be refused discharge, and further becoming potential ground for a motion of censure leading to its resignation as a body, seems rather theoretical for two main reasons.[33]

First, the Commission is generally given discharge each year despite a standing qualification of the legality/regularity of the EU expenditure by the ECA since more than twenty years.[34] In this respect, the delegation of managing functions to member states cannot be invoked as a justification since the "error rate" under "shared management" is nearly the same for expenditure managed directly by the Commission (European Court of Auditors 2016e, paragraph 1.33).[35]

A refusal of discharge has not been triggered either by serious criticism on EU spending's performance expressed recurrently by the Court in all policy fields. The main difficulties, summarized in Figure 9.2 below, refer to a lack of clarity about the purpose of the funding and its possible impact; the broad objectives and the absence of priorities; the lack of a specific EU dimension over and above current national measures; the non-availability of information about what was actually achieved and the benefits brought.

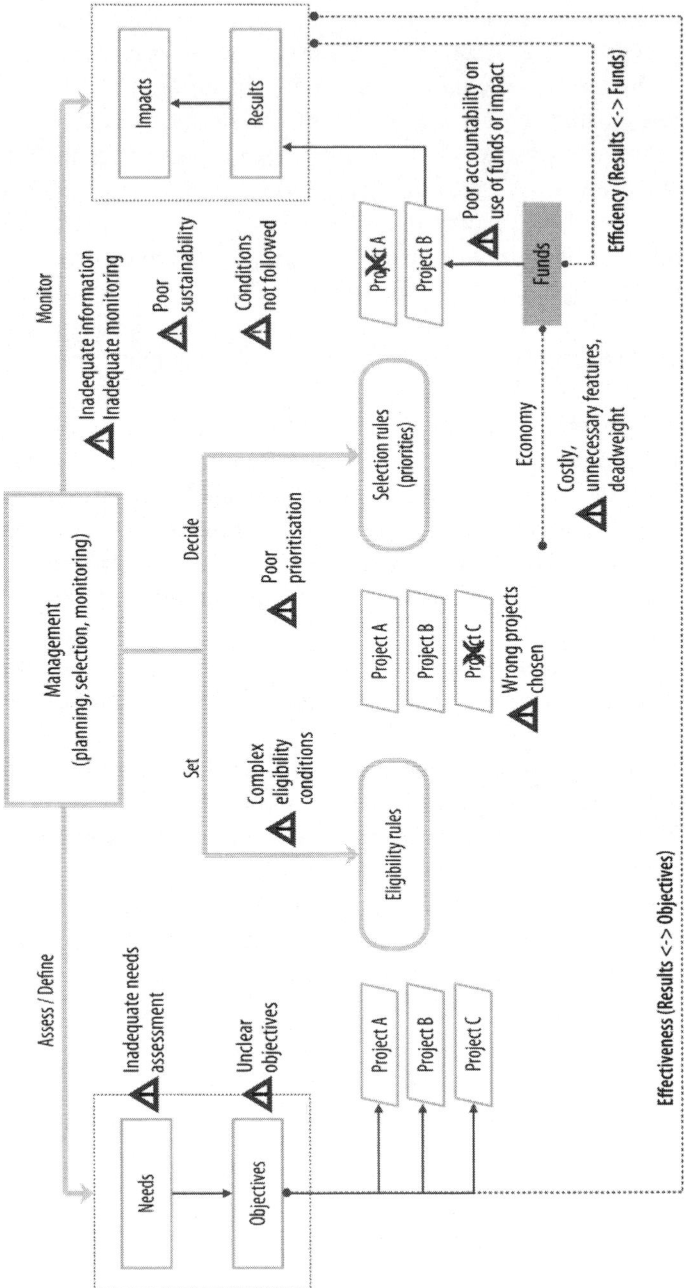

Figure 9.2: The most frequently reported problems in the Court's Special Reports
Source: European Court of Auditors 2014a, p. 24

Secondly, although the implementation of the budget may always provide an opportunity to justify a motion of censure with grounds unrelated to the budgetary implementation (Kannengießer 1995, p. 59), there is no automatism between a refusal to grant discharge and a motion of censure.[36] The latter is "a deterrent that cannot be exercised without threatening the destruction of the Community itself. Each Commissioner is protected from the wrath of the European Parliament by the consequences for all" (Williams 1991, p. 161; see also Bauer/Becker 2017, pp. 187-188). This may explain that no motion of censure has ever been approved.[37]

Accountability for what?

Member states bodies have a number of reporting obligations to the Commission, notably on legality and regularity of the expenditure managed, outputs achieved, funds' beneficiaries and controls carried out. This feeds into the Commission's own reporting in different ways. First, as part of the preparation of the budget for the following year, "programmes statements" should justify the operational appropriations requested for each spending programme.[38] During budget implementation the Commission reports periodically to the budgetary authorities on commitments and payments made.

After budget implementation, there are a number of financial and non-financial reporting requirements.[39] Directors-General annual activity reports are the main source of information. In their quality of AODs, Directors-General are required to state in these reports that, unless otherwise specified in any reservations, they have reasonable assurance that the resources made available have been used for their intended purpose and in accordance with the principles of sound financial management. Furthermore, Directors-General should provide an opinion on the effectiveness of existing control procedures to ensure the legality and regularity of the expenditure. As discussed earlier, Directors-General endeavour to ensure compliance of EU spending through *ex-post* clearance procedures, taking place often over several years. In this respect, they report on the overall amounts of financial corrections (disallowances of EU reimbursements) and projected risk by policy area.

Directors-General annual activity reports contain also general information on the progress towards the achievement of the policy objectives as provided by member states, without however taking responsibility for the reliability, completeness and correctness of the reported information on performance. The same applies to evaluations carried out on behalf of the Commission.[40] In particular, the attainment of policy objectives is considered to be outside the scope of the Commission's responsibility when EU action plays only a part in bringing about a given result (European Commission 2014a, p. 4). This is the case for most EU spending. Hence, the annual reports on the evaluation of the Union's finances based on the results achieved provide some indications as to the effectiveness and efficiency of the programmes, but they are not conclusive concerning the expected final results achieved by EU funds (for the 2015 financial year, see European Commission 2016a, section I).

Opaqueness about actual performance leads for example to a situation where there is no evidence for concluding that the common agricultural policy, representing about one-third of EU spending, has achieved the Treaty's objective of reducing the income gap between farmers and those in other sectors of the economy (European Court of Auditors 2016a, paragraphs 91-92). Similarly, while beneficiary farmers should comply in most cases with a broad set of rules (environment, climate change, animal welfare) in the aim of making the EU agriculture more sustainable, the Commission currently cannot be sure whether this is actually the case (European Court of Auditors 2016f, paragraphs 73-74).

It is in general not clear if the funds allocated to the different objectives are adequate to allow for the achievement of the results sought, not least due to the fragmentation induced by the use of multiple financing sources at EU and national level. One main reason is that, while pursuing numerous and broad objectives, the EU provides often "the icing rather than the cake".[41] Though, difficulties remain even when considerable funding is allocated to a policy. This is the case of Europe 2020, the EU's 10-year jobs and growth strategy launched in 2010 and associated with a number of targets, initiatives and objectives on employment, research, innovation, environment, energy, education, poverty. About 60 percent of the EU budget funds available are meant to contribute to the Europe 2020 strategy. In particular, European Structural and Investment Funds (ESI) should provide around three-quarters of the EU budget contribution through 11 thematic objectives. The ECA has observed that the political aspirations of Europe 2020 are not translated into useful operational objectives. There is an absence of linkage between the "programme statements" underlying the budget and subsequent stages of programming and reporting at the level of the Directorates-General. In particular, the eleven ESI thematic objectives have not an operational structure – with associated targets, milestones and indicators. Like the headline targets and flagship initiatives, the thematic objectives are high-level and broad by nature as they cover the entirety of the areas funded by the ESI funds whose scope goes wider than the Europe 2020 strategy. This reflects in a weak focus on results. Measuring and assessing the EU budget contribution towards Europe 2020 can only be done in a meaningful way if relevant, reliable and timely information, derived from a robust performance management and reporting system, is available to the Commission. This is not yet the case (European Court of Auditors 2015a, paragraphs 3.3-3.68).

Ultimately, most of the information available on the EU budget can be divided into four main areas: the budgetary execution (how much has been spent for each spending programme), the net-balances calculations (member states' contributions to the budget and payments received), the "error rate" of expenditure (the level of legality/regularity of spending) and the financial corrections (see note 23). This is the natural consequence of an input-based expenditure system whose best illustration is the development over the years of a series of "error rates" at the level of individual programmes. Used sometimes as a yardstick for performance, "error rates" are not an indicator of waste of fraud. They are no more than an estimate of the amount of money that should not have been paid out from the EU budget. Also, "error rates" do not cover the irregularities whose financial impact could not be quantified.

Acknowledging the difficulty to report reliably on results of EU expenditure, the Commission has launched in 2015 the "EU Budget Focused on Results" initiative, whose aim it is to ensure that resources are allocated to priorities and that every action delivers maximum performance and added value. In a recent proposal for amending the EU financial rules the Commission advocates a shift from disbursements towards results (European Commission 2016e). For example, it would be possible in all management modes to link funds to outputs instead of items of eligible spending (European Commission 2016e, Art. 121(1)e, p. 132). Yet, at the same time, the notion of SMART objectives (specific, measurable, achievable, relevant and timed objectives) for all sectors of activity would disappear from the information supporting the draft budget as well as from Directors-General annual activity reports (European Commission 2016e, Art. 31, 39(3)h, 73(9), pp. 76, 82-83, 102-103).[42] This sounds like giving up the possibility to set performance requirements and indicators (with baselines, milestones and targets) and to report on progress made in relation to the goals pursued, with a view to demonstrate the effects of the programme on beneficiaries and long-term changes in society triggered by EU expenditure.

In the absence of a correlation between performance information, based on discrete measurable objectives, and budgetary allocations it is hardly possible to judge what would have happened without EU spending, and so to demonstrate its value and performance compared to national spending alone. Such demonstration is however the *raison d'être* of the EU budget. Ultimately, the question is whether the EU budget should just distribute funds to be spent for contributing to high-level objectives or is deemed to achieve identifiable results: the "cake" or the "icing"?

The accountability gap and a possible way forward

Accountability for the EU budget draws its lines in sand. Diffused responsibilities create the conditions for a "no man's land" and for "immunity" of the management actors. This is first due to the Commission falling back on its specific tasks foreseen in sectorial legislation, hence reducing *de facto* its full responsibility to the financial management of the appropriations. Secondly, the inputs-oriented expenditure framework oriented towards funds absorption, the lack of critical mass for most spending programmes, which could make a difference for target groups, high-level and broad objectives pursued and the absence of meaningful performance indicators leave in uncharted territory the demonstration of results achieved by EU spending. There is ultimately no ownership and accountability for the results expected. Legitimacy towards taxpayers of the resources required is at stake.

If national parliaments have difficulties in ensuring accountability for the actions of their governments at EU level (Williams 1991, pp. 158-160; Goulard/Nava 2002, p. 38), the EP, "the only Union institution able and willing to hold the Commission to account for its conduct as an administration" (N.N. 1999, p. 271), lacks both the necessary information and a responsive counterpart.[43] As shown by the numerous and repetitive observations put forward from year to year, the discharge procedure does not seem to "change the price of fish". In the absence of appropriate information on performance, there is a tendency to make important what can be measured rather than to measure what is important. The focus on "error rates" creates the wrong incentives. What gets measured gets done. This encourages making of compliance an end in itself, at the expense of value for money.

Reforming the EU budget arrangements is everything but an academic issue. The current system reflects a consolidated sharing of roles between member states and the EU level. In that sense it represents a litmus-test of the EU integration process. A reform would mean finding a new balance between different views and interests at stake. Due to a certain "path dependency" (Becker 2017, pp. 109-110), the *status quo* is always a privileged option. Still, many believe that a reform is much needed.

What is the EU budget for?

Funds are limited. EU and national budgets compete for the same resources. Also due to its size, the EU budget cannot cover all critical needs in all sectors and geographical areas. The leitmotiv of the 2000 reform process, "doing less but better", is still valid. To avoid continuation of "business as usual", selective choices are needed, including setting negative priorities. The current "goals congestion" requires a careful assessment of the types of benefit and of the strength, longevity and sustainability of the intended effects (Tarschys 2011, pp. 14-15, 24, 26). Over-ambitious expectations and unrealistic impact assumptions can turn policy commitments into frustration. Making something happen that would otherwise not happen (or happen more slowly), concentrating on most effective results and, not least, realism, could represent three main drivers for identifying what ultimately the EU budget should be supporting.

"Impact assessments should cover the existence, scale and consequences of a problem and the question whether or not Union action is needed" (Interinstitutional agreement on better law-making of 13 April 2016, paragraph 12). They are a key instrument for providing to the EU political authorities the evidence and the logic for an efficient allocation of resources taking account also of the intervention areas that can be better dealt with by national policies, so that EU and national budgets "can deliver to best effect" (European Commission 2010b, p.28). In this respect, there is a fundamental difficulty if Commission's impact assessments are not properly considered by the co-legislators and "in the final stages of negotiations deals are found without taking full account of the direct and indirect impacts that compromise amendments may trigger" (European Commission 2015d, p. 8). One should also note however that the Commission did not support the establishment of EFSI, nor its proposed doubling, with a comprehensive and evidence-based impact assessment. As noted by the ECA, "the EFSI remains without an assessment and analysis of the causes of the investment gap and the market needs and how to best address them as well as of the complementarities with other programmes and financial instruments funded by the EU budget and how best to avoid undesirable overlaps" (European Court of Auditors 2016g, paragraph 22).[44] The revision of EU financial rules currently on-going is an opportunity for providing that when a proposal or initiative submitted to the legislative authority has been amended with appreciable implications for the budget, this should entail not only an update of the financial statement by the institutions proposing the amendment (European Parliament/Council of the European Union 2012, Art. 31(1)) but also an update of the *ex-ante* evaluation.

As policy initiator, the Commission is responsible for putting forward the MFF proposal and subsequently the corresponding legislative instruments. If spending programmes "must have a real impact, with the investment feeding through into action – action which is measured in terms of real impact, rather than in terms of the inputs involved" (European Commission 2010b, p.5), the intended results should be defined (relationship problems-objectives), made measurable (indicators for monitoring progress and performance) and achievable (objectives consistent with the available administrative and financial resources). Only if this occurs there could also be an adequate accountability process at a later stage.

Costing potential objectives and their alternatives through impact assessments would permit to reverse the current MFF logic. Instead of allocating funds to spending programmes as a result of quantitative arbitrages, MFF resources could be set transparently for each specific objective and be associated with meaningful indicators. This would allow subsequently for a better evaluation of their progress which, in its turn, would provide a key input for consideration when approving the annual budget[45] and during the discharge procedure. It would still be possible to set an overall multiannual ceiling for the EU budget, being the sum of the cost of specific objectives (Cipriani 2010, pp. 75-77, 2014, pp. 85-89).

Such an approach that could inspire some pilot testing within the impact assessment process would assist co-legislators in seeking consistency between specific objectives and resources, so that the EU "provide[s] itself with the means necessary to attain its objectives and carry through its policies" (Art. 311 TFEU). At the same time, this will clarify the scope of the EU intervention, and therefore the related expectations. In that way, citizens will better understand what the EU budget is for, encouraging them to pay greater attention to its implementation as suggested by the Commission (see European Commission 2016e, Art. 54(3), p. 91).

It takes two to tango

> "No matter how good a policy may be, it cannot succeed unless somebody implements it, and whoever implements has a key influence over what and how much is delivered, and to whom" (Levy 2000, p. 203).

A budget for Europe, placing public resources in common to achieve EU objectives above what individual countries could do by themselves, is a means to promote the EU general interest. For both aims, the Treaty has entrusted the Commission with specific responsibilities (Art. 17(1) TEU; Art. 317 TFEU; see also note 16). This is not without reason since the EU budget brings substantial and direct interests into play for the member states as stakeholders of policies whose day-to-day management is ensured by their own administrations. As indicated by the Commission, the "juste retour" approach "had a negative impact on the quality of delivery and reduced the EU added value" (European Commission 2010b, p.4; see also note 5). Full involvement by the Commission in the budgetary implementation, whatever the management mode, seems the most straightforward way to securing that funds are used to best effect and in line with EU common interests. The objective of shifting EU spending towards results reinforces the need for such a leading role by the Commission, not limited to establishing rules and guidance notes that are not a substitute for sound governance and management, to exert also a direct and close "after sales" supervision on the actual use of the funds. If a "regulatory" approach can work in a stable context and with adequate management capacities (Metcalfe 1992, p. 409), this is not sufficient when things, as in current times, are moving and new challenges emerge.

The Commission has historically focused its monitoring from the perspective of compliance rather than in terms of outputs, outcomes and impacts. A closer involvement by the Commission in the budgetary implementation would admittedly require rethinking the approach of *administration de gestion* discussed earlier and the "stream" towards increasing member states' responsibilities (see section "The Commission, a dual institution?"). Yet, it would be unrealistic to count exclusively on Commission's staff to manage the EU budget. Recourse to national bodies is potentially more effective, not least because of their experience in managing similar expenditure. Still, the process discussed earlier, based on specific objectives and results to deliver, requires ensuring that the right administrative structures (human resources, systems and management tools) are in place from the outset. Experience shows that this is not always the case.

The standing qualification by the ECA on EU spending and serious criticism of the performance achieved in all policy fields (see Figure 9.2

above) shows a lack of administrative capacity to set up intervention strategies, select viable and sustainable investments, and manage complex processes.[46] One example is the perennial difficulty to comply with public procurement rules, a significant source of error in EU cohesion expenditure. As noted by the ECA, there is no assurance yet that member states' public procurement systems meet the conditions required (European Court of Auditors 2015b, paragraphs 61-65). In addition, since these rules apply to expenditure on public works, goods and services representing around 20 percent of EU Gross Domestic Product (GDP), the effective enforcement of EU competition policy is also at stake. A similar situation occurs for compliance with State aids legislation, in particular concerning cohesion policy (European Court of Auditors 2016c).[47]

There are therefore grounds for considering that the designation of delegated national systems for EU funding, currently a sole member states' prerogative (European Parliament/Council of the European Union 2012, Art. 59(3)), should include an *ex-ante* assessment by the Commission at operational level (a vulnerability test adapted to the programme environment and beneficiary type), prior to them being allocated EU funds.

Such designation could be associated to pre-specified results and performance targets in line with the budgetary allocations, as well as monitoring by the Commission on a regular basis.[48] Limiting the current dissociation of the decision-taking aspect from the financial implementation will permit the Commission to report in full knowledge on the actual use of the funds and the results achieved. This, in turn, would make the Commission accountable for the whole implementation of the budget and would allow the discharge procedure to fulfil its institutional role (Cipriani 2010, pp. 77-80).

The audit and control environment

Audit is a basic means of ensuring that public organisations "are spending money raised from taxpayers in line with formal (often legal) requirements and, more recently, assessing whether they are providing services to citizens in line with published targets and standards" (Lapsley/Lonsdale 2010, p. 74).

Audit is however not only an element of the accountability process. If criticism on managers is an unavoidable "side-effect", audit is above all a learning process that acquires its best value (and credibility) when it succeeds in putting forward timely and operational recommendations.

Audit should not "put itself beyond empirical knowledge about its own effects" (Power 1999, p. 142). This requires sometimes from auditors a "cultural leap", enlarging the scope of their assessment beyond a description of what has gone wrong, something about which managers are most likely already acknowledgeable. For example, for each policy area the Commission's services are aware of the magnitude of irregular spending. The audit's main added value resides in understanding why the systems are not able to take timely corrective measures themselves and what could be done to address this problem. Such analysis could offer valuable advice to the legislative and the executive powers.

One may note for example that the ECA has produced in the last 15 years an impressive amount of audit reports in all policy fields, with more than 600 recommendations issued in 2012-2015. While the Court indicates that 73 percent of those recommendations had been implemented by the end of 2015 (European Court of Auditors 2016b, p. 47), there are a number of key findings (see Figure 9.2 above) whose repetitive nature suggests that the usual "cocktail" of remedial measures undertaken (action plans, rules' simplification, intensification of controls, financial corrections) is not sufficient to provide sustainable and effective solutions. On one hand, this confirms the necessity to ensure that management and control systems are fit to the task from the outset and that the *ex-post* disallowance of EU reimbursements provides at most a financial compensation, not a structural remedy. On the other hand, it suggests that the source of the problem may lie in the design of spending systems and their management arrangements.

There is a difficult balance to strike between audit intensity and its ultimate effectiveness. As observed by the ECA, "[a]ny control system is a trade-off between the cost of operating the defined intensity of checks on the one hand, and the benefit these procedures bring on the other" (European Court of Auditors 2004, paragraph 50). In its proposal for setting a level of tolerable risk of error per policy area, the Commission suggested to assess three parameters: the costs of control, the risk of error and the benefits (in particular, error-reduction/ recovery and the deterrent effect, European Commission 2010a, see also European Commission 2008). In fact, there is still uncertainty on those elements, in particular for the overall costs of control at member state level and the benefits in terms of increased compliance. Available estimates show significant discrepancies among policies, which may be due to methodologies applied.[49] In this respect, the Commission's intention to develop a common calculation for the cost of control in view of determining the relative cost-effectiveness of the control system in the different policy areas deserves to be pursued further (European Commission 2015f, p. 5).

The "efficiency effects of the multiplication of accountability mechanisms can remain indecisive" (Wille 2015, p. 478). Indeed, the number and variety of audit conclusions and opinions (above all the plurality of "error rates") do not necessarily result in greater accountability.[50] On the contrary, "too much control can result in policy inertia (over-bureaucratisation) since it can inhibit the capacity of organisations to act and to realise policies" (Wouters/Marx 2007, p. 3). There is a risk to "reinforce the existing conservatism of organisations which are aware of the unsympathetic political and media responses to perceived failure" (Lapsley/Lonsdale 2010, p. 86).

The "audit fatigue" generated by the multiplication of forms of oversight and scrutiny of EU policies is to a large extent the consequence of the diffusion of responsibilities induced by the shared management model. Controls tend to operate in isolation rather than in concert, in the name of independence but also due to a lack of trust among different political and administrative levels.

In order to avoid multiple layers of controls, the Commission envisages encouraging cross-reliance on audits when there is assurance equivalent to EU requirements, for example by relying on independent audits conducted on the use of the EU funds by international partners or member states (European Commission 2016e, Art. 123, p. 132). One may refer in this respect to Parliament's suggestion to put in place a "single audit" framework, where each level of control builds on the proceeding one (European Parliament 2002, paragraph 48). It is worth recalling that this proposition failed to materialise because of the insufficient reliability of member states' management and control systems (see also Cipriani 2010, pp. 26-34, 46-49). As discussed earlier, this difficulty persists.

Being responsible for the budget implementation, it is ultimately up to the Commission to decide whether and to what extent it can rely on delegated systems to validate EU spending. Therefore, putting in place an effective "single audit" framework depends on the capacity of internal control systems, primarily in the member states, to ensuring compliance of EU spending from the outset.

Notes

1 The opinions expressed by the author in this publication in no way commit his employer, the European Court of Auditors.

2 For the Commission's analysis of the "EU added value" concept see European Commission 2011. One may note that the European Parliament has asked the Commission "to produce a study on the savings achieved at national level by Member States as a result of policy action funded at EU level" (European Parliament 2016b, paragraph 71). Financial support may consist of grants, subsidies, loans, guarantees, direct budget support. There are "entitlement programmes", with EU disbursements based on meeting certain conditions. This is the case for example of student and research fellowships or direct aid for farmers. In the case of "cost reimbursement schemes", EU payments are based on inputs of eligible costs. Such schemes include, for example, research projects, investment schemes in regional and rural development, training schemes and development projects in third countries.

3 This is the role of *ex-ante* impact assessments undertaken by the Commission for gathering and analysing evidence to support policy making. Impact assessments are required for any initiative likely to have significant economic, environmental or social impacts. Between 2007 and 2014, the Commission produced over 700 impact assessments.

4 The current MFF was proposed by the Commission in June 2011, agreed by the European Council in February 2013 and finally adopted in December 2013. For the 2014-2020 MFF, see Council Regulation (EU, EURATOM) No 1311/2013 of 2 December 2013. See also Bauer/Becker 2016.

5 What is revenue for the EU represents expenditure for the member states. As a result, the MFF is highly influenced by the cash concept of "net budgetary balances", or the difference between member states' contributions to the EU budget and the payments they expect to receive from the various EU policies. The concept translates a zero-sum logic, where the accounting advantage of one member state is considered in practice to come at the expense of the other member states. For further details, see http://ec.europa.eu/budget/financialreport/2015/annex/3-/index_en.html (accessed 1 August 2016). For a critical analysis see Cipriani and Pisani 2004.

6 This explains for example that the level of the EU direct aid to farmers may vary considerably from one farm to another, from one country to another or from one region to another.

7 The principles of subsidiarity and proportionality (Art. 5(3)(4) Treaty on European Union, TEU) were set out by the Treaty of Maastricht (1992) as general principles of EU law. The overall approach has been developed by the conclusions of the Presidency at the European Council of Edinburgh (11-12 December 1992) and has been developed further by the Treaties of Amsterdam (1997) and Lisbon (2007). A Protocol (No. 2) annexed to the Treaties on the application of the principles of subsidiarity and proportionality provides that national Parliaments may express their opinions with regard to the compliance of a legislative act with the principle of subsidiarity and ask for it to be reviewed. The same protocol also provides for national Parliaments and the Committee of the Regions to bring suspected violations of the principle of subsidiarity before the ECJ. In its judgment of 4.5.2016 in case C-547/14 Philip Morris Brands and Others (paragraph 218), the ECJ held that its judicial review of compliance with the substantive conditions laid down in Article 5(3) TEU requires to "determine whether the EU legislature was entitled to consider, on the basis of a detailed statement (emphasis added), that the objective of the proposed action could be better achieved at EU level".

8 The concept of performance, or results, covers the outputs (specific deliverables), the outcomes (short and medium-term effects on direct addressees or recipients) and the impacts (long-term changes in society). See OECD 2002a.

9 The concept of sound financial management (or "value for money") has three dimensions: economy, efficiency and effectiveness. The principle of "economy" requires that the resources used shall be made available in due time, in appropriate quantity and quality and at the best price. "Efficiency" is characteristically a managerial value consisting in essence of maintaining a good ratio between resources employed and results attained. A related value is "effectiveness", which basically consists of ensuring that the performance of public administration is successful in achieving the goals and solving the public problems set for it by law and government (see Sigma 1999, pp. 13-14). These principles are part of EU financial (Regulation (EU, Euratom) No 966/2012 of the European Parliament and of the Council of 25 October 2012; European Parliament/Council of the European Union 2012, Art. 30(2)).

10 National bodies submit annually to the Commission, for acceptance, their accounts on the expenditure incurred and for which they have claimed a reimbursement from the EU budget. These accounts shall be accompanied by a management declaration confirming that the accounts are complete and accurate; that the expenditure was used for its intended purpose; and that the control systems guarantee compliance of spending. National bodies should also transmit an annual summary of audits and controls carried out. Those documents should be supported by an opinion of an independent audit body.

11 One may note in this connection that the Commission has proposed (see European Commission 2016e, Art. 250, p 205) to suppress the summary report by which member states should communicate their reaction to the findings of the Annual report of the ECA concerning the funds for which they ensure the day-to-day management (European Parliament/Council of the European Union 2012, Art. 162(5)). The Commission argues that this report comes too late for being considered in the discharge procedure. However, the details of the Court's findings on audited transactions are known by the Commission well before the publication of the Court's annual report.

12 National declarations are voluntary (see European Parliament/Council of the European Union 2012, Art. 59(5), last sentence). Only few member states establish such a declaration.

13 The Treaty (Art. 317 TFEU, first subparagraph) draws no distinction according to the form of management used. The Financial Regulation (European Parliament/Council of the European Union 2012, Art. 53(1) and 58(2)) states the Commission's ultimate responsibility irrespective of the implementation mode.

14 As pointed out by Ponzano (2009, p. 218) the general interest of the Union does not necessarily correspond to the addition of national interests, neither it equates the lowest common denominator of the different national stances. The Treaty itself recognises that national interests might not be in line with European ones. Hence, it provides that member states shall "refrain from any measure which could jeopardise the attainment of the Union's objectives" (Art. 4(3) TEU, third subparagraph).

15 The Treaty itself recognises that national interests might not be in line with European ones. Hence, it provides that member states shall "refrain from any measure which could jeopardise the attainment of the Union's objectives" (Art. 4(3) TEU, third subparagraph). In this respect, to avoid a legal gap, the Commission has

proposed to extend the obligation to prevent conflict of interests to all actors implementing EU funds, including at the level of member states (see European Commission 2016e, Art. 59, p. 93).

16 Pescatore (1978, p. 392) observes however that the Commission is probably the closest to the concept of executive or government usually understood according to the classical doctrine of the separation of powers.

17 To this end, different internal actions were undertaken by the Commission, such as "Sound and Efficient Management – SEM 2000" (1995), "Modernisation of Administration and Personnel – MAP 2000" (1997) or "Designing Tomorrow's Commission – Deocode" (1997).

18 The fund is financed by reducing planned spending on the Connecting Europe Facility by 2,8 billion euro and on Horizon 2020 by 2,2 billion euro and by using three billion euro from unallocated margins under the MFF expenditure ceiling. The Commission has proposed the doubling of the duration and financial capacity of the Fund (European Commission 2016d).

19 Therefore, the related assets are not accounted for in the EU consolidated annual accounts (see European Commission 2016b, p. 16).

20 According to the EIB statute (European Investment Bank 2013, Art. 19(6)), an unfavourable opinion of the Commission can be overruled only by a unanimous decision of the other members of the EIB Board of Directors. This represents a quasi veto-right.

21 In this respect, the Commission uses a materiality level of two percent (referred to the ratio of erroneous or irregular expenditure to the EU spending audited), beyond which financial corrections (disallowances of EU reimbursements) may apply. These measures can take place both before and after the Commission effects expenditure. They may be triggered by checks at any level of the control system in the member states or by the Commission, from audits of the ECA or from investigations of the European Anti-Fraud Office (OLAF). For a description see European Commission 2016c and European Court of Auditors 2016e, Figure 1.9.

22 In this connection, the perspective of the United Kingdom leaving the EU will need specific attention for a timely clearing of EU revenue and expenditure. According to current procedures compliance checks may extend into the post-Brexit period until at least 2023.

23 This framework was inspired by the concept of "new public management" emerged at national level since the 80s and characterised, on one hand, by the substitution of criminal liability with a political responsibility (Beaud 2000, p. 18) and, on the other hand, by the enhancement of responsibilities of civil servants, with the "transient" politicians only responsible for policy matters, not for management failures. See also Broeksteeg et al. 2008, pp. 275-287.

24 Comitology refers to a system of committees of member states' representatives to which the Commission submits draft implementing measures, in the aim to ensuring the widest possible support within these committees. The European Parliament and the Council have a scrutiny right and may indicate at any time that they consider the draft implementing act to exceed the powers conferred by the relevant legal basis to the Commission.

25 In the same mood, Parliament also grants discharge to a number of Institutions' Secretary-Generals (Council, Court of Auditors, Committee of the Regions, European Economic and Social Committee and Court of Justice).

26 One may recall (May 2016) the difficulties surrounding the appearance before the European Parliament Committee of Inquiry into Emission Measurements in the Automotive Sector of former Commissioner Verheugen who initially argued that only the Commission in office is entitled and capable to provide the required evidence. Verheugen finally accepted to appear before the Committee of Inquiry after intensive pressure from the presidents of the Commission and of the European Parliament.

27 The enforcement of individual responsibility is a matter for the president of the Commission who can ask a Commissioner to resign (Art. 17(6) TEU, last subparagraph). Parliament can ask the President of the Commission to withdraw confidence in an individual Commissioner (European Parliament 2016c, Annex XIII, paragraph II.5).

28 Parliament has reiterated this request lastly in 2015 (European Parliament 2015, paragraph 27). Also the ECA has recommended that the Commission, as an institution, adopts as its own AODs' management representations (see European Court of Auditors 2005, paragraph 1.57).

29 As from the 2015 financial year, the former "synthesis" report is part of the annual management and performance report (European Commission 2016b, section II).

30 OECD best practices provide that budget reports should "contain a statement of responsibility by the finance minister and the senior official responsible for producing the report. The minister certifies that all government decisions with a fiscal impact have been included in the report. The senior official certifies that the Finance Ministry has used its best professional judgement in producing the report" (OECD 2002, p. 14).

31 The lack of clarity as to whether the responsibility of the Commission as a whole encompasses responsibility for the actions of its Directors-General, or is distinct from it, has been pointed out by the ECA (2016d, paragraphs 21, 59).

32 For the 2015 financial year, see European Commission 2016a, section II.

33 Refusal of discharge only occurred twice, concerning the financial years 1982 and 1996.

34 It is worth mentioning that when examining the Court's first statement of assurance (financial year 1994), the Council pointed out that "many of the Court's remarks are recurrent and clearly show that the problem facing the Community is not one of a lack of funds, but of management" (Council of Ministers 1996, Annex 1, p. 8).

35 The "error rate", which represents an estimate of uncompliant payments, has a much stronger relationship with the basis for payment (reimbursement or entitlement schemes) than with the management mode.

36 Not unimportantly, while Parliament decides on the discharge by a majority of the votes cast (Art. 231 TFEU), a motion of censure shall be adopted by a two-thirds majority of the votes cast, representing a majority of members of Parliament (Art. 234 TFEU).

37 Though, in the case of the Santer Commission its resignation anticipated a likely censure by Parliament.

38 "Programmes statements" should contain information on the achievement of all specific, measurable, achievable, relevant and timed objectives previously set for the various activities, as well as new objectives measured by indicators. They should also present a rationale for intervention at Union level in accordance, inter alia, with the principle of subsidiarity.

39 These refer to the consolidated annual accounts (containing financial information on the activities of the institutions, agencies and other bodies of the EU); the report on budgetary and financial management (providing an analysis of the implementation of the year); the financial report (giving an overview of the sources of EU revenue and the allocation of funds to member states); the communication on the protection of the EU budget from illegal or irregular expenditure (presenting financial corrections and recoveries); the report on the protection of the EU's financial interests (covering antifraud measures); the Directors-General annual activity reports (containing financial and management information, including the results of controls), and the annual management and performance report (covering both compliance and performance information). In addition, there are annual monitoring reports for certain spending programmes like "Horizon 2020" (Research).

40 There are about one hundred evaluations a year, mostly ex-post. In general, a disclaimer indicates that they reflect only the views of the authors. One may also note that the Horizon 2020 Monitoring Report 2015, established by the Directorate-General for Research and Innovation, indicates that the information and views set out in that report do not necessarily reflect the official opinion of the Commission and that the accuracy of the data included is not guaranteed.

41 For example, only for twelve out of the over 50 spending programmes the average yearly amount available is more than one billion euro, while for 21 programmes yearly funds available vary from one million euro to 75 million euro. De Feo (2017, p. 285) observes that according to the Commission, 56 programs statements of the legislative package 2014-2020 have about 300 objectives and 700 indicators, between general and specifics, almost half of the programs have more than 10 objectives, some have more than 20 and a few more than 40.

42 For a comparison with current rules see European Parliament/Council of the European Union 2012, Art. 30(3), 38(3)e, i and 66(9), second paragraph.

43 The European Parliament claimed already in 1962 that it should be given the rights that the national parliaments have given up with the ratification of the EEC treaty, notably in the area of legislation and in budgetary power (European Parliament 1962, paragraph 20).

44 It is however positive that following the proposal (European Commission 2016d, Art. (1)(4)(d)), decisions approving the use of the EU guarantee for EFSI operations shall include the rationale for such decision, with particular focus on compliance with the additionality criterion.

45 In this connection Fuest et al. (2015, p. 6) suggest that the MFF should be limited to the budget ceiling, leaving to the annual budgetary procedure the decision on how to spend the money.

46 The difficulty of spending the funds available is also a symptom of insufficient administrative capacity. In 2015, the second year of the current MFF, more than three-quarters of operational spending still concerned the schemes of the previous MFF. The Commission estimates that less than 60% of available European Structural and Investment Funds under the current MFF will have been paid out by 2020 (European Commission 2016f, Annex 6, p. 58). D'Alfonso and Sapala (2017, pp. 206-207) observe that a delayed start of the MFF implementation for cohesion policy is a recurrent issue. This would plead for considering, for the post-2020 cohesion policy, not earmarking the full budget at the start of the programming period.

47 The Court noted that almost 20 percent of cohesion policy projects involving State aids were uncompliant in this respect (see Table 2 of the report). Also, infringements were mainly detected by EU audits rather than by national authorities (see paragraphs 74-77).

48 One may refer to the Commission's idea of a "Development and Investment Partnership Contract" with the member states, setting out the objectives to be achieved, how progress towards the achievement of these objectives will be quantified and measured and the allocation of national and EU resources among priority areas and programmes, taking account of the capacity to effectively utilise these resources (European Commission 2010b, p. 14). This idea is at the basis of the partnerships agreements through which the resources of the European Structural and Investment Funds are allocated for the seven year MFF period to thematic objectives and investment priorities, further developed in the individual operational programmes.

49 For example, the cost of management and control at the level of the member states in the field of agriculture and rural development is estimated at 7 percent of the total annual budget (European Commission 2015g, p. 142). This compares with 4,8 percent for the Social Fund (European Commission 2015b, p. 73); 4.3 percent for research spending (European Commission 2015a, p. 90) and 2.1 percent for the Regional Fund/Cohesion Fund (European Commission 2015c, p. 74). Further discrepancies can be noted in comparison to previous estimates (European Commission 2010a; see also European Commission 2008).

50 Moreover, "error rates" may have different meaning. For example, the Commission uses different indicators, such as the "amount at risk" (the level of error as an absolute amount), the "error rate" (the amount at risk divided by the expenditure or revenue considered) and the "residual error rate" (the amount at risk less implemented corrective measures, divided by the expenditure or revenue considered). See also European Commission 2016a, pp. 48-51.

References

Auditor General of Canada. 2002. *Modernizing accountability in the public sector*, Ch. 9, December: Ottawa.

Bauer, M. W., and Becker S. 2013. The Role of Middle Management and Directors-General. In *Accountability of the European Commission as administrator responsible of the management and the control of the EU budget over the last 10 years*, Committee on Budgetary Control paper presented at the Public Hearing of the EP Committee on Budgetary Control. http://www.europarl.europa.eu/meetdocs/2009_2014/documents/cont/dv/hearingdossier_/hearingdossier_en.pdf; 13 January 2017.

Bauer, M. W., and Becker S. 2017. Assessing the European Parliament's Power of the Purse: Rights, Capabilities and Strategies. In *The New Politics of the European Union Budget*, Eds. Becker, S., Bauer, M.W., and De Feo A., 173-194. Baden-Baden: Nomos Verlag.

Beaud, O. 2000. La responsabilité politique face à la concurrence d'autres formes de responsabilité des gouvernants. *Pouvoirs* 92: 17-30.

Becker, P. 2017. Reforming the European Multiannual Financial Framework – Looking for a Policy Window in a Path-dependent Environment. In *The New Politics of the European Union Budget*, Eds. Becker, S., Bauer, M.W., and De Feo A., 103-132. Baden-Baden: Nomos Verlag.

Begg, I., Enderlein, H., Le Cacheux, J. and Mrak M. 2008. Financing of the European Union Budget, Report to the Commission, Brussels.

Berlin, D. 1987. Organisation et fonctionnement de la Commission des Communautés européennes. In The European Administration, Eds. Berlin, D., Bourtembourg, C. and Pag S., 21-442. Maastricht: European Institute of Public Administration.

Broeksteeg, H., Van den Driessche, I., and Verhey, L. 2008. Political Accountability in the EU Member States: Different Concepts and Practical Implications. In *Political Accountability In Europe: Which Way Forward ? A Traditional Concept of Parliamentary Democracy in a EU Context*, Eds. Verhey, L., Broeksteeg, H., and van den Driessche, I., 271-298. Groningen: Europa Law Publishing.

Cipriani, G., and Pisani, S. 2004. The European budget: An alternative to budgetary balances to assess benefits for the member states. Società italiana di economia pubblica Working Paper No. 339. http://www.siepweb.it/siep/images/joomd/139-9116284339.pdf; 29 August 2016.

Cipriani, G. 2010. The EU Budget: Responsibility without accountability? Brussels: Center for European Public Studies.

Cipriani, G. 2014. Financing the EU budget: moving forward or backwards? Brussels/London: Center for European Public Studies/Rowman & Littlefield International.

Committee of Independent Experts. 1999a. *First Report on Allegations regarding Fraud, Mismanagement and Nepotism in the European Commission.* Brussels, 15 March 1999.

Committee of Independent Experts. 1999b. *Second Report on Reform of the Commission.* Brussels, 10 September 1999.

Council of Ministers Economy and Finance. 1996. *Rapport annuel de la Cour des comptes pour 1994 - Décharge à la Commission pour l'exercice 1994 - Déclaration d'assurance - in 1906e Session du Conseil - QUESTIONS ECONOMIQUES ET FINANCIERES, Bruxelles, le 11/03/1996.* doc. 5516/96. http://ec.europa.eu/dorie-/cardPrint.do?locale=en&&cardId=117589; 29 August 2016.

Council of Ministers Economy and Finance. 2005. *doc. 13678/058.* Brussels, 8 November 2005.

De Feo, A. 2017. The European Budget: Motor or Brake of the European Integration? A Walk through 40 Years of Budgetary Decisions. In *The New Politics of the European Union Budget*, Eds. Becker, S., Bauer, M.W., and De Feo A., 33-82. Baden-Baden: Nomos Verlag.

European Commission. 2000. *A White Paper*. COM (2000) 200 final. Brussels, 5 April 2000.

European Commission 2001. *A White Paper*. COM (2001) 428 final. Brussels, 25 July 2001.

European Commission. 2002. *A project for the European Union*. COM (2002) 247 final. Brussels, 22 May 2002.

European Commission. 2004. *Synthesis of Annual Activity Reports 2003 of DGs and Services*. COM (2004) 418. Brussels, 9 June 2004.

European Commission. 2007. *Report on the follow-up to 2005 Discharge Decisions (Summary) - European Parliament Resolutions*. COM (2007) 538 final. 19 September 2007.

European Commission. 2008. *Towards a common understanding of the concept of tolerable risk of error*. COM (2008) 866 final. Brussels, 16 December 2008.

European Commission. 2010a. More or less controls? *Striking the right balance between the administrative costs of control and the risk of error*. COM (2010) 261 final. Brussels, 26 May 2010.

European Commission. 2010b. *The EU Budget Review*. COM (2010) 700 final. Brussels, 19 October 2010.

European Commission. 2011. *The added value of the EU budget*. SEC (2011) 867 final. Brussels, 29 June 2011.

European Commission. 2014a. Synthesis of the Commission's Management Achievements in 2013. COM(2014) 342. Brussels, 11 June 2014.

European Commission. 2014b. *The Working Methods of the European Commission 2014-2019*. COM(2014) 9004. Brussels, 11 November 2014.

European Commission. 2015a. *DG Research and Innovation Annual Activity Report for 2014*. Brussels, 26 March 2015.

European Commission. 2015b. DG Employment, Social Affairs and Inclusion Annual Activity Report for 2014, Brussels, 31 March 2015.

European Commission. 2015c. *DG Regional and Urban Policy Annual Activity report for 2014*. Brussels, 13 May 2015.

European Commission. 2015d. *Better regulation for better results – An EU agenda.* COM (2015) 215 final. Strasbourg, 19 May 2015.

European Commission. 2015e. *Better Regulation Guidelines*. SWD (2015) 111 final. Strasbourg, 19 May 2015.

European Commission. 2015f. *Synthesis of the Commission's management achievements in 2014*. COM (2015) 279 final. Brussels, 3 June 2015.

European Commission. 2015g. *DG Agriculture and Rural Development Annual Activity Report for 2014.* Brussels, 12 June 2015.

European Commission. 2015h. *Report on the follow-up to the discharge for the 2013 financial year (Summary)*. COM (2015) 505 final. Brussels, 8 October 2015.

European Commission. 2016a. 2015 *Annual Management and Performance Report for the EU Budget*. COM (2016) 446 final. Strasbourg, 5 July 2016.

European Commission. 2016b. *Consolidated annual accounts of the European Union 2015*. COM (2016) 475 final. Brussels, 11 July 2016.

European Commission. 2016c. *Protection of the EU budget to end 2015*. COM (2016) 486 final. Brussels, 18 July 2016.

European Commission. 2016d. *Proposal for a Regulation on the extension of the duration of the European Fund for Strategic Investments as well as the introduction of technical enhancements for that Fund and the European Investment Advisory Hub*. COM (2016) 597 final. Brussels, 14 September 2016.

European Commission. 2016e. *Proposal for a Regulation on the Financial Rules Applicable to the General Budget of the Union*. COM (2016) 605 final. Brussels, 14 September 2016.

European Commission. 2016f. *Mid-term review/revision of the multiannual financial framework 2014-2020: An EU budget focused on results*. SWD (2016) 299 final, 14 September 2016.

European Court of Auditors. 2004. *Opinion N. 2/2004 on the "single audit" model (and a proposal for a Community internal control framework)*. Luxembourg, 2004.

European Court of Auditors. 2005. *Annual Report on the financial year 2004*. Luxembourg, 2005.

European Court of Auditors. 2013. *Annual Report on the financial year 2012*. Luxembourg, 2013.

European Court of Auditors. 2014a. *Making the best use of EU money: a landscape review of the risks to the financial management of the EU budget*. Luxembourg, 2014.

European Court of Auditors. 2014b. *Agriculture and cohesion: overview of EU spending 2007-2013*. Luxembourg, 2014.

European Court of Auditors. 2015a. *Annual Report on the financial year 2014, Luxembourg*. 2015.

European Court of Auditors. 2015b. Efforts to Address Problems with Public Procurement in EU Cohesion Expenditure Should Be Intensified. *Special report* No 10/2015. Luxembourg, 2015.

European Court of Auditors. 2016a. Is the Commission's system for performance measurement in relation to farmers' incomes well designed and based on sound data? *Special Report* No 1/2016, Luxembourg, 2016.

European Court of Auditors. 2016b. *Annual activity report 2015*. Luxembourg, 2016.

European Court of Auditors. 2016c. More efforts needed to raise awareness of and enforce compliance with State aid rules in cohesion policy. *Special Report* No 24/2016. Luxembourg, 2016.

European Court of Auditors. 2016d. Governance of the European Commission – Best Practice? *Special Report* No 27/2016. Luxembourg, 2016.

European Court of Auditors. 2016e. *Annual Report on the Financial Year 2015*, Luxembourg, 2016.

European Court of Auditors. 2016f. Making cross-compliance more effective and achieving simplification remains challenging. *Special report* No 26/2016, Luxembourg, 2016.

European Court of Auditors. 2016g. Opinion N. 2/2016 concerning the proposal for a Regulation of the European Parliament and of the Council amending Regulations (EU) Nos 1316/2013 and 2015/1017 and the accompanying Commission evaluation in accordance with Article 18(2) of Regulation (EU) 2015/1017, Luxembourg, 2016.

European Investment Bank. 2013. *Statute and other Treaty provisions.* http://www.eib-.org/attachments/general/statute/eib_statute_2013_07_01_en.pdf; 13 August 2016.

European Investment Bank. 2016. Evaluation of the functioning of the European Fund for Strategic Investments (EFSI), September, Luxembourg.

European Parliament. 1962. *Résolution du 18.10.1962 relative au Cinquième Rapport général sur l'activité de la Communauté économique européenne.*

European Parliament. 2001. *Resolution of 4.4.2001 on the discharge for implementation of the EU general budget for the financial year 1999.*

European Parliament. 2002. *Resolution of 10.4.2002 on the discharge for implementation of the EU general budget for the financial year 2000.*

European Parliament. 2005. *Resolution of 12.4.2005 on the discharge for implementation of the EU general budget for the financial year 2003, Section III.*

European Parliament. 2015. *Resolution of 29.4.2015 on discharge for the financial year 2013, Section III – Commission and executive agencies.*

European Parliament. 2016a. *Resolution of 28.4.2016 on the discharge for implementation of the EU general budget for the financial year 2014, Section III – Commission and executive agencies.*

European Parliament. 2016b. Resolution of 6.7.2016 on the preparation of the post-electoral revision of the MFF 2014-2020 : Parliament's input ahead of the Commission's proposal.

European Parliament. 2016c. *Rules of procedure.* http://www.europarl.europa.eu/sides/getLastRules.do?language=EN&reference=TOC; 13 August 2016.

European Parliament, and Council of the European Union. 2012. Regulation (EU, Euratom) No 966/2012 of the European Parliament and of the Council of 25 October 2012 on the financial rules applicable to the general budget of the Union. *Official Journal of the European Union* L 298/1: 17-96.

Fuest, C., Heinemann, F., and Ungerer, M. 2015. Reforming the Financing of the European Union: A Proposal. *Centre for European Economic Research (ZEW)* 2(May).

Goulard, S., and Nava, M. 2002. Un financement plus démocratique du budget européen: un défi pour la Convention européenne. *Revue Française de Finances Publiques* 80: 31-52.

Jenkins, R. 2007. The Role of Political Institutions in Promoting Accountability. In *Performance accountability and combating corruption*, Ed. Shah, A., 135-181. Washington: World Bank.

Kannengießer, C. 1995. Die Entlastung im Haushaltsrecht der Europäischen Gemeinschaft. *Die öffentliche Verwaltung* 2: 55-60.

Kassim, H., Peterson, J., Bauer M. W., Connolly, S., Dehousse, R., Hooghe, L. and Thompson, A. 2013. *The European Commission of the Twenty-first century.* Oxford University Press: Oxford.

N.N. 1999. Editorial Comments. *Common Market Law Review* 36.

Lapsley, I. and Lonsdale, J. 2010. The Audit Society: Helping to Develop or Undermine Trust in Government. In *Administrative Justice in Context*, Ed. Adler, M., 73-96. Oxford: Hart Publishing.

Levy, R. 2000. *Managing the managers: the role of the Commission in implementation. In At the Heart of the Union: Studies of the European Commission*, Ed. Nugent, Neill, 203-225. Basingstoke: Palgrave Macmillan.

Ludlow, P. 1991. The European Commission. In *The New European Community Decision making and Institutional Change*, Eds. Keohane R. O., and Hoffmann, S., 85-132. Boulder/Oxford: Westview Press.

Mecalfe, L. 1992. Après 1992: la Commission pourra-t-elle gérer l'Europe. *Revue Francaise d'Administration Publique* 63: 401-412.

Organisation for Economic Co-operation and Development (OECD). 2002a. *Glossary of Key Terms in Evaluation and Results Based Management.*

Organisation for Economic Co-operation and Development (OECD). 2002. *Best Practices for Budget Transparency.*

Pescatore, P. 1978. L'exécutif communautaire: justification du quadripartisme institué par les traités de Paris et de Rome. *Cahiers de droit européen* 4 : 387-406.

Pisani, E. 1956. Administration de gestion, administration de mission. *Revue française de science politique* 6(2) : 315-330.

Ponzano, P. 2009. Brèves considérations sur le rôle de la Commission européenne. *Revue du Droit de l'Union Européenn* 2 : 217-220.

Power, M. 1999. *The Audit Society.* Oxford: Oxford UP.

Schön-Quinlivan, E. 2011. *Reforming the European Commission.* Basingstoke: Palgrave MacMillan.

Sigma. 1999. European Principles for Public Administration. *Sigma Paper* 27.

Spinelli, A. 1974. Report to the symposium of 23-25.11.1972. In *La Commission des Communautées européennes et l'elargissement de l'Europe,* 275-278. Brussels : Editions de l'Université de Bruxelles.

Strasser, D. 1994. Les dispositions financières du Traité de Maastricht. *Revue française des finances publiques* 45 : 195-213.

Tarschys, D. 2011. European Public Goods: Which Selection Criteria for the Multiannual Financial Framework? In *The EU Budget. What should go in? What should go out?* Ed. Tarschys, D., 12-41. Stockholm: Swedish Institute for European Policy Studies.

Van Gerven, W. 2007. *Political, ethical and financial and legal responsibility of EU Commissioners.* http://www.europarl.europa.eu/meetdocs/2004_2009/documents-/dv/van_gerven_fin/van_gerven_final.pdf; 13 August 2016.

Vedel, G. 1974. Report to the symposium of 23-25.11.1972. In *La Commission des Communautées européennes et l'elargissement de l'Europe*, 235-243. Brussels : Editions de l'Université de Bruxelles.

Verhey, L. 2009. Political Accountability: A Useful Concept in EU Inter-Institutional Relations? In *Political Accountability and European Integration*, Eds. Verhey, L, Kiiver, P., and Loeffen, S., 56-70. Groningen: Europa Law Publishing.

Verhey, L., Claes, M., and Broeksteeg, H. 2008. Political Accountability in the European Union: Conceptual Analysis and Future Prospects. In *Political Accountability In Europe: Which Way Forward ? A Traditional Concept of Parliamentary Democracy in a EU Context,* Eds. Verhey, L., Broeksteeg, H., and van den Driessche, I., 299-344. Groningen: Europa Law Publishing.

Wille, A. 2015. Holding executive power to account. In *The Palgrave Handbook of the European Administrative system*, Eds. Bauer, M. W., and Trondal, J., 467-481. Basingstoke: Palgrave Macmillan.

Williams, S. 1991. Sovereignty and Accountability in the European Community. In *The New European Community Decision making and Institutional Change,* Eds. Keohane R. O., and Hoffmann S., 155-176. Boulder/Oxford: Westview Press.

Wouters, J., and Marx, A. 2007. *Efficiency of accountability instruments in international organisations*. Workshop on Governance in European Commission, Brussels, 3-4 October 2007, http://www.europarl.europa.eu/meetdocs/2004_2009-/documents/dv/paper_ep_efficien/paper_ep_efficiency.pdf; 13 August 2016.

Budget Consolidation and National Budget Policy Instruments

Uwe Wagschal and Georg Wenzelburger

After the recent economic crisis, most European countries and the rest of the world were hit by its severe consequences. Tax revenues fell below expectations and governments needed to avoid excessive fiscal deficits. As a result, many countries engaged in fiscal consolidation. These consolidation efforts followed, however, largely different strategies. On the one hand, the composition of the packages differed: some countries focused on the revenue side (tax hikes) and some on the expenditure side (austerity). On the other hand, the timing of the measures was different with some governments starting the consolidation right in the beginning of the mandate (frontloading strategies) and others adopting them toward the end of their term (backloading) (König/Wenzelburger 2016; Hübscher/Sattler 2016).

Parliaments, as one of the main subjects of this book, have different objectives concerning public finances. First of all they are responsible for adopting the budget law, the most prominent task of parliaments in the budgetary process. However, they are far more involved in public finances and yet are somehow overlooked as an institution. It is not only the executive which is solely responsible for the fiscal stance. The preferences of parliaments may also differ, especially when it comes to the expenditure. These may vary in terms of size and composition. According to the partisan theory (Hibbs 1977, p. 1473f; Castles 1984; Schmidt 1996) right wing parties tend to spend less than left wing parties. It is also possible to observe different preferences with regard to taxation (Wagschal 2004). Here, the size and structure of tax composition differs vastly according to the different political preferences. Also the influence of parliaments on public deficits and the level of public debt are discussed differently (Franzese 2002; Wagschal 1996).

Not only are crucial variables like public expenditures, taxation and the public deficit relevant, but also budget institutions, which give the parliaments power over the budget. The budget cycle is part of the execution as well as the transparency of the budget. Controlling the budget is important in terms of the forecast of the development of the budget and refers to long term planning of public spending and the required revenues. The second step of the budget cycle is drawing up the budget. In some parliaments the budget committees have a strong impact on this, though ultimately the parliament makes the final decision. Usually the parliament is not involved in the implementation process, except when short-term control is implemented. Also, the evaluation is usually done by - mainly independent - accounting offices of the government. However, the parliament also has some rights to control the budget. Furthermore, parliaments might use new instruments to control and evaluate the budget, for example benchmarking and best practices studies have gained in importance over the past years. To judge the strength of parliaments there are different indicators on the market (Molander 2001; Wagschal/Wenzelburger 2008, 2009; Wehner 2006). The empirical findings do not point in the same direction, e.g. Wehner (2010) talks about the myth of control.

The following article looks at different aspects of budget consolidation and their relation to the budget cycle and the various variables which might be influenced by the government, the parliament and other explanatory factors. The basis of this analysis is a cross country international analysis of the Organisation for Economic Co-operation and Development (OECD) countries. In the first part, we provide an overview on budget consolidation between 1980 and 2015. The second part considers the question: "at what times do governments consolidate?" Subsequently, successful strategies for sustainable consolidations are described in section four. Finally, the findings from the cross-country comparison are contrasted to the policies of the European Parliament (EP).

Budget consolidation

In the economics literature, numerous studies dealing with budget consolidations and their effects can be found (e.g. Alesina/Perotti 1995, 1996, 1997; von Hagen et al. 2002; Zaghini 2001; Brandner 2003; Larch/Salto 2003, Mulas-Granados 2006). These studies normally use the cyclically adjusted balance ratios (CAB) or the cyclically adjusted primary balances (CAPB) as indicators of discretionary fiscal policy. These measures adjust the budget data for changes in the macroeconomic environment and/or for the non-discretionary interest payments. Arguably, cyclical adjustment is desirable as it makes it possible to filter out the discretionary effects of fiscal policy. However, the methods of calculation vary so greatly that it is doubtful whether CAB ratios are in fact suitable indicators for determining consolidation periods (Wagschal/Wenzelburger 2008). International organisations use different methods for the cyclical adjustment of budget balances and the economics community is still discussing which of these is most appropriate (Girouard/André 2005). Even more problematic is the issue of data quality. For some countries, the adjusted fiscal indicators are only poorly correlated. Looking at different measurements of the CAB for Finland, data from the European Commission and data from the OECD (OECD 2005) for the period 1987-2005 only produce a correlation coefficient of r = 0.66. Moreover, the data differs to a large extent depending on whether one uses International Monetary Fund (IMF), European Union (EU) or OECD data. Therefore, the reliability of the CAB and CAPB data can be doubted.[1]

This paper introduces a new consolidation indicator which takes into account some of the critique against these standard approaches. First, we define the term consolidation by using the (non-cyclically-adjusted) primary balance ratios. The ordinary budget balance would also be misleading, because the interest payments, which cannot be influenced by governments, are included. Using this indicator avoids the discussion of the "right" method of cyclical adjustment and the associated data problems.

Most economic studies of consolidation use either one-year averages with high thresholds or two-(or more) year averages with lower thresholds to identify periods of budget consolidation. Here we use a more comprehensive indicator to evaluate consolidation performance in OECD-countries. The consolidation indicator[2] ranks the OECD countries on a scale from one to ten. A period covers two years, for example 2013 and 2014. However, the indicator is calculated for overlapping periods, so that it also covers 2014 and 2015. The calculation of the level of consolidation is based on three indicators:

- The level of the primary budget (% of Gross Domestic Product, GDP) measured by the average of the examined period (using moving averages).
- The development of public debt (% of GDP) during the examined period (= difference between the last year before the period and the last year of the examined period).
- A success criterion where the future development of public debt is taken into account. Consolidations are therefore designated as being successful or sustainable if the public debt ratio in the third year after the consolidation is at least at the same level as in the last year of the consolidation phase.[3]

Three different levels of consolidation can be distinguished:

1. No consolidation (one or two points): There is no consolidation, when a country has a negative primary budget and the level of public debt increases (= one) or decreases (= two) during the examined period.
2. Partial consolidation (three to six points): A partial consolidation is present, when the primary budget is positive and between zero and two percent of GDP. In case the public debt increases (decreases) during the examination period and there is also no success of the consolidation after three years a country gets three (four) points. When the primary budget is also between zero and two percent of GDP, but the consolidation was successful after three years, then a country gets five points when public debt increased and six points when public debt decreased during the examination period.
3. Substantial consolidation (seven to ten points): A substantial consolidation is present, when the primary budget is larger than two percent of GDP. In case the public debt increases (or decreases) during the examination period and there is also no success of the consolidation after three years a country gets seven (eight) points. When the primary budget is also larger than two percent of GDP, but the consolidation was successful after three years, than a country gets nine points when public debt increased and ten points when public debt decreased during the examination period.

Figure 10.1 shows the development of the OECD average of the consolidation indicator, with one of the best performers (Belgium) and two major European countries (Germany and the UK). The analysis of the indicator allows for long-term comparison of budget consolidation efforts between 1980 and 2015. It is important to note that indicators are based on two-year periods and that every two-year consolidation period already takes into account the development of public debt ratio three years later. For instance, the values of the indicator for the last consolidation period plotted in Figure 10.1 (2008-2009) include forecasts of public debt ratios in 2012. Figure 10.1 gives a clear picture of the impact of financial and economic turmoil on consolidation efforts in the OECD world (based on the latest forecasts available).

Consolidation performance in the OECD world between 1980 and 2015 varied remarkably over time (see Figure 10.1). The performance of the OECD-average was mainly driven by GDP growth, severe economic crisis (e.g. oil crisis of 1981, 1987-1988, 2000f, 2007f) and changes in the political framework such as the introduction of the euro or the collapse of the Soviet Union. For the 20 countries in Figure 10.1 where data is available from 1980 onwards it is obvious that the financial crisis after 2007 has had the biggest impact on consolidation. In 2009/2010 the indicator was at the lowest level for the entire period. The OECD average in Figure 10.1 further shows a clear positive effect of prospective Euro-membership on budget consolidation efforts. In the mid-1990s, consolidation efforts increased markedly, leading to a peak of the OECD-average in 1999 when the euro was finally introduced. After 1999, consolidation efforts declined, followed by another relative peak in the OECD-average in 2007/2008 at about 5,5 points just before the financial crisis began. These findings are similar to the findings that public debt was also driven – by a considerable amount – by the economic ups and downs and economic crisis.

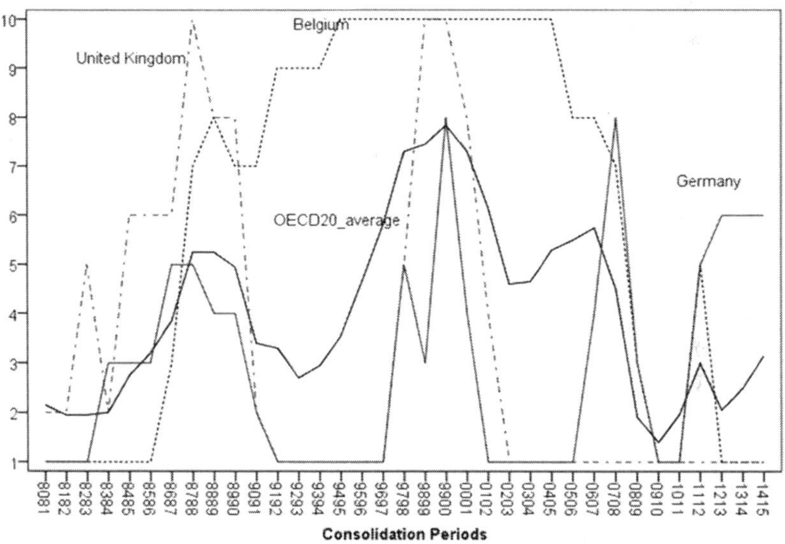

Figure 10.1: Budget consolidation in the OECD world (1980 to 2015)
Note: 10 = highest score for consolidation, 1 = lowest consolidation score. Data refers to 20 OECD countries where data is available for the whole period.

The aftermath of the last economic and financial crisis has already had dramatic consequences for public finances throughout the whole OECD world. For the 20 OECD-countries in Figure 10.1, the indicator for 2008-2009 has fallen by four points compared to two years ago. This was the sharpest decline in performance since 1980. Consolidation slumps of an even faintly similar magnitude occurred only after the economic crisis of

2001 following the dot-com bubble burst, when the average indicator fell by approximately three points within three years. The analysis of public debt ratios presents a similar picture. The OECD data displays an increase in the average public debt ratio of more than 30 percentage points for 2012 compared to the year before the crisis broke out (2007). This was an historically unique rise in public debt, never seen before in peacetime since 1945. The explosion of public debt is also causally linked to the decline in GDP growth as well as to the decline in the level of the GDP. In 2009, economic growth in the OECD world sank by 3.5 percentage points compared with the previous year. Compared to 2007, this leads to a difference of approximately six points of the consolidation indicator.

The frequency distribution (see Figure 10.2) of the ten-point consolidation indicator shows that in 52.4 percent of cases there is no consolidation. Further 21.7 percent of cases represent a partial consolidation and 26 percent a substantial consolidation. It should be mentioned that fiscal consolidation is not an end in itself. It might have high political costs in the short run. Some authors oppose consolidation in general arguing that it is a dangerous neoliberal idea (Blyth 2014). The consolidation of public finances is therefore a difficult task for governments. Any government that cuts social security benefits, increases taxes, or makes public service employees redundant will trigger protests from the groups concerned and jeopardize its chances of re-election. However, the development of the core economic indicators of unemployment and growth shows that more than in 80 percent of all cases the countries improved their economic situation further. The economies of the consolidators also improved compared to the benchmark of the OECD countries (Wagschal/Wenzelburger 2012). In the literature, these so-called non-Keynesian effects of consolidation (Giavazzi/Pagano 1996) are explained by the fact that the contractive effect of reducing expenditure is over-compensated by future earnings (income effect) (Bertola/Drazen 1993). This expectation hypothesis is particularly effective where credible (i.e. comprehensive) policy changes (especially expenditure reductions) are announced, which has been proven by empirical studies (Zaghini 2001). If these cuts in expenditure are then supplemented by only moderate wage agreements, there is an increased probability of a successful and sustainable consolidation with simultaneous strong economic growth.

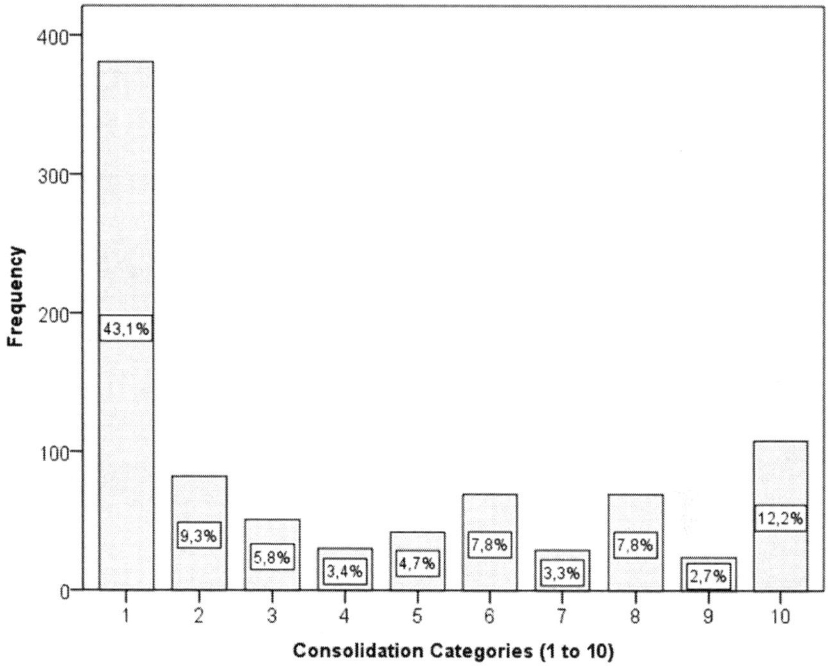

Figure 10.2: Frequency distribution of the Budget Consolidation Indicator in the OECD world (1980 to 2015)

Note: 10 = highest score for consolidation, 1 = lowest consolidation score.

The data and ranking of the OECD countries (see column one for 1980/81-2014/15) is displayed in Table 10.1. Also in Table 10.1 one can find the data for the sub-periods 1980/81-1996/1997 as well as for the period 1997/98-2014/15. The poorest performer in terms of the consolidation indicator is France followed by Austria, the United States and Japan. For the period since 1996 Japan is clearly the worst performer. For the overall period, especially small states highly integrated in the world market, performed best: Australia, Sweden, Finland, South Korea, Ireland, Belgium, Norway and Denmark as the overall champion. Peter Katzenstein (Katzenstein 1985) already demonstrated more than 30 years ago, that these small countries were forced to react much more flexibly than large countries.

Table 10.1: Country averages for the Budget Consolidation Indicator in the OECD world (1980 to 2015)

Country	Period 1980/81-2014/15 (1)	Period 1980/81-1996/97 (2)	Period 1997/98-2014/15 (3)	Difference (3) - (2)
Czech Republic	n.a.	n.a.	1.33	
Hungary	n.a.	n.a.	5.06	
Iceland	n.a.	n.a.	5.25	
Luxembourg	n.a.	n.a.	4.33	
New Zealand	n.a.	n.a.	5.78	
Poland	n.a.	n.a.	1.50	
Slovak Republic	n.a.	n.a.	1.44	
France	1.57	1.18	1.94	0.77
Austria	2.34	1.35	3.28	1.92
United States	2.49	1.94	3.00	1.06
Japan	2.57	4.12	1.11	-3.01
Spain	2.71	1.35	4.00	2.65
Germany	2.94	2.24	3.61	1.38
Portugal	3.00	3.65	2.39	-1.26
United Kingdom	3.23	3.71	2.78	-0.93
Netherlands	3.37	2.76	3.94	1.18
Greece	3.63	2.71	4.50	1.79
Canada	3.94	1.76	6.00	4.24
Italy	4.77	2.88	6.56	3.67
Australia	4.94	3.53	6.28	2.75
Sweden	4.97	3.29	6.56	3.26
Finland	5.23	4.47	5.94	1.47
South Korea	5.34	6.53	4.22	-2.31
Ireland	5.60	5.88	5.33	-0.55
Belgium	6.03	5.59	6.44	0.86
Norway	6.17	5.47	6.83	1.36
Denmark	6.26	5.76	6.72	0.96
Average	4.06	3.51	4.30	1.08

Note: The countries are ranked according to the values of column 1. The data is based on the consolidation indicator: 10 = highest score for consolidation, 1 = lowest consolidation score. Own calculations.

Dividing the time span into two sub-periods reveals another striking result: The consolidation performance differs to some extent, since the correlation between the two periods is only moderate (r = 0.398). If one looks closer at the correlation between the level of consolidation and the change of consolidation between the two periods, a medium strong correlation (r = -0.501) results. This means those countries that did more in the 1980s and 1990s were more relaxed with their consolidation efforts in the second period. However, country size still plays a significant role. Only Italy, one of the larger OECD countries, has been quite active in consolidating the budget after 1996. This activeness was mainly driven by Italy's aim to join the eurozone. Later the country became much more reluctant to fight public debt and deficits and currently has the third largest debt level of all OECD countries as well as a strong increase in overall debt over the examined periods (see Figure 10.3).

In general, consolidation has become much more relevant since the early and mid-nineties. One reason was the overall increase of debt level, which reached levels that have never been seen before during peacetime. This led to consolidation processes, because the drag of interest payments and growing vulnerability by the capital markets started to become a problem. As can be seen in Figure 10.3, some of the OECD countries managed to reduce their debt levels significantly, such as New Zealand, Denmark, Sweden, the Netherlands and Belgium.

Sweden presents a particularly interesting case. Göran Persson, who had taken over from Ingvar Carlsson as prime minister in 1995 supported budget consolidation in Sweden. Persson had previously been the Minister of Finance and had incorporated the reform of the budget process that he had developed in his previous ministry into the budget negotiations in spring 1996 (Wenzelburger 2006). As Minister of Finance, he was forced to go to Wall Street and to negotiate vigorously with the financial market, because Sweden was a major borrower. Later he commented that he would never go there with the same financial situation again. Therefore the political will and skill of politicians to conduct consolidation is an important factor. Other key figures were Dehaene in Belgium, Douglas in New Zealand or Thatcher in Britain.

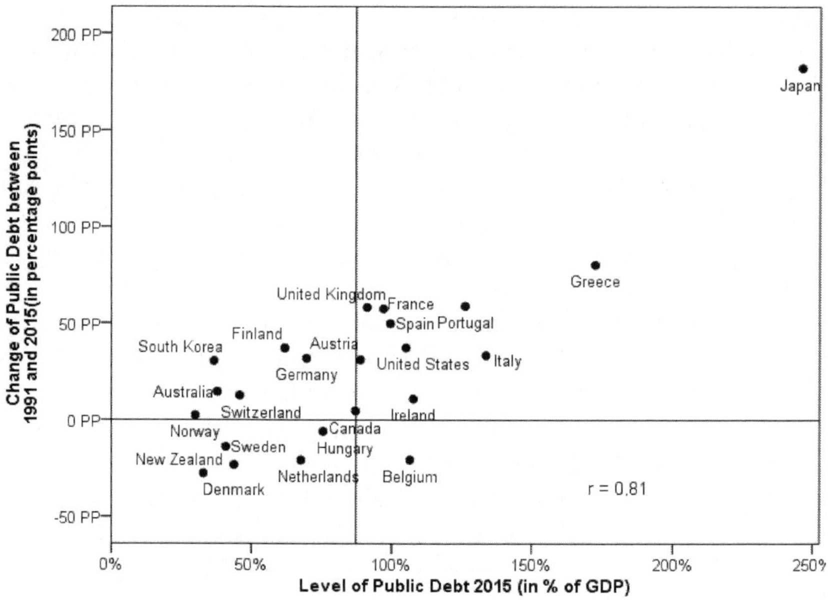

Figure 10.3: Level and change in public debt levels (1991 to 2015)

The impact of entering the eurozone was also highly relevant. Some budget consolidations are closely linked to the dynamic that was triggered by the decision over the Maastricht criteria in the mid-90s. However, the success of consolidations can only be partly explained by this debt rule as well as of national debt brakes. The European stability criteria of the Maastricht Treaty and the European Stability Pact were especially relevant before entering the eurozone. Once accepted into the eurozone, the countries reduced their efforts drastically. Calculating the correlation coefficient between the Fiscal Rules Index of the European Union and the consolidation index from Figure 10.1, shows only a pearson correlation of 0.2 for the period 2001-2009 (we left the aftermath of the financial crisis out). Since 1999 the debt rule of the Maastricht treaty was violated in around 55 percent of all cases and the deficit criteria in around 40 percent of the cases. Therefore, one might conclude that the impact of financial rules and the ownership of these regulations within the eurozone are only of minor importance.

When do governments consolidate?

What drives budget consolidations? The empirical findings, on the basis of theoretical approaches and hypotheses derived from these theories, led to the following findings (Wagschal/Wenzelburger 2012, 2009; Mulas-Granados 2006). First, socio-economic factors have a significant influence on consolidation probability. Strong economic growth during the consolidation episode is positively associated, whereas a strong demand for social security expenditures (because of rising unemployment or population ageing) is negatively related to the probability of a consolidation episode. The indicators for socio-economic problem pressure – the misery-index and the level of the lagged (by one year) debt-ratio – show that governments are more likely to consolidate public finances when they are confronted with economic pressure. Countries start to consolidate when they are in bad economic shape and their public debt has reached high, and probably not sustainable levels. This result confirms the theoretical expectations as well as the empirical results of other studies (von Hagen/Strauch 2001; Mulas-Granados 2006).

Do parties matter when it comes to budget consolidation policy? The results of the empirical analysis suggest a rather weak connection at best. The findings for the partisan variables show only a very small effect, pointing to the outcome that right-wing cabinets perform a little worse in budget consolidation. However, even if there is some evidence that right-wing parties hinder budget consolidation, while left-wing parties enhance their likelihood, the empirical result is not very strong.

With respect to the institutional variables, it is possible to observe quite a significant influence of the veto-player index: the more veto-players (Tsebelis 2002), the smaller the probability of budget consolidation. This finding is in line with the theory. It suggests that veto-players support the status quo, block policy reforms and thus hinder budget consolidation.

The theoretical expectation for the influence of path-dependency of the social security system on budget consolidations is strongly confirmed. Countries where the social insurance principle plays an important role in the social security system (strong path-dependency) have a smaller probability of consolidating their public finances. This can be explained by the rights-conferring nature of social contributions. In contrast, the analysis offered here demonstrates absolutely no support for the view that open economies are more successful in consolidating their budgets than closed ones.

To sum up, our analysis suggests that strong problem pressure, institutional arrangements with few veto-players, a tax-financed social security system, a decreasing share of unemployed and seniors in the population and high economic growth during the consolidation episode increase the chances that a country consolidates its public finances. Mixed, but generally rather weak, evidence is found for the partisan influence and of the influence of trade unions on budget consolidations.

Strategies for sustainable consolidations

In a study, which was based on quantitative analyses as well as qualitative case studies (Wagschal/Wenzelburger 2008), we argued that there is no ideal way or consistent pattern for consolidation. Individual countries have chosen different paths and strategies for consolidating their budgets.

Nevertheless some findings can be generalized. A first aspect of budget consolidation worth investigating is their composition. Whether consolidation should be revenue-based or expenditure-based and which strategy is the most sustainable in this respect is a matter of debate (Alesina/Perotti 1997; Zaghini 2001). Daily political discussion generally focuses only on the direct short-term effects and notes that you should not "save to the point of harming the economy". For a sustainable consolidation strategy, however, the dynamic and medium to long-term aspects are crucial (Giavazzi/Pagano 1996).

The findings are clear-cut: First, all consolidators cut their public expenditures more than the benchmark group of all OECD countries. Second, expenditure decreased much more in the group of sustainable (i.e. successful) consolidators than in the group of non-sustainable consolidators. A further and obviously complementary question is whether there is a link between the sustainability of consolidations and the change in government revenues, i.e. either a reduction or increase in taxes, contributions and other non-tax revenues. On average there is virtually no difference between the change of the revenue ratio (i.e. in percent of GDP) of the consolidators and the OECD benchmark, i.e. all the other OECD countries.

However some successful consolidation cases showed that moderate tax increases were implemented, particularly for higher earners. The revenues generated were not extraordinarily high but by using such measures the implementation of the reform could be cushioned and given broader support in terms of policy. With this type of tax policy, the costs and benefits of consolidations would be better distributed and easier to communicate.

Any policy that involves cuts will be unpopular; this policy follows the "blame avoidance" model (Pierson 1994) and thus reduces the risk of the government being subsequently punished by the electorate.

These displayed findings reveal that reductions in public expenditures are an important cornerstone of successful budget consolidations. In addition, expenditure-based measures are more successful than revenue-based measures (i.e. tax increases). Especially the non-sustainable consolidations have mainly relied upon a revenue increase.

A third – and more detailed – perspective takes the changes in the composition of public expenditure over time into account. This is possible with the Classification of the Functions of Government (COFOG) data that summarises public expenditure in ten expenditure categories: general public services; defence; public order and safety; economic affairs; environmental protection; housing and community amenities; health; recreation/culture/religion; education; and social protection (see Castles 2007 for a detailed analysis of the COFOG data). Looking at the COFOG data there are some similarities but also huge differences between the consolidators and the non-consolidators. First, expenditure cuts have been larger in the group of consolidators than in the group of non-consolidators except for defence. Second, whereas both groups have made significant expenditure cuts in the areas of general public services, economic affairs (notably subsidies, slightly less investment) and defence, huge differences in the expenditure profile during the consolidation episodes can be observed, especially for social spending: the non-consolidators increased their social expenditures by over 20 percent, while the consolidators have reduced their social spending on average by 1.4 percent.

A fourth aspect of consolidation strategies relates to the timing of the consolidations. Are they initiated after major changes in the party complexion of government or are they just as likely to occur at any stage in the life of a government? In response to this question, we examined the starting point for each consolidation government and identified how long after a change in the partisan complexion of government a consolidation commenced and how long that consolidation lasted. Almost two thirds of the consolidations were started at the latest one year after the change of power. Consolidations obviously have a good chance of success if they are carried out soon after a substantial change in the party complexion of government. In this case the period of consolidation is also longer. This finding, which is referred to in the literature as the "honeymoon" effect" (Williamson/Haggard 1994), shows that as a consequence of the enhanced legitimacy conferred by election victory, reforms can be implemented more easily and with a higher level of credibility when the parties in government have just changed. For parties in power for a longer period of time, however, the probability of being able to implement radical reforms is drastically reduced. In the remaining time of a first legislature period, only very few reforms are initiated. Thus, it seems crucial that budget consolidations are carried out soon after a change of government. This frontloading of reforms is important for two reasons: First, the opportunities for policy implementation are increased. Second, the reform governments have a better chance of deriving positive effects from a reform and not getting punished at the ballot box.

Another important aspect of the political-economic literature links different institutional arrangements to the budget consolidation performance. Generally speaking, the key point of the argument is that strong and stable governments, especially single party governments, perform significantly better – in terms of consolidation – than minimal winning coalitions, surplus and minority governments. The reason is because they are less hampered by coalition negotiations and do not have to satisfy as many special interests. Moreover, it is argued that stable governments have more room in which to manoeuvre when it comes to consolidations (Persson/Svensson 1989; Roubini/Sachs 1989). The empirical findings do not support this theoretical argument, since there are only a few cases where single majority governments have carried out successful consolidations. Countries with minority governments like Sweden, Denmark, Norway and New Zealand managed their public finances quite well.

In addition to the size of government it is also argued that the size of parliaments matters. On the one hand the size of parliament is assumed to have a tendency to increase expenditure. This is caused, among other things, by the so-called "common-pool" problem (Weingast et al. 1981; Hallerberg/Hagen 1999).

The role of parliaments is also analyzed in connection with budget consolidation. Four variables lie in the heart of this branch of research: the fragmentation, the size, the number of chambers and the strength of the parliaments. Fragmentation of parliaments is strongly associated with the electoral system. Countries with proportional representation put slightly more emphasis on consolidation over a constant level of revenues or a moderate increase in such revenues. For example, the countries with proportional representation reduced their revenues slightly (in terms of GDP) during the consolidation period whereas countries with majority representation systems remained stable. This can be explained by the fact that proportional representation systems ultimately represent broader society interests both in the parliament as well as in the government and are normally coalitions, which is why revenue-side loads can be distributed more widely.

The expansion of welfare states during the so-called "Golden Age" up to 1973 meant that the state activity and social security benefit ratios rose drastically. The different levels of the expenditure profiles (Schmidt 1997) as well as the revenue profiles (Wagschal 2005) can be attributed to the different institutional features of the OECD countries. The veto player theory played a major role in explaining the differences between different nations. Veto players can hinder or even block reforms and therefore slow down political change (e.g. expansion of the welfare state) (Tsebelis 2002). However, this variable was not relevant in the empirical analysis. Therefore it is not surprising the existence of a second chamber – especially with large power – also has no real impact on consolidation.

The size of parliament is – from a political economy perspective – another factor that could have an impact on consolidation. The hypothesis is that large parliaments (indicator: members of parliament in relation to inhabitants) usually produce higher deficits and therefore also have a weaker consolidation performance. Empirically, one can find in international comparisons a slight significant effect that the size of parliaments increase expenditures and produce higher deficits. This also holds true for the local communities in Germany as well as for the German states. Why do large parliaments lead to more expenditure? The theoretical reason is that pork barrel politics tend to produce higher expenditures, because the politicians want to be re-elected. A second argument is that of the common pool resource problem. The more decision makers in politics the more likely the outcome is to be spending. However, calculating correlations for the members of parliament (non-standardized and standardized in percent of the population), one cannot find an association. Since the correlation is close to zero one can conclude that there is no evidence for the USA (see Figure 10.4). This might be because of more efficient debt brakes or supermajorities in the budget process, when a deficit has to be adopted by the legislature.

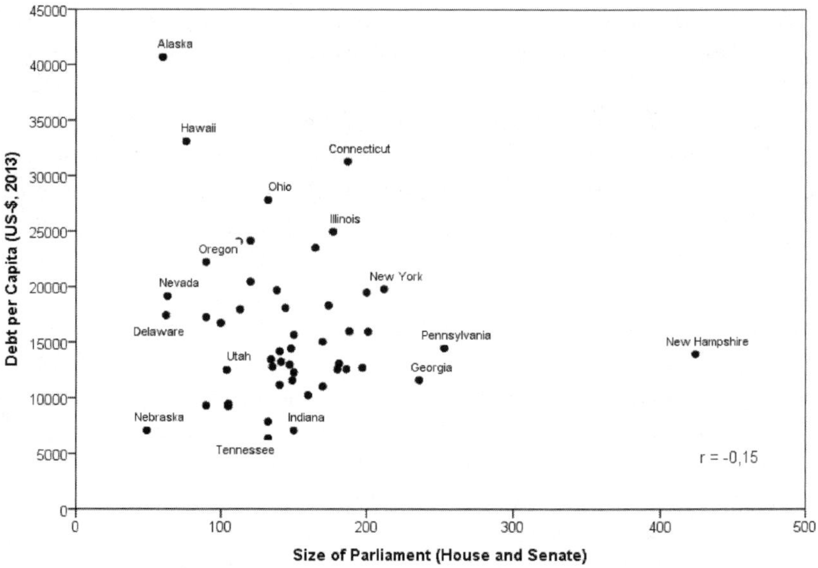

Figure 10.4: Size of legislature and public debt in the United States (2013)

Measuring the strength of parliaments Wehner (2010) finds consistent evidence that powerful legislatures are associated with higher public spending than those with limited authority. This is against the conventional wisdom in the political economic literature, but nevertheless plausible in the way Wehner derives his results. For the Strength of Parliament Index of the European Union (Fish/Kroenig 2009) and the deficit also finds a slight positive correlation (see Figure 10.5). Wehner also applied multivariate analysis with more detailed findings, which does not change much in the outcome. A new approach was recently published by Auel et al. (2015). Their new indicator measures parliamentary strength and activity in EU Affairs. They have seen a change in parliamentary strength after the financial crisis, but so far no one has used this new indicator in the analysis of public debt and deficits as well as for the analysis of budget consolidation.

Despite this poor performance of institutions for consolidation, a specific institutional aspect does matter for effective consolidation strategies. Consolidators often shifted their budget process from a "bottom-up" to a "top-down" model. The pioneering work by Jürgen von Hagen (1992) and subsequently by Hallerberg and von Hagen (1999) and Hallerberg, Strauch and von Hagen (2009) focused on the importance of budget institutions in the individual countries. In the consolidation process it is important to note whether a country follows a so-called "delegations" or a "commitment" approach. Typically, majority systems concentrate more on the delegations approach, which includes a strengthening of the position of the Minister of Finance, than countries that are organised on the basis of a consensus democracy. Successful consolidators – according to the data of 1992 (von Hagen) and 2001 (Hallerberg 2003) – substantially reformed their budget institutions. Especially countries like Canada and Italy strengthened the "delegations institutions", while Belgium and the Netherlands went for a commitment strategy and some countries like Sweden chose a mixed strategy.

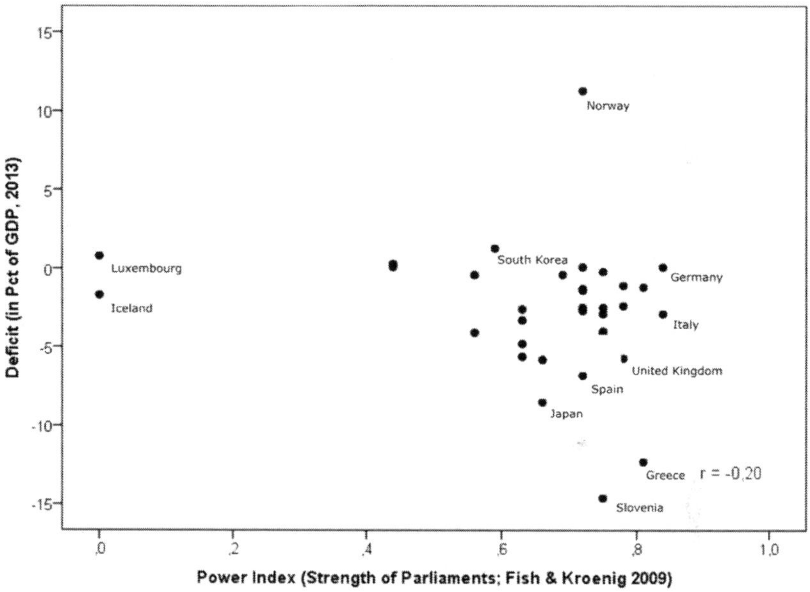

Figure 10.5: Strength of parliaments and public deficit (2013)

Note: Own calculations based on OECD data and the Power Index from Fish and Kroenig (2009).

Conclusion

Budget consolidation is not an end in itself. Consolidation creates more room for manoeuvre in terms of policies, in order to shape the common good in a sustainable way for subsequent generations. The main findings of our article, in which we analysed the politics of budget consolidations from different angles, can be summarized as follows:

- First, we have presented a new budget consolidation indicator which enables us to judge the performance of countries between 1980 and 2015. The indicator which varies between one (no consolidation) and ten (substantial and successful consolidation) has revealed substantial over-time variation in the overall consolidation performance of Western industrialized countries. Clearly, the ups and downs in the performance are closely related with the economic cycles and economic crisis.
- Second, the overview of empirical analyses of budget consolidation in recent years has shown that while country specific causes for successful budget consolidation do also exist, several important determinants of consolidations that hold true across various countries can be distilled from the existing literature. Important drivers of consolidations are strong economic growth and decreasing unemployment during the consolidation period, the existence of high public debt in the years before the consolidation or the aim of many European countries to join the eurozone. Moreover, the budget process has been shown to strongly affect consolidation performance.
- Third, we have shown that consolidation is also a realistic prospect if expenditure cuts and revenue increases can be achieved at the same time and if they are accompanied by institutional reforms in the medium term. However, against some theoretical arguments found in the literature, constitutional rules have only minor effects in our analyses.

What can be learned from these results for the case of the EP? Going by the results from the consolidation literature on the importance of the budget process and clear spending limits, it is evident that the fixed budget with a ceiling of available resources and the restriction not to issue public debt or even own bonds was (and is) a successful barrier against the accumulation of deficits on the European level. However, the finances of the EU are tight and Brexit will put even more pressure on them. Multiannual budgets, neglecting the loss of flexibility, were a solution to create more flexibility in the medium term perspective in some countries. However, the past negotiations for the EU budget have shown that these parts of the budget are rather difficult and redistribution is hard to achieve.

Some advices from our analysis might be to generate windfall profits through prudent budget estimates and growth forecasts. Underestimating growth and prudent budgeting has been a strategy in many countries that managed to consolidate public finances, because if growth turns out to be better than estimated, the windfall profits can be used to improve public finances. Moreover, this strategy made it easier to manage the budget and protected it against unpleasant surprises. Using a "golden hamster" rule, according to which unexpected surpluses must be used to reduce public debt (or in the case of the EU to set other priorities), the prudent estimates also directly resulted in greater leeway.

Related to this issue is the problem of unreliable forecasts. Some countries have improved their forecasts and had therefore less problems with unexpected surprises. This means also that the multiannual fiscal planning is a rather strict plan. The reserves within the EU budget should therefore be increased.

Minor, but also important factors, are strict auditing systems and independent fiscal institutions which can help to plan the budget. Auditors might help to circumvent deadlocks. Benchmarking studies could also reduce large costs and help to get rid of inefficient spending. Finally, the EP could also opt for a much stricter top-down budget process following the example of Sweden with overall spending targets and clear priorities firmly set at the very beginning of the budget process. Only with such a qualitative judgement of the most relevant spending categories and a firm rule that binds the subsequent budget process to numerical spending targets, can the EU institutions improve the current situation.

Notes

1 In a recent study, the IMF criticises the existing literature – and more specifically the last contribution of Alesina/Ardagna (2010) – for the use of cyclically adjusted deficits (IMF 2010: 96): "The change in the CAPB-to-GDP ratio is an unreliable guide regarding the presence of fiscal consolidation. The standard approach tends to select periods associated with favourable outcomes but during which no austerity measures were actually taken. It also tends to omit cases of fiscal austerity with unfavourable outcomes."

2 This indicator is also used for the Sustainable Governance Indicators of the Bertelsmann foundation: http://www.sgi-network.org/2016/Policy_Performance/-Economic_Policies/Budgets/Budget_Consolidation.

3 This means that for the years 2013 to 2015 we must rely on forecasts. Data base for the analysis is predominantly IMF data, but for reasons of data availability OECD data is used for some countries and years.

References

Alesina, A., and Perotti, R. 1995. The Political Economy of Budget Deficits. *IMF Staff Papers* 42 (1): 1-31.

Alesina, A., and Perotti, R. 1996. Reducing Budget Deficits. *Swedish Economic Policy Review* 3: 113-134.

Alesina, A., and Perotti, R. 1997. Fiscal Adjustments in OECD Countries: Composition and Macroeconomic Effects. *IMF Staff Papers* 44 (2): 210-248.

Alesina, A., and Ardagna, S. 1998. Tales of fiscal adjustment. Why they can be expansionary. *Economic Policy* 13(27): 488-545.

Alesina, A., and Ardagna, S. 2010. Large changes in fiscal policy: taxes versus spending. *Tax policy and the economy* 24: 35-68.

Auel, K., Rozenberg, O., and Tacea, A. 2015. Fighting Back? And if Yes, How? Measuring Parliamentary Strength and Activity in EU Affairs. In *The Palgrave Handbook of National Parliaments and the European Union*, Eds. Hafftler, C., Neuhold, C., Rozenberg, O., and Smith, J., 60-93. London: Palgrave Macmillan.

Bertola, G., und Drazen, A. 1993. Trigger Points and Budget Cuts. Explaining the Effects of Fiscal Austerity. *American Economic Review* 83 (1): 11-26.

Blyth, M. 2015. *Austerity: the history of a dangerous idea.* Oxford: Oxford University Press.

Brandner, P. 2003. Budgetpolitik der Niederlande, Finnlands und Schwedens – Lehre für nachhaltige Konsolidierungen? *Wirtschaftspolitische Blätter* 50 (2): 183-204.

Castles, F. G. 1982. The Impact of Parties on Public Expenditure. In *The Impact of Parties*, Ed. Francis G. Castles, 21-96. London and Beverly Hills: Sage.

Castles, F. G. (Ed.). 2007. *The Disappearing State? Retrenchment Realities in an Age of Globalization.* Cheltenham: Edward Elgar Publishing.

Fish, S. M., and Kroenig, M. 2009. *The Handbook of National Legislatures: A Global Survey.* New York: Cambridge University Press.

Franzese, R. J. 2002. *Macroeconomic policies of developed democracies.* Cambridge: Cambridge University Press.

Giavazzi, F., and Pagano, M. 1996. Non-Keynesian Effects of Fiscal Policy Changes. International Evidence and the Swedish Experience. *Swedish Economic Policy Review* 3 (3): 67-103.

Girouard, N., and Andre, C. 2005. *Measuring cyclically adjusted budget balances for 0ECD countries.* Paris: OECD Economics Department Working Papers 434.

Hallerberg, M., and von Hagen, J. 1999. Electoral Institutions, Cabinet Negotiations, and Budget Deficits within the European Union. In *Fiscal Institutions and Fiscal Performance*, Eds. Poterba, J., and von Hagen, J., 209-232. Chicago: Chicago University Press.

Hallerberg, M., Strauch, R., and von Hagen, J. 2009. *Fiscal governance in Europe.* Cambridge: Cambridge University Press.

Hibbs, D. A. 1977. Political Parties and Macroeconomic Policy. *The American Political Science Review* 71 (4): 1467-1487.

Hübscher, E., and Sattler, T. 2016. Fiscal consolidation under electoral risk. *European Journal of Political Research*: online first.

International Monetary Fund (IMF). 2010. *Recovery, Risk, and Rebalancing, IMF World Economic Outlook October 2010*. Washington D.C.: IMF.

Katzenstein, P. J. 1985. *Small States in World Markets: Industrial Policy in Europe.* Ithaca: Cornell University Press.

König, P., and Wenzelburger, G. 2016. Honeymoon in the crisis? A comparative analysis of the strategic timing of austerity policies and their effect on government popularity in three countries. *Comparative European Politics:* online first.

Larch, M., and Salto, M. 2003. *Fiscal rules, inertia and discretionary fiscal policy.* Brussels: Europ. Commission, Directorate-General for Econ. and Financial Affairs.

Molander, P. 2001. Budgeting Procedures and Democratic Ideals: An Evaluation of Swedish Reforms. *Journal of Public Policy* 21(1): 23-52.

Mulas-Granados, C. 2006. *Economics, politics and budgets: the political economy of fiscal consolidations in Europe*. Basingstoke: Palgrave.

OECD. 2005. *Central Government Debt: Statistical Yearbook 1994-2003*. Paris: OECD.

Persson, T. and Svensson, L.E.O. 1989. Why a Stubborn Conservative Would Run a Deficit: Policy with Time-Insconsistent Preferences. *Quarterly Journal of Economics* 104 (2): 325-346.

Pierson, P. 1994. *Dismantling the Welfare State? Reagan, Thatcher, and the Politics of Retrenchment.* Cambridge: Cambridge University Press.

Roubini, N., and Sachs, J. D. 1989. Political and Economic Determinants of Budget Deficits in the Industrial Democracies. *European Economic Review* 33: 903-938.

Schmidt, M. G. 1996. When Parties Matter: A Review of the Possibilities and Limits of Partisan Influence on Public Policy. *European Journal of Political Research* 30 (2): 155-183.

Schmidt, M. G. 1997. Determinants of Social Expenditure in Liberal Democracies: The Post World War II Experience. *Acta Politica* 32: 153-173.

Sustainable Governance Indicators. 2016. *Has the government successfully consolidated the budget?* http://www.sgi-network.org/2016/Policy_Performance/ Economic-_Policies/ Budgets/Budget_Consolidation; 2 November 2016.

Tsebelis, G. 2002. *Veto Players. How Political Institutions Work.* Princeton: Princeton University Press.

Von Hagen, J., Hughes Hallett, A., and Strauch, R. (Eds.). 2001. *Budgetary consolidation in EMU.* Brussels: Europ. Comm., Directorate-General for Economic and Financial Affairs.

Von Hagen, J., Hughes Hallett, A., and Strauch, R. 2002. Budgetary Consolidation in Europe: Quality, Economic Conditions, and Persistence. *Journal of the Japanese and International Economies* 16(4): 512–535.

Von Hagen, J. 1992. *Budgeting procedures and fiscal performance in the European Communities.* Brussels: Directorate-General for Economic and Financial Affairs, Commission of the Eropean Communities.

Wagschal, U., and Wenzelburger, G. 2008. *Successful budget consolidation. An international comparison.* Gütersloh: Verlag Bertelsmann-Stiftung.

Wagschal, U., and Wenzelburger, G. 2009. Determinants of budget consolidations in the German „Länder" (1992–2006). *Zeitschrift für Vergleichende Politikwissenschaft* 3 (1): 33-58.

Wagschal, U, and Wenzelburger, G. 2012. When do Governments Consolidate? A Quantitative Comparative Analysis of 23 OECD Countries (1980–2005). *Journal of Comparative Policy Analysis* 14 (1): 45-71.

Wagschal, U. 1996. *Staatsverschuldung. Ursachen im internationalen Vergleich.* Opladen: Leske + Budrich.

Wagschal, U. 2005. *Steuerpolitik und Steuerreformen im internationalen Vergleich. Eine Analyse der Ursachen und Blockaden.* Münster: LIT-Verlag.

Wehner, J. 2006. Assessing the Power of the Purse: An Index of Legislative Budget Institutions. *Political Studies* 54 (4): 767-785.

Wehner, Joachim. 2010. *Legislatures and the Budget Process. The Myth of Fiscal Control.* Palgrave: Basingstoke.

Weingast, B. R., Shepsle, K. A., and Johnson, C. 1981. The Political Economy of Benefits and Costs: A Neoclassical Approach to Distributive Politics. *Journal of Political Economy* 89 (4): 642-664.

Wenzelburger, G. 2006. *Wege der Konsolidierung – Die Haushaltssanierungen von Schweden, Kanada und Österreich im Vergleich.* Master Thesis. University of Munich.

Williamson, J., and Haggard, S. 1994. The Political Conditions for Economic Reform. In *The political economy of policy reform*, Ed. Williamson, J., 527-596. Washington: Inst. for Internat. Economics.

Zaghini, A. 2001. Fiscal adjustments and economic performance: a comparative study. *Applied Economics* 33 (5): 613-624.

EU Budget Politics: Looking Forward

Alfredo De Feo

This volume has tried to capture the various dynamics in the new politics of the EU budget. The institutional modifications of the Lisbon Treaty have introduced the most comprehensive reform of the budget system since the "budget treaties" of the 1970s. Political events have transformed the political context of EU budget politics: challenges for new policies but also pressure to dismiss old policies to respond to new needs, the necessity of more financial resources but also a growing hostility in a large part of European public opinion and, last but not least, the consequences of the UK referendum on the British exit from the European Union.
The various chapters in this edited volume have offered a contribution to better understanding of the new politics of the EU budget and its contribution to European integration. This final chapter highlighting the challenges which the new EU budget politics have to face in the near future does not have the ambition to offer tailor-made solutions but to focus on some of the main challenges which will be on the agenda in the near future.

The challenges ahead

The contributions in this volume touch many of the themes of relevance to the future of EU budget politics and policy: the impact of Brexit on the EU budget (Brunsden/Robinson 2016) and the EU reform to better respond to the worries of public opinion and the financing of policies to relaunch the EU. The financial and economic crisis, the management of the migration flux, security of the EU external borders, the stability of neighbouring countries, relations with Russia, commercial relations with the United States, the energy issue, and the reduction of emissions to limit climate change are only some examples of the transnational challenges that Europe has to face. Nationalistic and populist tendencies are gaining ground in many EU countries, offering the illusion of national solutions.

At the same time, European leaders have difficulties in showing a new vision of European integration. Solutions to the challenges based on *business as usual* are not perceived by public opinion as adequate for the current challenges. The outcome of the British referendum renders maintaining the status quo even more unacceptable. To respond to disaffection with European ideals, political leaders have to offer to European public opinion a new vision, a political courage and supplementary financial resources.

The aim of this volume is not to offer solutions to the big challenges, but to analyse the contribution that the EU budget could make to some of the problems on the table. EU own resources are, for instance, one of the crucial topics which could contribute to supporting new strategies and policies to face the challenges, and also to give European citizens a perception of what Europe can do. A better use of EU funds more focused on results can be a second pillar to re-launch European integration and face the new challenges. Enhanced monitoring and scrutiny of European Policies by the EU institutions is the third element, which would allow a better assessment of EU policies.

The Brexit impact on the EU budget

The first challenge EU leaders have to handle with care is the UK's exit from the EU. It will be a very complex operation, which could also be a motor stimulating further reform of the EU. The official narrative, so far, tells us that there will be no impact of the UK for the next two years after the triggering of Art. 50 of the Treaty on the Functioning of the European Union (TFEU). This is formally true, but the reality seems to be more complex and it would be wise for EU Leaders to acknowledge some key principles involving the British government as soon as possible.

An issue to be clarified is whether the commitments made by the EU (at 28) will be honoured, in terms of dissociated payments, a few years after the legal commitment and after the formal exit. Respect for commitments is a self-evident principle, which should be respected by all the Member States. The United Kingdom should remain bound to honour past and future commitments made until its formal exit from the EU. This principle has a particular relevance for all new EU (dissociated) expenditure in favour of UK beneficiaries and also for the UK staff of the institutions recruited between 1973 and 2018, in particular for the cost of their pensions, to which the UK government should contribute. The Commission might be tempted to freeze all new long-term expenditure in favour of UK beneficiaries in the absence of a clear commitment by the UK government on this issue.

This is probably only one of the problems to be settled in negotiations. In any case, the EU budget will lose the UK contribution (House of Commons 2016). The UK contributes about ten percent of the Member State financing of the EU budget (about ten billion euro) and it is a net contributor by about 4,9 billion (in 2014, European Commission 2016). This gap, *rebus sic stantibus*, should be filled by the other MS unless the 27 decide to downgrade the EU contribution for some policies, which should imply the agreement of the 27 MS. Even in this case, the situation could be complicated by the likely UK participation in some EU policies (e.g. Common Foreign and Security Policy, environment policies, etc.) through the European Economic Area or through other special arrangements, which could be negotiated by then.

On the own resources side, Brexit should, in principle, affect all correction mechanisms, with relief especially for the countries financing the double rebates. The current own resources system will become fairer as it will be financed purely by Gross National Income (GNI) contributions. The absence of the UK might also stimulate the creation of EU taxation to replace the current system of financing, opening a supplementary window of opportunity for the recommendations by the Monti group.

Multiannual financial planning has always been the place for negotiating reform towards a budget that is less redistributive and more oriented to investments. The UK has always been in the lead in this battle (Blair 2005), with some (modest) success. The absence of the UK leader at the European Council risks reducing the impact of the forces aiming to reform the budget, unless EU Leaders find other motivations for the reform.

The reform of own resources

Traditionally, the own resources issue came to the attention of public opinion and EU institutions in periods of crisis when the ceiling was reached and more resources were necessary. This time is different. The EP has raised the problem of the replacement of own resources with *more transparent, simple, fair and democratically accountable ways to finance the EU,* independently of the size of the budget.

The High Level Group on Own Resources (HLGOR) is entering its final phase, a very comprehensive study commissioned by the HLGOR has been published (Núñez Ferrer et al. 2016) and a meeting with national parliaments is scheduled for 7-8 September 2016 in order to finalise the final report to be presented to the European Council by the end of 2016. The final report will arrive on the table of the institutions in a moment when the need to develop new European policies might require more resources. The problem of the quality and quantity of the own resources cannot be dissociated from the needs and the policies to be developed.

Academic literature offers many suggestions for new EU taxes[1] together with the assessment criteria to evaluate the sustainability of each individual tax. The first report by the HLGOR identified the weaknesses of the current system to be redressed: lack of simplicity, of transparency, of fairness and of democratic accountability. In addition to a deep analysis of the problems, the study commissioned by the group offers many ideas and potential solutions which could inspire not only the HLGOR but also the EU leaders. The study presents a well-documented analysis of the pro and cons of various options for political decisions.

The story of European own resources is marked by a limited number of events often linked to a crisis. The Treaty of Rome abandoned the idea of the Coal and Steel Community (ECSC) of a supranational body with full fiscal autonomy. The problem of the financing of the European Community (EC) was on the table in the mid-60s when the Commission proposed a package of proposals which included the own resources, the financing of the agricultural policy and reinforcement of the competences of the European Parliament (EP). This proposal led to the *empty chair* crisis, and modifications only came in the margins of the 1970 Treaty with a decision, as there was no agreement to modify Art. 201 EC (Council decision 70/243/ECSC, EEC, Euratom). Agriculture levies and common custom duties were topped up in 1975 with a third resource, a portion (one percent) of value added tax (VAT).

1984 and 1988 are two other key dates, the first one for allowing the UK to have a substantial discount on its contribution (about 66 percent of its "normal" share) and the second for increasing the revenue of the EC with the introduction of the so-called fourth resource, a percentage of the Gross National Product (GNP). With these resources the Member States were back in the driving seat of the own resources. The fourth resource amounted to ten percent of the total revenue in 1988 and it was over 72 percent in 2016. The idea of autonomous resources was abandoned. The period until 2013 was marked by adjustments and rebates of the rebates – all measures which made the system less transparent and more unfair.

In spite of many criticisms, the mechanism has guaranteed stability and sufficiency of resources to finance EU activities. It also guarantees fairness among Member States as the richer States pay more than the poorer.

The debate around the introduction of new taxes is complicated by the fact that it should be framed in the perimeter of the current Treaty, as a reform of the Treaty for a new EU fiscal capacity is probably desirable but difficult to conceive in the short (medium) term.

Abundant academic literature, including proposals by the Commission, offers a number of potential tax candidates to replace at least part of the current sources (Schratzenstaller 2013; European Commission 2011a). A consensus is emerging on the criteria for assessing the validity of a tax in the medium/long term, i.e. visibility and simplicity, financial autonomy, a contribution towards an efficient allocation of economic resources, yield, and cost efficiency with regard to tax administration, revenue stability and equitable gross burden. Most of the taxes suggested fulfil all the criteria but the perfect tax does not exist. The first assessment report by the HLGOR concludes that reform of the EU mechanism "should be based on the merging of national interests with a higher European interest" (HLGOR 2014).

Some consider that the current VAT tax is one of the causes of the complexity and the lack of transparency of the current system and they consider that it should be replaced with new taxes. Others see that VAT could guarantee the financing of the whole EU budget (similarly to an EU federal system, see Cipriani 2014).

Since 1998 the Commission has advanced various proposals for European taxes which still have some validity, such as:

- Emission Trade system;
- Financial Transaction Tax;
- Financial activity tax;
- Air transport tax;
- EU VAT;
- EU energy tax;
- EU Corporate income tax.

Two other proposals are worth mentioning: a tax on the digital economy and a tax on European Central Bank (ECB) gains (*droit de seignorage*). Tarschys (2015) sees the digital economy, like other multinational activities, as particularly agile at escaping traditional sources of taxation and often being beyond the reach of Member State fiscal authority, especially considering that the digital economy has no solid territorial link – who knows exactly where the revenues from downloaded apps go? A European tax would be more efficient than national attempts to tap these companies.

The EU "*is strong enough to confront the powerful actors that are experienced masters of evasive fiscal manoeuvres*" (Tarschys 2015, p. 7).

The second proposal is a tax on ECB profits, which are about 25 billion euro per year (Lamassoure 2007; Haug et al. 2011). According to a study by Willem Buiter at Citigroup and Huw Pill of Goldman Sachs, "the present value of all of the future income which the ECB can earn from investments financed by seigniorage is in the region of €2,000-3,000bn" (Davies 2011; Soros 2012). If these figures were confirmed, the ECB could contribute not only to the financing of the EU budget but also be more active in supporting the governance of the euro.

In the panorama of options for reform, we need to also mention the minimalistic, but also realistic, approach of other authors who support the idea that it is not necessary to reform the system and that a supplement to revenue can easily derive from more efficiency in management, the revision of policies, and eventually the extension of co-financing to some of the current policies, such as agriculture expenditure (Heinemann 2016).

A reform of own resources is important not only to replace the current obsolete mechanism, to abandon the "*juste retour*" approach, but also to open potential avenues to supplementary financial means for the EU.

Reform of EU own resources should not be a revolution, and it is unthinkable that the EU will reach full fiscal autonomy independently of the Member States. EU taxes should top up the GNI contribution, which, in my view, should be maintained. This will leave a double protection for the Member States.

A realistic reform should be conducted within the current Treaty with a revision of the own resources decision. Many reasonable proposals are on the table, but none of them are perfect. My modest conclusion would be to include as many potential taxes in the revision of the own resources decision and leave the decision to the normal community method: during the annual procedure take a decision according to the rules set by the Treaty.

To conclude, reform of the EU own resources cannot be totally untied from the expenditure side of the budget and its efficiency, which will be the subject of the next section.

A budget focused on results

In times of economic crisis and instability, there is an increased need for the mobilization of public funds to stimulate growth, but at the same time there is scarcity of resources. This situation stimulates the search for more efficiency and effectiveness, and ultimately a better use of resources in terms of concentration of funds and focusing on results. Because of its size, the EU budget has a limited macro-economic impact, but its leverage effect and its capacity to mobilize resources through co-financing are important and can make a difference.

The Multiannual Financial Framework (MFF) 2014-2020, in spite of the global reduction of resources, has continued this (slow) evolution rebalancing between redistribution and investments. Agriculture was reduced by more than 13 percent with respect to the previous period, Cohesion policy was reduced by about eight percent, while the heading Competitiveness for growth and jobs, which includes research and innovation, education and training, trans-European networks in energy, transport and telecommunications, social policy, and development of enterprises, etc., has been increased by more than 35 percent. This trend was already initiated in 2007-2013 with respect to the previous programming period.

Until recently, the targets of the Commission in implementing European policies were double: spending the allocation and complying with the various rules established in the financial and legislative regulations. Even the European Court of Auditors (ECA) and the Parliament until recently were particularly focused on respect for these two elements.

The Treaty of Lisbon (Art. 318) reinforces the relevance of the efficiency and effectiveness of the policies financed by the budget. The Commission now has to submit an annual Report on the *"evaluation of the Union's finances based on the results achieved"* (European Commission 2015). The ECA has drawn the attention of the institutions to the necessity of enhancing the assessment of the quality of the expenditure since 2010.

The renewal of all legislation with a financial impact for the period 2014-2020 has allowed the introduction into the "spending" regulations of a number of performance objectives, indicators and macro-economic conditionality, together with evaluation and reporting arrangements. In particular, in the case of structural funds there is the possibility to draw supplementary funds from a "performance reserve". According to the Commission, 56 programme statements in the 2014-2020 legislative package have about 300 objectives and 700 indicators, either general or specific, almost half of the programmes have more than 10 objectives, some have more than 20 and a few more than 40. Are these too many for effective control? The Commission has to report on legality, regularity and compliance with the indicators in the Annual Activity Reports and in the report ex art 318 TFEU (see, for example, European Commission 2015), but more relevance is given to "the value resulting from an EU intervention which is additional to the value that would have been otherwise created by Member State action alone" (European Commission 2011b, p. 2), which can be assessed on the basis of three criteria: effectiveness, efficiency and synergy.

The complex EU decision-making process in the preparation, decision, implementation and control of the EU budget involves many actors. A change of culture can only be achieved if there is collective ownership of the new approach more focused on outputs than inputs. The Commission, under the leadership of the responsible Commissioner Kristalina Georgieva, has taken the initiative to lead this profound change of culture by involving all the stakeholders involved in the budgetary process, starting with the staff of the Commission, EU institutions and the Member States. The organization deployed by the Commission to implement this new approach looks solid and structured and could open the way for a profound change in the financial and legislative activities of the EU, as important as the Delors reform of 1988. [2]

Performance budgeting is the method which takes into consideration the relation between inputs and the outputs and services achieved to measure the efficiency of public spending. Performance budgeting implies a choice of shared indicators to measure the outputs and outcomes of a programme, taking into account the external factors and the time lapse which might influence the results. It also implies more flexibility and autonomy in the management of programmes. The EU Financial Regulation should therefore be adapted. Experience shows that high investment, especially in administration but also at the political level, is necessary to implement a performance budgeting method.

Measuring the output of implemented legislation could be a treacherous exercise: either it is left to technocrats, with the risk of transforming the budgetary exercise into a "perfect algorithm", or the decision defining the metrics is given to the legislator, with the risk of achieving good compromises but not viable indicators. Using the performance budgeting model to establish the EU budget could expose it to risks and reduce the political impact of the budget.

The evolution toward a performance budgeting approach is a necessary step to make EU disbursements more effective and visible to the citizens in terms of European added value. A generalised implementation of performance indicators should measure the effectiveness of European decisions and be a component of future budgetary decisions.

The scrutiny of budget implementation

Enhancement of the measurement of outputs in the allocation of resources in the annual procedure should reinforce the role of control and budgetary authority. Scrutiny of legislation should not be a sole prerogative of the budget committees of the EP and of the Council but should involve the legislative committees in both institutions. The leading role in this scrutiny procedure should be left to the legislative and budgetary authority with the active support of the ECA. A new interinstitutional agreement (IIA) could frame the monitoring of legislation and its link with the annual budgetary and discharge procedure and the allocation of funds. In fact, scrutiny should not be an exercise in itself but should produce political decisions on the allocation of resources.

The need to have legislation which can bring European added value and which should be implemented to achieve its targets should be shared by all the institutions, which should be ready to adapt their working methods. Performance budgeting should not become a technocratic exercise but a tool which can influence the allocation of resources and reinforce the European dimension of legislation. This cultural change can only be achieved if all the actors, EU institutions and also Member States, agree to put in place this new evaluation procedure.

The mid-term review of a five-year multiannual framework could become the moment to assess results after two/three years of monitoring and to take concrete decisions in terms of the financial envelopes of programmes translating positive and negative priorities also based on concrete outputs and performances. It is important that the decisions in this new monitoring system are not taken annually but at a precise moment. Apart from exceptional cases, annual decisions on the performance of programmes can be disruptive for their implementation. Annually, the discharge and budgetary authority may issue recommendations to draw attention to eventual poor performance of some policy areas.

Finally, this new approach should put an end to the pre-allocation of funds to specific Member States. That projects should be financed on their own pure merits and not as part of a national envelope is a model to be generalised, following the mechanism successfully put in place for the European Fund for Strategic Investments (EFSI).

To conclude, driving the EU budget into a performance budgeting method is an ambitious but necessary objective which can only be reached if the main stakeholders feel ownership of the project and they are ready to sustain the change of culture. A new IIA could remodel the cooperation of all the institutions to achieve a shared decision. The Commission has the opportunity to lead a fundamental reform and put the budget at the centre again, as the motor of European integration.

Final remarks

This overview tells the story, necessarily incomplete, of the contribution of the EU budget to the construction of European integration. Over this period, the EU budget has been the crossroads of institutional dialogue and struggles between two visions of European construction: the community and the intergovernmental method. I will conclude with some remarks on the research questions raised at the beginning of this chapter.

The EU budget, in spite of conflicts, has guaranteed the financing of policies which have favoured the integration process, but at the same time the budget has slowed down this process because of scarcity of resources and the difficulty for the institutions to reform the budget for a better use of financial resources. The identification of negative priorities or obsolete policies has been an objective that (all) the institutions have failed to achieve. New policies have been financed, generally, through redeployment, or more rarely with supplementary funds. The Council has generally been successful in imposing redeployment but in most cases the EP has managed to limit the redeployments. However, especially in recent times both arms of the budgetary authority have shared the political priorities of the new policies put in place.

Increases in resources and inter-institutional balance have been the major drivers of the evolution of the budgetary procedure while, up to now, structural reform of the budget has only been marginal.

As the various contributions to this volume show, the budgetary domain has certainly been one of the most dynamic sectors in the European process. The rise over time in the influence of the EP has obliged the other institutions, but in particular the Council, to change their attitude: Parliament was no more a procedural step to be fulfilled but became a partner with whom it is necessary to dialogue. The EP also changed its attitude: from conflict to cooperation. The conflicts since 1988 have developed new interinstitutional relations, as the evolution of the IIAs show, but they have never put the adoption of the budget in danger. The financial provisions of the Lisbon Treaty reinforce the position of the institution aiming at a lower budget. In consequence, the EP – traditionally more inclined to increase expenditure – has less influence over final decisions and it has a reduced negotiating power.

Europe today faces major challenges – the economic crises and the governance of the euro, the migration flux and neighbouring relations, the security of its own territory and protection of the external border – at a moment when public opinion shows a clear disaffection and disillusion with the European project. European leaders, and a part of public opinion, know that the major challenges cannot be overcome individually by each single country but only with a strong European position and a will to reform. The step forward will pass, once again, through budgetary decisions.

Supplementary resources will be necessary and alternative ways of financing must be identified. The legislative and budgetary scrutiny of the legislation adopted is the area where more dynamism is necessary. The EP could develop a new role of scrutinising the budgetary implementation of EU legislation if this exercise could be linked to budgetary decisions (increasing or reducing allocations as a function of performance). The initiative of the Commission for budgetary results is certainly a step in this direction.

The fact that own resources and efficiency of EU spending are both high on the agendas of the budgetary circles of all the institutions proves that, even in this deep European crisis, the budget is doing everything possible to ignite the motor of European construction. Looking back at the history of the last forty years is encouraging, even if the direction and vision of the Europe of the future generation can only be set by our European leaders.

Notes

1 Extensive references can be found in De Feo and Laffan (2016).

2 A first conference was organised in September 2015 and a follow-up conference is foreseen for September 2016. A group of EU institution experts and Member states has been established together with a dedicated website: (http://ec.europa.eu/budget/budget4results/index_en.cfm).

References

Blair, T. Speech to the European Parliament. *The Guardian*. http://www.theguardian.com/politics/2005/jun/23/speeches.eu; 18 August 2016.

Brunsden, J., and Robinson, D. 2016. EU budget: the post-Brexit challenges for London and Brussels. *Financial Times*. http://www.ft.com/cms/s/2/84cba658-3eda-11e6-9f2c-36b487ebd80a.html?siteedition=intl#axzz4FrmjFwcZ; 18 August 2016.

Cipriani, G. 2014. *Financing the EU budget: moving forward or moving backwards?* Brussels: CEPS.

Council of the European Union. 1970. *Council Decision of 21 April 1970 on the replacement of financial contributions from Member States by the Communities' own resources.* http://publications.europa.eu/en/publication-detail/-/publication/d0a020-b9-0544-4eb0-86e8-f87bd0d7942a/language-en; 18 August 2016.

Davies, G. 2011. Does the ECB really have a silver bullet? *Financial Times*. http://blogs.ft.com/gavyndavies/2011/11/10/does-the-ecb-really-have-a-silver-bullet/; 18 August 2016.

De Feo, A., and Laffan, B. (Eds). 2016. *EU Own Resources: Momentum for a Reform?* Florence: European University Institute. doi:10.2870/176147

European Commission. 2011a. *Financing the European Union: report on the operation of the own resources system.* http://ec.europa.eu/budget/library/biblio/documents/fin_fwk1420/proposal_council_own_resources__annex_en.pdf; 18 August 2016.

European Commission. 2011b. The added value of the EU budget. *Commission Staff Working Paper* SEC (2011) 867 final. http://ec.europa.eu/budget/library/biblio/-documents/fin_fwk1420/working_paper_added_value_EU_budget_SEC-867_en.p-df; 18 August 2016.

European Commission. 2015. *Report from the Commission to the European Parliament and the Council on the evaluation of the Union's finances based on the results achieved (Article 318 Report).* http://ec.europa.eu/smart-regulation-/evaluation-/docs/2014_report_en.pdf; 18 August 2016.

European Commission. 2016. *EU expenditure and revenue 2014-2020.* http://ec.europ-a.eu/budget/figures/interactive/index_en.cfm; 18 August 2016.

Haug, J., Lamassoure, A., and Verhofstadt, G. 2011. *Europe for growth: for a radical change in the revenue of the European Union.* https://www.ceps.eu-/publications/-europe-growth-radical-change-financing-eu; 18 August 2016.

Heinemann, F. 2016. Strategies for a European EU budget. In *The future of the EU-Finances*, Eds. Buettner, T., and Thöne, M., 91-108. http://www.le-figaro-fr/conjoncture/2012/04/22/20002-20120422ARTFIG00166-so-ros-l-europe-pourrait-financer-seule-sa-relance.php; 18 August 2016.

High Level Group on Own Resources. 2014. *First Assessment Report.* http://ec.europa-.eu/budget/mff/hlgor/library/reports-communication/FirstAssessme-ntReport-December2014.pdf; 18 August 2016.

House of Commons. 2016. *EU budget and the UK's contribution.* http://researchbriefings.parliament.uk/ResearchBriefing/Summary/SN06455; 18 August 2016.

Lamassoure, A. 2007. *Report on the future of the European Union's own resources.* European Parliament Session Document A6-0066/2007. http://www.europarl.europa.eu/sides/getDoc.do?pubRef=-//EP//NONSGML+REP-ORT+A6-2007-0066+-0+DOC+PDF+V0//EN; 18 August 2007.

Núñez Ferrer, J., Le Chacheux, J., Benedetto, G., and Laffan, B. 2016. *Study on the Potential and Limitations of Reforming the Financing of the EU Budget.* http://ec.europa.eu/budget/mff/hlgor/library/highlights/hlgor-studies-external-study-onfinancingofeu-budget-june-2016_en.pdf; 18 August 2016.

Schratzenstaller, M. 2013. The EU own resources system: reform needs and options. In *Intereconomics* 48(5): 303-313.

Soros, G. 2012. L'Europe pourrait financer seule sa relance. *Le Figaro.* http://www.lefigaro.fr/conjoncture/2012/04/22/20002-20120422ARTFIG00166-soros-l-europe-pourrait-financer-seule-sa-relance.php; 18 August 2016.

Tarschys, D. 2015. Entering a world of footloose tax bases: can the EU generate its own income? *European Policy Analysis* 2015(8). http://www.sieps.se/sites-/default-/files/2015_8epa_eng_A4_korr2.pdf; 18 August 2016.

About the Authors

Michael W. Bauer is Jean Monnet Professor and holds the chair of Comparative Public Administration and Policy Analysis at the German University of Administrative Sciences in Speyer. He is interested in international and multilevel public administration as well as in the comparative analysis of public policy-making. Recent publications comprise "International Public Administration: A New Type of Bureaucracy? Lessons and Challenges for Public Administration Research" (2016, Palgrave Series on Public Organizations), "Bureaucratic autonomy of international organizations' secretariats" (2016, Special Issue of the Journal of European Public Policy) and "The State, the Economy, and the Regions: Theories of Preference Formation in Times of Crisis" (2016, JPART).

Peter Becker works as a senior associate in the Research Division EU/Europe of the Stiftung Wissenschaft und Politik in Berlin, which is an independent research institute that advises the German Bundestag and the German government as well as international organisations on questions concerning foreign, European and security policy. His major research topics include European budgetary policy, European cohesion policy as well as European economic and social policies. His latest publication on the issue of European budgetary policy is *Das Finanz- und Haushaltssystem der Europäischen Union. Grundlagen und Reformen aus deutscher Perspektive*, Springer VS, Wiesbaden 2014.

Stefan Becker is a research associate at Chair of Comparative Public Administration and Policy Analysis at the German University of Administrative Sciences Speyer. He holds a BA and a BSc in European Studies and Public Administration (Münster/Enschede) as well as an MA in International Relations (Berlin/Potsdam). His research focuses on European institutions, economic governance and political dimensions of bureaucracy.

Gabriele Cipriani joined in 1978 the European Court of Auditors where he has spent his whole career holding several managerial positions, lastly as Director of the Audit Chamber responsible for 'Structural Policies, Transport & Energy'. Gabriele is the author of publications on various aspects of EU finances. His core research interests focus on the reform of the EU budget and its accountability arrangements.

Manuele Citi is Associate Professor at Copenhagen Business School - Department of Business and Politics. He received his MRes and PhD in Political and Social Sciences from the European University Institute in Florence. Before joining CBS, he was lecturer in EU Politics at James Madison University.

Alessandro D'Alfonso works as a policy analyst at the European Parliamentary Research Service (EPRS) in Brussels. He regularly writes on EU budgetary affairs. Many of his publications are available on the website of the Think Tank of the European Parliament.

Alfredo De Feo is currently a fellow at the European University Institute, Robert Schuman Centre for Advanced Studies and Professor at European College of Parma. Most of his career was spent at the European Parliament, his last positions Director of European Parliamentary Research Service (EPRS) and Budgetary Affairs. He is a panelist and speaker at many European events. His research interests and teaching experience focus on European integration, the history of the European Parliament, its budgetary powers and its organization.

Magdalena Sapała is an expert on the EU budget and EU cohesion policy and works as a policy analyst at the European Parliamentary Research Service (the think tank of the European Parliament) in Brussels. She holds a PhD in economics with a specialisation in European integration.

Linn Selle is a policy officer at the Federation of German Consumer Associations (vzbv) since 2015. Prior to that, she was a PhD student (2013-2016) and a Research Associate (2013-2015) at the European University Viadrina, Frankfurt/Oder. She studied Political Science, Sociology and European Studies at University of Bonn, Sciences Po Paris and European University Viadrina.

Anne Vitrey is Director of Budgetary Affairs within DG Internal Policies of the Union at the European Parliament (2008-present). She is responsible for the EP work linked to the preparation of the EU Budget and Budgetary Control. She oversees the work of the teams responsible for providing assistance to interinstitutional negotiations (annual budgets, MFF, High Level Group on Own Resources, OLAF etc.). She joined the Parliament in 1985, initially working as an administrator in the DG for Information and Public Relations and then the DG for Committees and Delegations and later for the Committee of Women's rights. She was then nominated as Head of Unit to the secretariat of Budgets. Anne Vitrey contributed to the drafting of the first and second reports of the Expert Committees on the Reform of the European Commission and afterwards headed the secretariat for the temporary Committee on Financial Perspectives 2007-2013 (2005-2006).

Uwe Wagschal is Professor for Comparative Politics at the University of Freiburg. He received his M.A. in Political Science (1992), his Diploma in Economics (1993) and his PhD in Political Science (1996) from the University of Heidelberg. In 2003 he became Professor for Public Policy and Empirical Methods at the University of Munich and in 2005 he joined the University of Heidelberg as professor for Comparative Politics. His main research areas are Public Finances, Direct Democracy and Public Policy.

Georg Wenzelburger is Juniorprofessor for Political Science (Political Economy) at the TU Kaiserslautern, Germany. His main research interests are in the area of comparative public policy with a focus on the welfare state and the politics of welfare state reforms, fiscal policies as well as law and order policies. Recent work has been published in the British Journal of Political Science (on law and order policies), the Journal of Public Policy (on the myth that cutting welfare leads to successful adjustments) or the Journal of European Public Policy (on the validity of replacement rate data).

November 2016